Gipsy Moth IV

A legend sails again **Paul Gelder**

GIPSY MOTH IV

Gipsy Moth IV

A legend sails again Paul Gelder

 BICENTENNIAL 1807 WILEY 2007 BICENTENNIAL

 WILEY NAUTICAL

To Laura
'If you want a rainbow, you gotta put up with the rain.' Dolly Parton

In memory of John Williams, who died living his last adventure.

Published by
John Wiley & Sons Ltd, The Atrium, Southern Gate, Chichester,
West Sussex PO19 8SQ, England
Telephone (+44) 1243 779777

Email (for orders and customer service enquiries): cs-books@wiley.co.uk
Visit our Home Page on www.wileynautical.com

Other Wiley Editorial Offices
John Wiley & Sons Inc., 111 River Street, Hoboken, NJ 07030, USA
Jossey-Bass, 989 Market Street, San Francisco, CA 94103-1741, USA
Wiley-VCH Verlag GmbH, Boschstr. 12, D-69469 Weinheim, Germany
John Wiley & Sons Australia Ltd, 42 McDougall Street, Milton, Queensland 4064, Australia
John Wiley & Sons (Asia) Pte Ltd, 2 Clementi Loop #02-01, Jin Xing Distripark, Singapore 129809
John Wily & Sons Canada Ltd, 22 Worcester Road, Etobicoke, Ontario, Canada, M9W 1LI

Wiley also publishes its books in a variety of electronic formats. Some content that appears in print may not be available in electronic books.

Anniversary Logo Design: Richard J. Pacifico
British Library Cataloguing in Publication Data
A catalogue record for this book is available from the British Library

ISBN 978-0-470-72443-9

Design by PPL Design + Print
Illustrations by Maxine Heath/Yachting Monthly & Greg Filip/PPL
Picture research by PPL Photo Agency
Printed and bound in Italy by Trento

This book is printed on acid-free paper responsibly manufactured from sustainable forestry in which at least two trees are planted for each one used for paper production.

Contents

BUCKINGHAM PALACE

The campaign to restore *Gipsy Moth IV* and sail her round the world again has been a bold adventure which celebrates not only the spirit and determination of Sir Francis Chichester, but has inspired a new generation of young people. Sir Francis, with his courage and determination, was an inspiration to a generation of yachtsmen and women As Patron of the UK Sailing Academy, the new custodians of *Gipsy Moth IV*, I have followed her 40th anniversary adventures with great interest, and was delighted to sail aboard her in Sydney Harbour last year, when I opened a *Gipsy Moth* Exhibition at the Australian National Maritime Museum.

Just as Sir Francis faced many challenges on his solo voyage round the world in 1966-67, so, too, have the young crews today, and I have been able to meet some of the young people who took part in the 28,000-mile voyage, many of whom had life-changing experiences aboard the yacht. One of the most exciting aspects of the voyage is the way it has mixed many challenges for the young crew with an increased awareness of the environmental challenges affecting our oceans.

I hope you will join with me in supporting this shining example of education in action and in helping to keep the spirit of adventure alive in the hearts and minds of a new generation of young people.

Anne

HRH Princess Royal

Gipsy Moth *'will help to keep the spirit of adventure alive in the hearts and minds of a new generation of young people,'* said Princess Anne

Inspired by
Gipsy Moth IV...

Dame Ellen MacArthur

I have read stories of Sir Francis Chichester and *Gipsy Moth* since I was young. The adventures of this great boat and this great sailor inspired me to follow my dreams to one day take to the sea on my own, but I never imagined that I would have the opportunity to sail onboard her. As a kid, I remember visiting her as she sat entombed in concrete. What a sad end to a historic boat that could have been.

So it was a great honour to be asked to join lead skipper Richard Baggett and his crew of young people on Sunday 3rd June 2007 for the final part of *Gipsy Moth IV*'s global adventure as she sailed into her new home port of Cowes to join the UKSA's fleet of yachts.

In her day, *Gipsy Moth* was at the height of modern technology and seamanship. She really is the most beautiful boat and it is fantastic to see her back out on the water in her full glory – Sir Francis Chichester would be very proud.

I am delighted that *Gipsy Moth IV* will continue to take young people, including children from the Ellen MacArthur Trust who are on the road to recovery from cancer, leukaemia and other serious illnesses, on challenging sailing experiences in the Solent and beyond. This amazing project that *Yachting Monthly*, the UKSA and many others have worked so hard to achieve, will allow new generations to learn about her past and share in her future.

Ellen, pictured below with some of Gipsy Moth's *young crew at Greenwich in 2005 and (right) with Giles Chichester at the opening of Skandia Cowes Week 2005.*

Barry Pickthall/PPL

Barry Pickthall/PPL

A legend relaunched

Giles Chichester

The safe return of *Gipsy Moth IV* from her second globe-girdling adventure – 40 years to the day since my father completed his solo circumnavigation – was the culmination of a tremendous effort and achievement to bring her back to life. A much better fate than befell the *Golden Hind* in which Sir Francis Drake became the first Englishman to sail round the world. She rotted away at Rotherhithe on the Thames and barely lasted 50 years after her triumph.

Gipsy Moth IV was rescued from a similar fate in dry dock at Greenwich by a great co-operative effort sparked off by Paul Gelder, the editor of *Yachting Monthly*, and carried forward by David Green and the United Kingdom Sailing Academy, with help and support from thousands of people and organisations. The Maritime Trust played a crucial role by agreeing to 'sell' *Gipsy Moth* for a symbolic pound and a gin and tonic.

The most exciting aspect of *Gipsy Moth IV*'s second circling of the world has been the way so many young people have been involved as crew members. Her passage along the trade wind route and through the two great canals of Panama and Suez has given a new generation a taste of life at sea and a sense of adventure. I rather fancy *Gipsy Moth IV* preferred the trade wind sailing to the empty wastes of the Southern Ocean and Roaring Forties.

Like every proper adventure there have been setbacks, including one which attracted a lot of publicity when a navigation blunder put the boat aground on a coral reef in the Pacific. I guess my father would have tut-tutted at the poor navigation – although I can remember him getting pretty unpopular with my mother for going aground in the Solent. He would certainly have taken his hat off to the successful recovery of *Gipsy Moth*.

He would also be intrigued that *Gipsy Moth* has gone down to the lonely sea and the sky (*pace* Masefield) again and is enjoying a second life with all sorts of new kit not available to him, GPS and modern communication systems in particular, while showing a new generation what he achieved in the ketch.

'I fancy Gipsy Moth *preferred trade wind sailing to the empty wastes of the Southern Ocean.'*

Making a dream come true

Introduction Paul Gelder

If this book has a theme, it's triumphing against the odds, just as Chichester did. Having a dream to see *Gipsy Moth IV* liberated from 37 years' entombment in dry dock at Greenwich and sailing round the world again, was the easiest part of this five-year project. Making the dream come true needed an army of true believers to keep the faith.

The key players included millionaires, knights of the realm, disadvantaged youngsters living in condemned inner-city tower blocks, retired shipwrights, captains of industry and teenagers battling cancer. They all shared one ultimate aim: to see *Gipsy Moth* back in the water with a second life, sailing round the world.

We all shared one ultimate aim: to see Gipsy Moth *back in the water with a second life.*

The sea is a great leveller and no ego could be allowed to eclipse the star of the show – *Gipsy Moth IV* and her indomitable partnership with Sir Francis Chichester. Their inspirational adventure was always the centrepiece of this project, and its catalyst.

I could never have imagined quite how far the ripples would spread from one small stone thrown in the water in February 2003, when I wrote to The Maritime Trust asking them to support a campaign by *Yachting Monthly* to save the iconic ketch.

Since then, thousands of column inches have been written in newspapers and magazines all over the world. Hundreds of hours of TV and radio were broadcast from the UK, Tahiti, Auckland and Sydney – and from countries that *Gipsy Moth IV* had never even visited.

Fewer people have sailed on *Gipsy Moth IV*, even after her second circumnavigation, than have been into outer space – and in rough weather some crew may have felt they were going into orbit! For everyone involved, it's been a privilege to gain an insight into one man's amazing singlehanded achievement against the odds.

The message is, if you believe in something strongly enough, you can make it happen. Chichester's slogan was: 'I hate being frightened, but, even more, I detest being prevented by fright.' In today's language he was saying: 'Go for it!'

Graham Snook/Yachting Monthly

Fewer people have sailed in Gipsy Moth than have been in outer space.

The Chichester spirit of adventure

The media called it 'The Loneliest Journey in the World'. At an age when most 65-year-old men are collecting a free bus pass, Francis Chichester made the fastest circumnavigation of the globe in 1966-67.

One of the most unforgettable pictures in the history of small boats sailing across big oceans is *Gipsy Moth IV* rounding Cape Horn under bare poles and spitfire jib. To starboard lay a horrifying white crater: the death of a giant wave, one and a half times the length of the *Gipsy Moth*'s 53ft hull. Back in the 1960s it was a voyage on the far frontier of sailing endeavours and Chichester became the most celebrated British sailor since Nelson.

'Wild horses could not drag me down to Cape Horn and that sinister Southern Ocean again in a small boat,' he said later. 'There is something nightmarish about deep breaking seas and screaming winds. I had a feeling of helplessness before the power of the waves came rolling down on top of me.'

Yet it was never any good expecting Chichester to take things easy, or drift into retirement. He had a spirit that was driven to seek new things. He should have died long before in the wreck of a crashed seaplane in Japan, or a London cancer ward.

What motivated this single-minded, rebellious and romantic adventurer? Born in Devon in 1901, his father was a sombre, stern Anglican clergyman who made it clear that Francis was the *least favourite* of his four children. Thus the boy grew into a shy loner... with an impetuous streak.

Chichester later said his father 'seemed to be disapproving of everything I did... waiting to squash any enthusiasm.' On one occasion, when young Francis was bitten by a snake near the family rectory at Shirwell, his father admonished him: 'What a thing to bring an adder home! It might have bitten your sister!' he roared, instructing his son to 'Get out on your bicycle at once and go to the infirmary in Barnstaple.' It was four miles away up and down steep hills.

From the age of 13 to 17, Chichester was sent to Marlborough College. 'Its iron discipline was prison-like,' he said. 'The diet 150 years out of date.'

A hero's welcome for Francis Chichester as he returns to Plymouth after 119 days and 15,517 miles.

Chichester Archive/PPL

Gipsy Moth *sails past Cape Horn*
under bare poles and spitfire jib.

Aged 18, he left England on a steamship, bound for New Zealand, with just ten gold sovereigns, a gift from his father. He worked his passage as an assistant stoker – calling himself 'George', in case Francis sounded cissy – and vowed not to return until he had a fortune of £20,000.

He found jobs as a sheepshearer, lumberjack, coal miner, gold prospector, writer and door-to-door newspaper salesman. It was property, first as a land agent, then a developer, that made his fortune. He and a partner planted a million trees and sold off small lots as sites for weekend cottages. He then took to the air, selling joyrides – 6,000 passengers at ten shillings a head. He took flying lessons himself and became hooked and was nicknamed 'Chich'.

On a visit home to England, he secretly resolved to buy a plane and fly back to Australia. The plane was a Gipsy Moth, and a few months later, having mastered astro-navigation, he became only the second person to fly the 12,000 miles from London to Sydney solo, arriving after 19 days and 22 stops, including surviving a crash landing in Libya.

At the age of 28 he was acclaimed a hero of the skies and wrote a book about his experience, *Solo to Sydney*. Later, he fitted floats to make Gipsy Moth into a seaplane and made the first solo flight across the Tasman Sea to New Zealand. Landing at tiny islands to refuel was 'like trying to find a penny in a field.' If his fuel had run out certain death would have followed. His next daring plan, to fly round the world, did end in disaster, when he flew into telephone wires taking off from a small harbour near Yokohama, Japan. Miraculously he survived the crash – but with 13 broken bones.

The 30-year-old daredevil settled down to a quieter interlude. But the urge to circle the world 'lay dormant in me, like a gorse seed which will lie in the earth for 50 years until the soil is disturbed,' he said.

Back home in England, he married Sheila Craven and, having been turned down as a fighter pilot because of poor eyesight, he became a researcher at the Air Ministry during the Second World War. After the war, he set up business as a map publisher. He came late to sailing and was already well into his fifties when he advertised his services as a navigator and found a crewing opportunity with a retired P&O commodore.

His first voyage, to Holland, was not a happy experience. He wrote home: 'I really am a little schoolboy again with a very strict "headmaster" who gives me hell at all hours. In spite of all this, the trip is great fun.'

Smitten by sailing, in 1953 he bought a day cruiser, *Florence Edith*, for £1,150. Nervously, he rang Sheila. 'I've bought a boat!' and was amazed when she exclaimed, 'How wonderful, I've always wanted one!'

Renamed *Gipsy Moth II*, in tribute to the fragile plane whose wreckage he'd left in Japan, she had a waterline length of 7.3m (24ft) and displaced 8 tons. He kept her on an East Coast mooring at Brightlingsea. The first time Sheila went to meet him for a sail, she was left waiting at the jetty after he'd put her aground on the Buxey Sands. He didn't reach harbour until the following morning.

Shaving aboard Gipsy Moth IV, with her notorious roll was a risky operation

Chichester Archive/PPL.

Together they converted her from sloop to cutter rig for ocean racing. After a first Channel crossing in 1954 with son Giles, Chichester joined the Royal Ocean Racing Club and entered his first race across the North Sea. At the start he ran aground and lost his kedge anchor, but he managed to sail 2,510 miles in his first season.

By 1957 Sheila decided it was time to have a new boat, and Robert Clark was asked to design *Gipsy Moth III*, 12.1m (39ft 7in) LOA. She was built at Jack Tyrrell's boatyard in Arklow, Ireland, with an iron keel 'for bouncing off coral reefs in the Pacific' – because Chichester still wanted to circle the world.

'Few yachts can have been less visited by the owner during their building,' Chichester said in his book *The Lonely Sea and the Sky*. The reason? In 1958 Chichester was diagnosed as having carcinoma and told he would die without an operation to remove his lung. Some doctors claimed it was a lung abscess or a shadow on the X-Ray. Sheila, who had a strong belief in natural remedies and the power of prayer, refused an operation. Later, during a visit to the Royal Ocean Racing Club, next

Sir Francis Chichester's achievements with *Gipsy Moth IV*

- *Fastest voyage around the world by any small vessel – approximately twice as fast.*

- *Longest passage made by a small vessel without a port of call – 15,500 miles.*

- *More than twice the distance of the previous longest passage by a singlehander – 15,500 miles compared to 7,400 miles.*

- *Twice broke the record for a singlehander's week's run by more than 100 miles.*

- *Set a singlehanded record by covering 1,400 miles from point to point in 8 days.*

- *Twice exceeded the singlehanded speed record for a long passage – 131.75 miles per day for 107 days, and 130.25 miles per day for 119 days.*

- *Third true circumnavigation by a small vessel via Cape Horn.*

Rust-streaked and salt-stained, Gipsy Moth *sails into Plymouth after 119 days.*

Chichester Archive/PPL

door to his office, Chichester spotted on the notice board a proposal for a solo yacht race from Plymouth to New York.

His willpower and Sheila's self-devised holistic and macrobiotic diet meant that in 1960, more than two years after being taken ill, Chichester was one of four competitors to cross the start line in *Gipsy Moth III* in the first-ever solo transatlantic race. He finished in first place after 40 days – 16 days faster than the previous record. Ocean racing, it seemed, was good medicine and an avalanche of publicity engulfed him. He wrote a book, *Alone Across the Atlantic*. He also remained a vegetarian for the rest of his life, which lasted 14 years beyond the doctors' six-month death sentence.

In 1964 Chichester again competed in the OSTAR (Observer Singlehanded Transatlantic Race), but this time he was beaten by Frenchman Eric Tabarly sailing *Penduick II*, which had been specially built for the race.

A patriotic Lord Dulverton decided Chichester needed a 'proper, fast boat for the next race'. Thus the 53ft ketch *Gipsy Moth IV* was born, designed by Illingworth and

Primrose. But Chichester wanted to attempt 'the Everest of the sea' – a solo round the world race against the clock, via the three Great Capes of Good Hope, Leeuwin and Horn. He wanted to beat the best time of 100 days logged by the Australian wool clipper ships sailing to and from Sydney.

A month after setting off, in August, 1966, he celebrated his 65th birthday, wearing his famous green velvet smoking jacket that had been across the Atlantic with him six times and drinking champagne and brandy cocktails. After 107 days he arrived in Sydney, exhausted and with a litany of complaints about the yacht. His friend, Commander Erroll Bruce, thought the boat 'a masterpiece'.

But for Chichester, describing her as 'cantankerous' and 'needing an elephant to move the tiller', the voyage to Sydney had turned out to be a nightmare. A press campaign advised that he should end his voyage and 'cease to tempt fate'.

But in January 1967, he sailed *Gipsy Moth IV* from Australia in the teeth of a storm, 'a real Tasman terror'. The yacht capsized. 'Everything

A one shilling souvenir programme from May 1967, celebrating Chichester's homecoming after his circumnavigation.

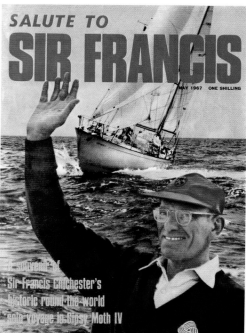

SALUTE TO **SIR FRANCIS**

MAY 1967   ONE SHILLING

A souvenir of Sir Francis Chichester's historic round-the-world solo voyage in Gipsy Moth IV

Chichester Archive/PPL

Chichester Archive/PPL

The lone sailor finds company — flying fish were frequent visitors to Gipsy Moth's *scuppers on both her circumnavigations. Good fried for breakfast.*

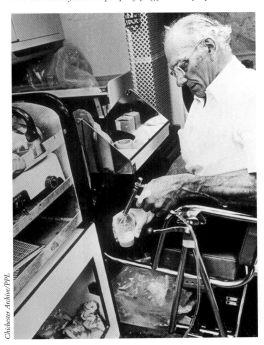

Chichester Archive/PPL

Chichester's gimballed chair, where he could eat and drink on the level — he's seen here pouring a Whitbread beer.

Chichester Archive/PPL

Waving to the crowds and hundreds of welcoming craft on his arrival in Sydney Harbour, after 107 days and 14,000 miles.

seems wrong about this voyage. I hate it and I'm frightened,' Chichester wrote. He rounded Cape Horn, swept along in a raging gale, and reached Plymouth in May, having made the fastest ever round-the-world voyage in a small yacht (226 days). He broke a host of other sailing records.

When the *New York Times* asked Chichester what drove him to take on such desolate, solitary voyages, he said he took tremendous satisfaction from being the first man to achieve something. 'And I like to do them alone … when I'm alone I perform twice as efficiently. I don't have to defer to other people's opinions. I'm just a loner, I suppose.' Was this the legacy of his stern upbringing?

Chichester's final solo voyage was in a new *Gipsy Moth V*, in the 1972 OSTAR. Seventy years old and weakened by a cancerous tumour on his spine, he was forced to turn

back. 'Where is he going?', 'New riddle?' were the news headlines.

'Weak and cold. Want rest,' transmitted Chichester.

Eventually, Giles and John Anderson, a journalist and sailing friend, were winched from a helicopter to a Navy frigate and transferred to *Gipsy Moth V* to help sail her the last 250 miles back to Plymouth.

Sir Francis died two months later, just before his 71st birthday, on 26 August 1972. At the funeral service in Plymouth his coffin was carried by Giles and flag officers of the Royal Western Yacht Club. He was buried in Shirwell churchyard, where he had been christened. As biographer Anita Leslie wrote: 'Sheila stood in the golden evening light. So much was over for her – the toughness, the tantrums, the tenderness. It would be strange for her and Giles to return to St James's Place without him.'

Sir Francis Chichester surveying damage onboard Gipsy Moth V during his solo transatlantic speed challenge.

Chichester Archive/PPL

At the memorial service at Westminster Abbey, Prime Minister Edward Heath, spoke from the heart of this fellow sailor's great achievements.

Sir Chay Blyth recounts how, as a young paratrooper fresh from rowing the Atlantic, he queued for more than two hours at the 1968 London Boat Show to get a signed copy of *Gipsy Moth Circles the World*. Just as he got to within two places from his table, Chichester suddenly pronounced. 'Right. That's it, I'm off to lunch.'

Sir Robin Knox-Johnston recalls: 'I met him several times and we would often talk on the phone. One day I telephoned and asked him what he was up to and he answered… "I'm certainly not going to tell you….You would only try to do it first!"

The shy schoolboy, who furiously peddled his bicycle to hospital on a life-and-death mission to survive a deadly snake bite, had become one of Britain's greatest 20th century heroes. Forty years on, *Gipsy Moth IV* is assured to carry forward the legend of Francis Chichester, survivor, rebel and adventurer, to a new 21st century generation.

Chichester's five Gipsy Moths

The first Gipsy Moth, was the aeroplane made from wood and linen and weighing just 88 lbs, which Chichester bought in 1929.

Gipsy Moth II, the 24ft 8-ton wooden yacht built in 1938, was the vessel on which Chichester learned ocean racing. He bought her for £1.150.

Gipsy Moth III, a classic wooden yacht designed by Robert Clark, won the first singlehanded transatlantic race in 1960. She was a sea-kindly yacht, with a novel windvane invented by Chichester, which he called 'Miranda'.

Gipsy Moth IV the 53ft ketch designed by Illingworth and Primrose for Chichester's solo voyage around the world was cold-moulded and sat in dry dock at Greenwich for more than 35 years before *Yachting Monthly* began a campaign to restore her in 2003.

Gipsy Moth V, a 57ft wooden ketch designed by Robert Clark for Chichester's last solo adventure at the age of 70. She was wrecked on Gabo island, off Australia, by another solo sailor during another round the world race.

Why Gipsy Moth IV had to be saved

'Why save a boat rotting away in dry dock for 37 years that drove her skipper to despair and needs hundreds of thousands of pounds spending on restoration?' many people have asked.

Even Sir Francis Chichester, the part-owner of *Gipsy Moth IV*, who sailed her solo round the world to a triumphant homecoming, said: 'She has no sentimental value to me at all. Now that I have finished, I don't know what will become of her. I only own the stern, while my cousin (Lord Dulverton) owns two thirds. For my part, I would sell any day. It would be better if about a third were sawn off. She is cantankerous and difficult and needs a crew of three – a man to navigate, an elephant to move the tiller and a 3ft 6in chimpanzee with arms 8ft long to get about below and work the gear!'

When *Yachting Monthly* launched the campaign to save *Gipsy Moth* in September 2003, one curmudgeonly correspondent wrote: 'What *Gipsy Moth IV* needs is a gallon of paraffin and a box of matches!' Another said: 'Not worth preserving… she was built for a stunt with no intention of durability. Burn her. Spend the money on something worthwhile, like the *Cutty Sark*.'

A few weeks later, some vandals did try to set fire to *Gipsy Moth*, but were thwarted – unlike the *Cutty Sark* incident, which followed in the summer of 2007.

Even in Greenwich dry dock, Gipsy Moth IV inspired people. But beneath the surface, her timbers were rotting away, thanks to deck leaks and rainwater.

Chris Laurens/PPL

The fact is, *Gipsy Moth* is one of the world's most famous small boats. She warmed the hearts of the most hard-bitten modern racing sailors and grizzled old seadogs and she was, and is, a vital part of Britain's maritime heritage.

When *Gipsy Moth*'s keel was laid in 1964 she was to be the 'best yacht money could buy'. No expense was spared and there were no statutory regulations governing design, construction or equipment.

She was the first custom-designed yacht for fast solo sailing around the world – hoping to achieve a passage target of 100 days from Plymouth to Sydney, Australia. She was the Open 60 of her day and Sir Francis was the pathfinder and pioneer. No one had designed a boat which could be close-winded, fast and light-displacement, yet strong enough to stand up to a knowndown in the Southern Ocean.

Designer John Illingworth later said they could have designed a heavier, beamier boat which would have sailed more upright, but she would have been much slower.

True, others had sailed singlehanded round the world before Chichester, like Joshua Slocum (1895-98). But theirs were leisurely cruises, often taking years. Chichester's was a defiant, harrowing race against the clock, in a bold attempt to beat the time of the Victorian clipper ships, including the *Cutty Sark*. *Gipsy Moth IV* was then the biggest boat conceived for solo sailing – a 53ft ketch for a man aged 64!

In nautical terms, she was like a Battle of Britain Spitfire – inextricably a part of Britain's finest hour at sea. Chichester's record-breaking circumnavigation inspired many of today's sailing stars – including Dame Ellen MacArthur, Sir Robin Knox Johnston and Sir Chay Blyth, all of whom followed in his illustrious wake as solo round the world record-breakers. As a schoolgirl Ellen MacArthur would take the best-selling book, *Gipsy Moth Circles the World*, out of the library and re-read it with the same

In nautical terms, Gipsy Moth *was like a Battle of Britain Spitfire – part of Britain's finest hour at sea.*

Chichester Archive/PPL

sense of excitement that today's teenagers have for the Harry Potter books … and the Southern Ocean could prove just as malevolent as Lord Voldemort.

'Wild horses could not drag me down to Cape Horn and that sinister Southern Ocean again in a small boat,' wrote Chichester after his voyage. 'There is something nightmarish about deep breaking seas and screaming winds… I had a feeling of helplessness before the power of the waves came rolling down on top of me.'

Between 27 August 1966, when Chichester sailed from Plymouth, and 28 May 1967, when he returned, via Cape Horn, after one stop in Sydney, Australia, he effectively re-wrote the Guinness book of ocean sailing records. But more than that, his solitary, heroic feat was said to have restored the illusion of British mastery of the Seven Seas. He was the new conqueror, like Scott of the Antarctic or Hillary of Everest – for his voyage was the sailor's Everest.

A quarter of a million people lined Plymouth Hoe on a spring evening to welcome home the man who had sailed faster than anyone before him. On the way, he'd celebrated his 65th birthday with a champagne cocktail wearing his green velvet smoking jacket. 'My only 'slip-up is that I left my bow-tie behind…' he wrote in his logbook.

This was the era of the Swinging Sixties, with hippies, drop-outs, flower power and free love and one commentator wrote that 'Sir Francis stood as a living refutation to the seedy claims of sex, drugs and rock and roll.'

When the Queen knighted him at Greenwich, with the same sword that Elizabeth I used to knight Sir Francis Drake in 1580, thousands watched on TV in pubs and homes across the country. 'People found something to celebrate in themselves,' wrote Jonathan Raban in his introduction to Chichester's classic book of his voyage, *Gipsy Moth Circles the World*. 'Their new stooped, short-sighted knight reminded them of the salt in their veins, their brave historic past, their English mettle.'

Britain had a new sporting super hero to celebrate. You could say, perhaps, that Chichester was the David Beckham of his day – even if he was old enough to be Beckham's grandfather!

In the 21st century, the reverberations of Chichester's achievement still stand the test of time. Others half his age set off to break his record, often in greater comfort and with better equipment. But Chichester will always be the first. After his voyage, *Gipsy Moth* was exhibited at the London Boat Show in Earls Court in January 1968, and then offered by Lord Dulverton to the Greater London Council, who undertook to put her on display to the public at the river-side Cutty Sark Gardens as a permanent memorial to the epic voyage and her bid to beat *Cutty Sark*'s 100-day record. A public appeal was launched so Sir Edward McAlpine's firm, which built the dry dock for *Cutty Sark*, could now do the same for this doughty ketch. Thus *Gipsy Moth* was 'embalmed' in her concrete tomb. For many years she was open to the public and continued to inspire visitors.

Chichester knighted by the Queen at Greenwich with Sir Francis Drake's sword in July 1967.

Chichester Archive/PPL

Vandals and louts hurled rubbish onto Gipsy Moth's *deck and a few years after her first refit she was in a sorry state again.*

But in August 2001, on one of many visits to Greenwich, I stood alongside the land-locked ketch and saw her peeling paintwork encrusted with bird droppings. A lager lout's beer can lay on the sidedeck and burger containers had been lobbed into the cockpit. It seemed nothing less than the desecration of a maritime monument. I felt a special affinity to the Moth, since she had been 'born' in my home town of Emsworth, Hampshire, where her designers, John Illingworth and Angus Primrose, had an office at 36 North Street.

Boats like *Gipsy Moth* belong in the ocean. Rainwater rots them. They are meant to be sailed, not entombed or exhibited in museums. A wooden boat is a living entity, imbued with the spirit of those who built and sailed them.

Seven years earlier, in 1995, I had seen *Gipsy Moth* restored to a pristine state. The Maritime Trust, her owners since 1973, had arranged for her to be taken by road to the Maritime Workshop in Gosport, where shipwrights lovingly restored her. Two decades in dry dock with London's polluted air and acid rain lying in puddles on the deck and in the bilges, plus thousands of tourists tramping feet stepping aboard, had left their mark on her.

I went to Gosport to report for *Yachting Monthly* on the £30,000 refit being funded by the Trust and Nauticalia, a company which sells maritime artefacts, including models of *Gipsy Moth IV*.

A new plywood deck had been made and the cold-moulded Honduras mahogany hull, coachroof and cockpit were being refurbished and repainted. I discovered letters had arrived from nautical souvenir hunters as far away as America, asking for pieces of her old deck. I was given a piece myself by Bill Puddle, Managing Director of the workshop, which I kept on my desk in pride of place. Appropriately, Bill had begun his apprenticeship as a boat-builder aged 15 at Camper & Nicholsons, less then two miles away, where *Gipsy Moth* was built. Many of Camper's shipwrights who had helped to build her stopped by to re-examine their craftsmanship. The new deck was covered with a layer of hi-tech epoxy saturated matting to keep the London rain from rotting her when she returned to Greenwich in the spring.

Now, six years later in 2001, she was back in a sorry state once again, with rot in her coamings and the aft part of the cockpit. It would be a tragedy and a scandal if this relic of Britain's maritime heritage rotted away.

In September 2001, we had reported on a proposal to get *Gipsy Moth IV* sailing again as a 'flagship' for the International Sailing Craft Association (ISCA), making passages to its collection of historic craft at various sites around Britain.

But months on nothing had happened. The London Borough of Greenwich was demanding that the yacht couldn't be moved until a guarantee was given that the dry dock basin was filled in – at a cost of some £60,000! The Maritime Trust and ISCA simply didn't have the money. It was an impasse – and *Gipsy Moth* was the innocent victim.

Captain Simon Waite, Superintendent of Ships for the Maritime Trust and Master of the *Cutty Sark*, said *Gipsy Moth* was deteriorating because his workforce was so small. 'Apart from washing down her decks and airing her out occasionally, little is being done to look after her,' he admitted. There wasn't even any money for a part-time 'curator' so paying visitors could tour the ketch. It had been years since a member of the public had been below

Gipsy Moth leaves Greenwich, after almost 20 years, for her first re-fit in 1995.

Ray Little

Gipsy Moth's cracked decks. It had cost the Trust £10,000 a year to open the yacht to the public with only £5,000 gained in revenue.

In 2002, when I became editor of *Yachting Monthly*, the seed of an idea began to grow. In four years' time it would be the magazine's 100th birthday and I was looking for something special to mark the occasion. What better than a circumnavigation?

I discussed the idea of finding a suitable yacht which we could sail round the world with *Yachting Monthly* Features Editor Dick Durham. We were sure that one of the big manufacturers, like Jeanneau, Bavaria, or perhaps even Najad or Hallberg Rassy, might lend us a boat for the publicity they would gain. But shouldn't we be sailing and promoting a British boat from Rustler, Rival or Northshore?

What about re-fitting a second-hand yacht, with the bonus of a series of articles. But what sort of boat? Then the penny dropped. Supposing we could get our hands on *Gipsy Moth IV*? As soon as I discovered that 2006 was also the 40th anniversary of Chichester's voyage, as well our birthday year, all the pieces fell into place. If *Yachting Monthly* could find a suitable sponsor to foot the bill, we would have a fantastic story to cover and most of our readers were sailors, who, like me, had been inspired by Chichester.

The next day I rang Peter Seymour, one of the directors of the Blue Water Round the World Rally, an event *Yachting Monthly* had reported on for 10 years, to see if he would accept *Gipsy Moth* on the 2005-07 event. He was very enthusiastic and, after consulting with fellow directors, immediately offered to waive the rally fees, some £12,000 – including the costs of transiting the Panama and Suez Canals.

The rally would leave Gibraltar in October 2005 returning to the Mediterranean in spring 2007, just in time for a 40th anniversary homecoming.

Of course, this tradewind route with more than 20 stopovers, from the Caribbean to Tahiti, Australia, Singapore, Bali and Phuket, was perhaps not as adventurous as a Southern Ocean voyage. But a 22-month cruising circumnavigation through a tropical

Left: Bill Puddle from The Maritime Workshop, Gosport, with Gipsy Moth's tiller.

A new plywood deck, with epoxy saturated cloth, was installed on Gipsy Moth *during a 1995-96 refit at The Maritime Workshop.*

The author sits in the famous gimballed chair, where Chichester stayed level-headed while the boat heeled at crazy angles

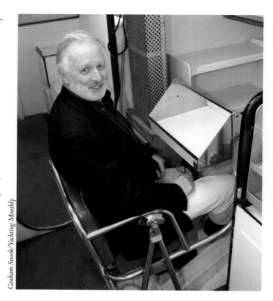

paradise seemed audacious enough for a 40-year-old lady, rather than a hair shirt, lonely passage via Cape Horn. The route would also offer more media coverage for sponsors, with plenty of exotic stopovers to change crew and introduce them to a variety of cultural experiences and climates. Plus the route was designed to take account of avoiding hurricane and tropical cyclones.

Before things went any further, it was time to speak to my publisher, Jessica Daw. Her first comment, perhaps understandably, was: 'We're in the business of publishing magazines, not restoring old boats!'

The phrase rang through my head for months to come as I promised her that the staff would not be deserting their desks to go blue water sailing in the trade winds and the magazine would not suffer. But I did need to find a reliable skipper who could take 22-months off work to sail the boat around the globe.

Yachting Monthly's freelance consultant editor James Jermain, who did much of the magazine's boat testing, and, like me, was from the generation inspired by Chichester's feat, seemed the ideal candidate. I phoned him to see if he might be interested. A few days later he admitted: 'I nearly bit the phone in my enthusiasm to be the first aboard the project. It's the chance of a lifetime!'

Next it was time to talk to *Gipsy Moth*'s owners. I rang Richard Doughty, Chief Executive and Director of Fund-raising at The Cutty Sark Trust, and secretary of the Maritime Trust, and invited him to lunch. Over pizza and a bottle of wine I outlined the scheme.

I was confident that *Yachting Monthly* would have no problem finding a sponsor to support a major refit of the yacht. We were ideally placed to guarantee the publicity they would want. The original builders, Camper & Nicholsons, might even be persuaded to take on the work. And surely British marine industry suppliers would leap at the chance to be involved in such a worthwhile project,

using it as a platform to promote their latest products? Many of *Gipsy Moth*'s original suppliers – like Lewmar, B&G, Blakes, International Paints, Avon dinghies, Henri-Lloyd and Kelvin Hughes – had grown into hugely successful companies and *Gipsy Moth* was a living advert for the longevity of their equipment.

If I couldn't spare *Yachting Monthly* writers, or pay freelance writers, for the voyage, we could offer places to deserving youngsters. We could run a competition in the national newspapers. Crewing the yacht with disadvantaged young people would add a new dimension to the project and give it a depth of purpose in the hunt for a sponsor.

The 40th anniversary voyage appealed to Richard. Something bold and imaginative was desperately needed, he said, to revive interest in the yacht's future. *Gipsy Moth* was the last small vessel in the Trust's original historic collection of 35 boats, which once included the steam-sail ship *The Warrior*, Captain Scott's *Discovery* and *Cambria*, the last Thames barge to trade under sail. Richard faced an uphill bid for fund-raising to restore *Cutty Sark*. He simply didn't have the resources in money or manpower to cope with Chichester's old yacht.

He invited me to visit *Gipsy Moth*, now locked up from public view. My first visit had been some 30 years before, when a 'curator' showed sightseers all the points of interest – from Chichester's snug quarter-berth and his ancient Marconi Kestrel radio (from which he made his twice weekly calls to the *Times* newspaper), to the Aladdin pink paraffin heater which kept him warm in the Southern Ocean and even the flannel, on which he grew his mustard and cress – a source of vitamin C at sea. I sat in the red gimballed chair where Chichester drank his beer and ate his meals. The cabin was 'haunted' by Chichester's presence … a time capsule in which the old man of the sea had sailed round the globe in solitary confinement … a prison cell just a few feet long and less than 5ft wide below decks. Fitting a full crew into a yacht designed for one man wouldn't be easy, but there were five berths, plus two pipe cots in the fo'c'sle.

By coincidence Ginnie Chichester, Giles's wife, visited the yacht that week with the entire staff of the Francis Chichester Ltd map and guide company. When told in confidence of our proposals their verdict was very favourable.

But I had to wait anxiously for several days before Richard rang me to say that a meeting of the trustees had also unanimously approved our plan to refit the yacht for *The Yachting Monthly-Gipsy Moth IV* Birthday Voyage (2005–2007).

The approval was subject to securing enough money to reinstate *Gipsy Moth* to a seaworthy condition.

It was thrilling that we had successfully negotiated the first hurdle. We had a scoop on our hands! Dick even ventured to say that rival sailing magazines would be jealous of our coup in getting a 'claim' on such a prime piece of Britain's maritime heritage. It was a marketing man's dream – and a publisher's nightmare!

Interestingly, I discovered that another famous sailor had campaigned to get his hands on *Gipsy Moth* – but had been turned down by the trustees at the Cutty Sark Society.

Donald Crowhurst campaigned unsuccessfully to charter Gipsy Moth IV *for his ill-fated entry in the 1969 Golden Globe Round the World Race.*

Donald Crowhurst, who became famous as the protagonist in what Chichester called 'the sea drama of the century', had written to the Town Clerk at Greenwich in January 1968 when he heard *Gipsy Moth* was to be put in dry dock. It would be madness, he said, 'to put the yacht to sleep' and he pleaded with the council to let him sail her non-stop round the world in *The Sunday Times* Golden Globe Race – an event organised as a follow-up to Chichester's feat. He promised to hand over all the money he expected to make from the race.

His letter was convincing: 'I know myself to be competent to undertake this voyage in a seamanlike manner …There are risks in such a project, but I ask you to share them with me, not only because they are acceptable but also because our tradition as a seafaring nation demands that we accept them.'

Mr Doble, the Town Clerk, passed Crowhurst's letter to the Cutty Sark Society, which was responsible for putting *Gipsy Moth* on display in dry dock. However, their plans were already well advanced and they decided to take no action.

Crowhurst didn't give up. He spoke to Frank Carr, chairman of the Ship Management Committee, and offered an immediate £5,000 donation, plus any prize money won, plus £10,000 insurance cover.

Carr thought it 'unwise to risk such a notable heroic symbol on the oceans' and said the boat was unsuitable, quoting Chichester's own scathing criticism of her. Also, £17,000 had already been committed to building the dry dock and Crowhurst's offer didn't begin to match the value of the boat.

A determined Crowhurst intensified his doomed campaign by lobbying some influential figures. He got the backing of Angus Primrose, the co-designer of *Gipsy Moth IV*, and some top yachting journalists. Bernard Hayman, editor of *Yachting World*, and Anthony Churchill of *Yachting & Boating Weekly*, thundered that boats, even famous ones, were meant for sailing, not museums.

Chichester was consulted but could find no evidence of Crowhurst's competence as a sailor from a third party. Crowhurst even offered to sail a solo passage of a few hundred miles as 'free trial without obligations' to prove he was worthy. But in the battle of wills, he lost his chance to 'borrow' *Gipsy Moth* and the Cutty Sark Society lost the goodwill of the yachting public, who contributed meagrely to the Gipsy Moth Fund.

Crowhurst eventually sailed off alone in an ill-prepared trimaran, *Teignmouth Electron*, into one of the biggest maritime mysteries of

modern times. Eight months and 10 days later his boat was found drifting in mid-Atlantic with no sign of him. Later, from his logbooks, it was deduced that the stresses of solo sailing an unfit boat had triggered a mental breakdown. In 16,000 miles of sailing, Crowhurst had never left the Atlantic. His logbooks showed he had faked his positions. No one knew for sure if he had committed suicide or fallen overboard, though the turmoil of his last log entries suggested the former. A compassionate account of the tragedy is told in the book, *The Strange Voyage of Donald Crowhurst*, by Nicholas Tomalin and Ron Hall. A documentary film, *Deep Water*, was also released in 2006.

I was conscious of the implications of Carr's comment to Crowhurst that 'it was unwise to risk such a notable heroic symbol on the oceans'. After all, another solo sailor had borrowed Chichester's *Gipsy Moth V* for another round the world race – the 1982-83 BOC Challenge – and come to grief when he fell asleep off Australia and the yacht ran onto the rocks at Gabo lighthouse. As the wooden yacht broke up, pounded by the surf, Desmond Hampton borrowed a chainsaw from the lighthouse keeper to salvage winches, hatches and deck gear. By next morning the yacht was driftwood. Less than 400m (1,200ft) was all that separated *Gipsy Moth* and her deadly course onto the barren outcrop of rocks on this south-east extremity of Australia from the open sea.

Even though we were sailing around the world on a trade wind route – the so-called 'coconut milk run' across the Pacific – and we would have a crew of at least six, I had sailed twice myself in French Polynesia and heard and read enough stories about shipwrecks on low-lying coral reefs to have a nagging voice in the back of mind echoing Carr's concerns.

How would it look if *Yachting Monthly*'s campaign to rescue *Gipsy Moth* from rotting away in dry dock ended with her being pounded to pieces in the surf on some remote atoll hundreds of miles from any rescue attempt?

Chichester's Gipsy Moth V *was wrecked in the 1982-83 BOC Challenge solo race when she ran into Gabo island after the skipper fell asleep.*

Ace/PPL

Bill Shaw, one of Camper & Nicholsons top shipwrights discovered extensive rot on his first visit to Greenwich in 2003

Before we went public with the campaign, at Southampton Boat Show in September 2003, it was time to write to Giles Chichester, Sir Francis' son. I wanted to be assured of all the support we could get for the voyage, with all its risks. I invited him to be a patron of our campaign and Richard invited him to join the steering group.

At this stage all the details of our project were confidential. We wanted all the loose ends tied up and everything in place before launching the campaign to find a title sponsor.

Giles, now a Conservative MEP for the European Parliament, with special responsibility for Devon and Cornwall, wrote back enthusiastically saying, 'Gipsy Moth has languished ashore for too long and needs a good run at sea. Judging by my father's experience in the trade winds, she will go round the world very well in those conditions. I hope Camper's get their sums right this time, having significantly overrun on cost when they built the yacht in the first place!'

When I mentioned the shipwreck of *Gipsy Moth V*, I took heart from Giles' comment that a shipwreck on a brave ocean adventure was preferable to *Gipsy Moth IV* rotting away ignominiously in a land-bound dry dock. Four years later, those words offered comfort when I got a phone call on a Sunday morning to say *Gipsy Moth* was shipwrecked on a coral reef 200 miles from Tahiti.

Now the next job was to get *Gipsy Moth* surveyed, to find out the cost of making her seaworthy again – and whether, in fact, it was possible or cost-effective. I approached Pat Lilley, then Managing Director of Camper & Nicholsons, owned by Nautor's Swan, who had built the boat for Chichester and his cousin, Lord Dulverton. Pat generously offered to come to Greenwich and look over the boat himself with an expert for no fee. The expert was Bill Shaw, one of the C&N's top shipwrights. I was to see a lot more of Bill over the months to come.

'Spike testing' the stern sections of Gipsy Moth's hull revealed wood as rotten as a soft pear

Clipper Ventures

Challenge Business

Veteran solo circumnavigators Sir Robin Knox-Johnston and Sir Chay Blyth backed Yachting Monthly's *campaign to save* Gipsy Moth IV.

I also invited *Yachting Monthly* columnist Tom Cunliffe to be present. He is a wooden boat aficionado, and owner, who had served on the technical sub-committee of the Historic Ships Committee for six years at the stage when the core collection was being decided. He had also offered to be a relief skipper on the voyage in the event that James Jermain found 22-months away from home too arduous! James came along, too, to get a close-up of what might be his new home for many months.

We all met up at Greenwich on 9 May 2003. Using ladders to climb down into the dry dock, Tom produced a yachting knife and stuck it into the sternpost. It disappeared up to the hilt. The wood was as rotten and as soft as a pear. Bill Shaw prodded other parts of the hull and discovered the rot was extensive. It was worse than I'd hoped. We all adjourned to the *Cutty Sark* for a pow-wow in the plush surroundings of the panelled Master's Cabin, where Richard Doughty had laid on a buffet lunch.

Pat Lilley was understandably upset at the state of *Gipsy Moth*'s decline just seven years after her refit. Having found one of Chichester's original frying pans in the bilges, along with a beer keg, he wondered how much work had been done before she was laid up in dry dock some 35 years ago.

The biggest problem was where leaks through the new deck, possibly made worse by a vandal who had kicked in a cockpit coaming, had allowed rainwater into the bilges.

One thing was clear, if something wasn't done soon, *Gipsy Moth* would be lost to the nation forever, beyond any economic repair, let alone the possibility of ever putting to sea again.

Six days later Bill Shaw returned to Greenwich to carry out a more thorough survey and submitted a three-page report. The good news was that much of the ketch had survived intact, especially the cold-moulded hull. The forepeak, chart space and galley area appeared to be in good order. But when the new plywood deck was fitted, the coachroof and cockpit coaming had not been removed. The old deck was cut out some 200mm outside the coaming and the new one butted up to it. There was extensive rot in many places. The stern post was rotten and the hull area around it needed major surgery: over 1,000 hours. The cockpit and companionway needed total renewing: another 600 hours work.

In total, the initial estimate was that *Gipsy Moth IV* required about 2,500 hours of shipwright's work. The repair bill would be at least £100,000, plus further costs incurred in replacing the engine and the rigging, surveying the masts, making new sails plus all

University of Greenwich

Graham Snook/Yachting Monthly

Richard Doughty, from the Cutty Sark and Maritime Trust, got approval for our campaign and Marie-Helen Bowden helped in the long search for suitable sponsors.

the new gear she would need. Considering the original cost of building *Gipsy Moth* was around £33,000 it was one hell of a boatyard bill. But how can you put a price on history?

I reckoned we'd need at least £400–500,000 to secure the refit and cover the cost of the circumnavigation – this included the stopover in Sydney, Australia, which was not part of the Blue Water Rally route. There was no shortage of enthusiasm, but what we desperately needed was a rich sponsor!

By now, Sir Robin Knox-Johnston had agreed to become a patron of the campaign and Ellen MacArthur the first member of our supporters' club. At 24, she had already been catapulted to stardom as the fastest woman sailor and the youngest person solo round the world (94-days) in the 2000-2001 Vendee Globe. In 2005 she'd do it in 71 days in the trimaran *B&Q*.

Sir Robin had certainly been inspired by Chichester's voyage and recalled in his book, *A World of My Own*, a conversation with his father in 1967, wondering if French sailor Eric Tabarly was going to beat Chichester's record by sailing a trimaran round the world – perhaps non-stop. 'That's about all there's left to do now, isn't it?' said his father. The words 'non-stop' gave Robin the idea to enter *The Sunday Times* Golden Globe Race.

'Chichester was really the catalyst for me,' he said. 'I was in South Africa when *Gipsy Moth*

passed the Cape of Good Hope and I really felt that his voyage left only one thing to be done. Sadly, as you know, I was unable to gain sponsorship for the Golden Globe, which means I may not be a good person as patron!'

Others added their weight to the campaign. Sir Julian Oswald, Admiral of the Fleet, and chairman of The Maritime Trust, said: '*Gipsy Moth IV* and Sir Francis Chichester are sailing legends at the centre of Britain's remarkable heritage of sail. We are proud to have this exciting opportunity to let this historic boat break free from her dry berth of the last 37 years.'

Roy Clare, director of the National Maritime Museum at Greenwich, also offered enthusiastic backing and support in kind – even crew volunteers! 'Your idea challenges logic, but it has romance that gives it strength and deserves full support. Go for it!' he wrote to me.

Giorgio Bendoni, who had taken over as Managing Director at Camper & Nicholsons, also offered his support to help restore the yacht, but the company was not in a position to do it free of charge.

'C&N has built many of the world's most famous yachts, but few have captured the hearts and imaginations of the public as *Gipsy Moth IV*,' he acknowledged. 'Now she needs urgent work if she is to survive.'

In July we put the finishing touches to the campaign launch in the October issue of *Yachting Monthly*, which went on sale at Southampton Boat Show. A new section of our website went 'live' at the same time, highlighting the history of *Gipsy Moth* and her sad decline.

The most heartwarming outcome of the launch was the sheer number of offers of help, large and small, from yachtsmen. Many emailed, wrote letters and phoned to say how much they owed to Chichester's inspirational voyage.

The press hailed it was one of the most exciting maritime heritage projects of our time. *The Times* headline was 'MacArthur joins bid to steer *Gipsy Moth* back to sea' and *The Western Morning News* in Plymouth headlined their story: 'Dream to recreate *Gipsy Moth* voyage'. There were TV and radio interviews spreading the news far and wide. Sailors at the Cruising Yacht Club of Australia and the Sydney Royal Yacht Squadron offered a welcome 'as big as the one given to Francis Chichester in December 1966.'

Our sailing website forums buzzed with debate on the pros and cons of restoration. Two independent TV companies wanted to make a documentary on the restoration. Offers of help from the marine industry included a new teak deck, electronic instruments, oilskins, and all the stainless steel work we needed. Readers offered donations.

By the time of our next issue we reported that The Maritime Trust had agreed that whoever paid the bill for *Gipsy Moth IV*'s refit could become her new owner, subject to securing enough funds for her long-term future. Ownership would be transferred to an individual, a corporation or a consortium – anyone prepared to take responsibility for her long-term survival and preservation. Ideally, this would be as a sailing boat rather than a static object.

Within days I was amazed to receive two generous offers from readers, in return for ownership. One for £200,000, came from a company director John Clarke, who, like Chichester, was a pilot and a sailor. He wanted to join the circumnavigation with his partner. The other offer, for £100,000, was from another yachtsman who wrote: 'My interest stems from a great admiration for Chichester and *Gipsy Moth* and the possibility of being involved in saving a magnificent piece of sailing history.'

I met John with James Jermain and there were discussions with Richard and The Maritime Trust. John was willing to allow public access to *Gipsy Moth* after the voyage and while still in his ownership.

Alas, the money was not enough for the refit and offered no guarantee of securing the long-term future of the yacht. The idea of the yacht going into private ownership seemed fraught with problems.

Later John and Pam bought their own 53ft ketch, a French Super Maramu called *Kaimin*, got married and sailed off on the next Blue Water Round the World Rally (2007–09).

The search for a title sponsor went on. Scores of letters and phone calls were made. Proposals were sent out to top company executives who were sailors: men like Charles Dunstone, of Car Phone Warehouse, and well-known philanthropist Mike Gooley, who set up Trailfinders and has donated millions to charity.

At Annapolis Boat Show in America, I met Richard Matthews, boss of Oyster Marine, who had shown interest. His company, Southampton Yacht Services, had undertaken the refit of the classic J-class yacht *Velsheda*. I also met Paul Strzelecki, Joint Chief Executive of Henri-Lloyd, the company which supplied Chichester's oilskins. He declined to be a title sponsor but agreed to supply clothing at favourable rates. Skandia Life Assurance, sponsors of Cowes Week, and Schroders UK, sponsors of London Boat Show, were also approached. Interest was shown by Peter Harrison, the GBR Olympic Team backer, and news of the restoration had reached Buckingham Palace where the founding president of The Maritime Trust, HRH the Duke of Edinburgh, expressed his delight that the 'next chapter in the yacht's history was about to begin.'

But was it? The campaign had created tremendous interest, with many generous offers, but none was big enough to take on the task.

In January at the 2004 London Boat Show at ExCel I approached Leonardo Ferragamo, scion of the Italian shoe and fashion house, and boss of Nautor's Swan, owners of Camper & Nicholsons. Since *Gipsy Moth* was one of their most iconic yachts, could they be persuaded to become a title sponsor?

Georgio Bendoni, C&N's new MD, decided to undertake a second, more detailed, survey before they made any decision.

The second survey, eight months after the first, showed that *Gipsy Moth* was deteriorating fast. The number of shipwrights' hours had shot up from 2,500 to 3,200. And some jobs were guesswork, because areas of the yacht were not accessible. At a meeting at C&N in Gosport I pressed our case and screened a DVD of the TV coverage the project had received so far. Present were Marie-Helene Bowden, from The Maritime Trust and Nicia Carter-Johnson, IPC Marine Media's Assistant Publisher, who explained the business plan and the tax breaks.

While title sponsorship was out of the question, Giorgio said that the company would agree to undertake the restoration as a charitable project at cost price – as soon as we could find a sponsor.

Seven months after the campaign was announced, another *Yachting Monthly* reader, Terry Lundberg, had a proposition. Terry, a keen sailor with a Bavaria 40, had set up a registered charity, The Youth Yachting Trust, to teach sailing to disadvantaged young adults. He was about to make a 'substantial' grant application to Sport England and thought a collaboration with the *Gipsy Moth* project could be beneficial to both of us.

Terry's vision to help under-privileged teenagers was a perfect match for the project, but he had no premises and no funding and,

like us, was looking for a backer. We met three times but it was a chicken-and-egg situation.

More than 12 months of letters, emails, phone calls and meetings had failed to find a suitable sponsor and we were running out of time. It seemed we would need a miracle if we were to make the start of the Blue Water Rally in Gibraltar in just 13 months.

Just as I was beginning to despair, the cavalry came riding over the hill in the shape of David Green, the CEO at the UK Sailing Academy in Cowes.

David had a dream, too.

David Green and Frank Fletcher from the UK Sailing Academy shared the dream so save Gipsy Moth IV

UKSA

The restoration and relaunch

The first time I met David Green he was standing next to Princess Anne. As a patron of the UK Sailing Academy, she was visiting their Cowes HQ to name a new yacht in the fleet. I was there with Marie-Helen Bowden, Development Director of the Maritime Trust, to promote the *Gipsy Moth IV* project. It was September 2004, exactly a year after we had launched the campaign at Southampton Boat Show.

The Princess, herself an enthusiastic sailor with a Rustler 36, showed keen interest in *Yachting Monthly*'s proposal. 'But shouldn't you be at the boat show?' she joked. This was the first of eight occasions when I would meet the Princess over the coming two-and-a-half years. Seven of them were at Green's instigation. She was an ardent supporter of *Gipsy Moth IV.*

'Three cheers for Gipsy Moth IV!' was called from a deckful of supporters on the Cutty Sark.

Graham Snook/Yachting Monthly

David Green grasped the ethos of the project immediately. Like others before him, he could see it was a fantastic promotional vehicle for the UKSA, handed to him on a plate: Save an iconic vessel. Celebrate a legendary sailor. Give young people a life-changing journey.

Unlike others before him, he was in the perfect position to make it happen. He was boss of a big sailing school with a fleet of over 300 craft. The UKSA was a registered, non profit-making charity set up in 1987. *Gipsy Moth IV* would be a 'flagship'. She would be used and cared for. They even had a workshop, where they trained people in maintenance. And when the voyage round the world was over, she would have the guarantee of a secure after-life, being used, not neglected.

In the following days, discussions went on between Richard Doughty and Marie-Helene at the Maritime Trust and the UKSA, culminating in a landmark lunch in October at the SE10 restaurant in Greenwich, where we toasted our new sponsor. David Green admitted: 'A few tears have been shed by our staff in Cowes at the thought of being involved in saving such a national treasure.'

The UKSA would buy *Gipsy Moth* for a symbolic £1 and a gin and tonic. The drink symbolised the spirit of Chichester, who revealed that the lowest moment on his epic voyage was when the gin ran out! The UKSA would also inject £40,000 cash to the restoration fund. The Trust had already pledged a further £10,000 when a sponsor was found.

Graham Snook/Yachting Monthly

Staff from Yachting Monthly *and the UK Sailing Academy at Greenwich on November 17, 2004, when* Gipsy Moth IV *finally left to begin her second life.*

Now the serious fund-raising could begin. Once the yacht was taken from Greenwich, other people would start to believe this dream could come true. The plan would gather its own momentum. I was confident the marine industry would rally round. Giorgio at Camper & Nicholsons had been ready and waiting to get started on the refit for some months.

David also was eager to get his hands on *Gipsy Moth IV*. There was almost a jealous rivalry between us, like two men fighting over a mistress. And *Gipsy Moth IV* was certainly that – and a demanding one, too! Having turned down other 'suitors', I was thrilled we'd found her a suitable partner, but at the same time it was hard to let go of the project I'd nurtured for 18 months. As the new owner of *Gipsy Moth IV*, David would now call the shots. He also had the staff to sail *Gipsy Moth IV* around the world and although it was part of our 'memorandum of agreement' that *Yachting Monthly* was guaranteed a berth for a writer on each leg of the voyage, James could no longer be the skipper. The project, however, would be a partnership between the UKSA, *Yachting Monthly* and The Maritime Trust.

But first we had to find out if *Gipsy Moth* could be made seaworthy. The first of many meetings was held at C&N at the beginning of November. A 'mission statement' for the restoration had to be written by the UKSA – we agreed the refit would retain as much of the original gear for seagoing use as possible – and a contract drawn up. Labour would be charged at 'cost' (£25 per hour plus VAT). I bought in Paul Jeffes, a marine surveyor and then *Yachting Monthly*'s technical editor, as a consultant. The boat would have to be coded for sail training by the Maritime & Coastguard Agency. It was agreed that the findings of a 'deep survey' would be reported at a meeting in three weeks on 10 December.

There were 1001 things to do. The UKSA and C&N had VAT and tax issues to sort out, including the status of companies donating products free of charge. Suppliers had to be chosen and we set up another meeting to discuss fund-raising, a supporters' club, media coverage and PR opportunities. The Royal Albert Yacht Club and Royal Naval Club in Portsmouth let us use their library for a meeting.

Bob Bradfield

The first public donation to the restoration fund was £15,000 from offshore yachtsman Stephen Thomas, 51, who had been inspired by Chichester and sailed around the world with his wife, Catherine, and son James in the 1995–97 Blue Water Rally, then called the Trade Winds Rally.

A successful computer software designer, Stephen, from Cambridge, was also a rally director. He made his donation by email from his yacht, *Magic Dragon*, in Chile, en route to Patagonia and Antarctica. Tragically, a few weeks later he was killed when he fell down a crevasse. In his memory The Stephen Thomas

Left to right: Paul Gelder, Ginnie Chichester, Richard Doughty, C&N's Giorgio Bendoni and David Green with Noel Lister (seated) from the UKSA.

Graham Snook/Yachting Monthly

Sailing Bursary was set up for 16 to 20 year olds to sail on *Gipsy Moth*. Catherine and son James would both come to Gibraltar a few months later in 2005 to see *Gipsy Moth*'s departure on her round-the-world voyage.

On 17 November, a month after our SE10 lunch to toast the new sponsor, *Gipsy Moth IV* was craned out of dry dock to headlines in the world's yachting press: '*La renaissance de* Gipsy Moth IV' in France; '*La Vuelta al mundo del* Gipsy Moth' in Spain and 'Gipsy Moth *weer in de vaart*' in Holland.

The cost of this operation alone was more than £10,000. An aluminum trackway had to be laid across Cutty Sark Gardens to spread the crane's load and prevent the weight of the boat and lorry cracking the paving or worse: falling through into the underground car park below! Barriers had to be erected for public safety. The Maritime Trust were concerned about any mention of 'concrete tombs' or 'graveyards' and wanted to keep the occasion low-key. They were worried Greenwich Council might raise the question, again, of the £60,000 bill to fill the hole in the ground. But how could we keep this special day low-key?

This would be the first time I'd witness David Green's showmanship and one of his trademark military-style operations.

The UKSA sent a coach load of staff. They bought Plymouth gin, Mumm champagne and Mount Gay rum to celebrate (all these companies would later help to lubricate our way round the world). Project Manager John Walsh, Development Director Jon Ely and Partnership Manager Frank Fletcher, arrived early to unstep and undress the masts, with Richard Baggett and Steve Rouse, later to become two of the yacht's skippers. Veteran rigger Harry Spencer, 80, who set up *Gipsy Moth IV*'s original rig, came to help and offered his iron-grip handshake. Tony Grimes, MD of C-Guard, whose adhesives were used in the yacht's cold-moulded hull construction, attended. He had written to me months ago offering to donate more glue to help put the boat together again. Giorgio Bendoni, from

Camper & Nicholsons came too, as did the Mayor of Cowes, Alan Wells. The Mayor of Gosport came to greet her on arrival at C&N. Greenwich's Mayor seemed conspicuously absent. Was it embarrassment, perhaps, that one of the town's star attractions had been allowed to fall into a state of such shameful neglect though lack of funds?

As *Gipsy Moth IV* was craned out of her hole, a section of her portside bulwark collapsed under the squeeze of the lifting strops: it was as rotten as a pear. Her white topsides were smeared with city grime and her coamings splintered by vandals' boots. Yet nothing could mar the dignity of *Gipsy Moth IV*. As the crane 'disinterred' her, the lines of a 53ft thoroughbred were silhouetted against the sky for the first time.

Cameras flashed and camcorders whirred as spectators filmed one of the world's most famous yachts in the first stages of deliverance. Her bow swung from west to east and she was put onto a low-loader with the care of an eggshell, for her journey back to her birthplace. From the deck of the tea clipper *Cutty Sark*, more than 100 enthusiasts raised three cheers.

Before her 114-mile journey to Camper & Nicholsons, there was a gathering in the hold of the *Cutty Sark* to toast her good health. Among those raising their glasses were most of *Yachting Monthly*'s editorial staff, Chichester's daughter-in-law Ginnie, wife of Giles, and Jane Chichester, a cousin. Noel Lister, the founder of the UKSA, was there in a wheelchair with his nephew David, one of the UKSA trustees. Noel had suffered a stroke some months before, but it didn't stop him later climbing aboard *Gipsy Moth* at Camper and Nicholsons during the refit.

The Duke of Edinburgh, president of The Maritime Trust, sent a letter expressing his 'best wishes and delight' that the 'next chapter' in the yacht's history was about to begin. Months earlier, when first told of the plan, I'd heard he thought the idea of taking *Gipsy Moth* around the word again was 'cuckoo'.

Richard, CEO of the *Cutty Sark*, recalled that Chichester himself had learned some of his navigational skills aboard the square rigger and that the *Cutty Sark* was used as the control centre where his 29,630-mile voyage was plotted daily from Marconi radio signals.

By late afternoon, as the winter sky darkened, *Gipsy Moth IV* was waiting patiently on her low-load trailer. I'd already booked a place for myself and Dick Durham as 'crew' on

Graham Snook/Yachting Monthly

The thoroughbred lines of Gipsy Moth IV *are revealed as she is craned out of dry dock on to the lorry's cradle.*

The author and Dick Durham join Gipsy Moth IV as 'crew' on her voyage home to Gosport, via the M25 and A3.

Graham Snook/Yachting Monthly

her first 'voyage' home. Before we climbed into the cab of Terry Ollerton's 430hp DAF Super Space truck, I shook hands with Richard and Marie-Helen, who had done so much to get us this far.

There was a cheer as a path was cleared through the traffic by our escort van, marked '*Voiture Pilote, Convoi Exceptionnel*' – Terry does a lot of work hauling Bénéteaus back from France. To the policemen holding back the traffic, *Gipsy Moth* was just an 'abnormal long load'. But as her sleek hull rolled past shoppers and office workers heading home at the start of rush hour, she was an icon. One pensioner stood to attention and saluted.

This was the second time Terry had moved *Gipsy Moth IV* – last time was in 1995 for her original refit. 'I'm flattered to be asked again,' he said. 'I was at primary school in short trousers when Chichester set off round the world!'

Added to *Gipsy Moth*'s 53ft LOA and 11 tons was Terry's cab and trailer – an all-up weight of 31 tons – quite a snake to weave round the corners of waterside Greenwich.

Soon we were speeding along the M25 at 50mph and Terry's CB radio crackled into life: 'The self-steering gear is flapping around a bit, Terry!'

It was the voice of our 'pilot car' driver, Alan Wood, 57, with crew James Bates and Frank Greenfield – all boating people from Terry's Shoreline Yacht Transport based, appropriately, in Chichester, West Sussex.

'I reckon she'll be all right, Alan, we'll stop at the next service station,' said Terry.

We pulled into Clacket Lane Services to lash Hasler's self-steering gear, more used to the Roaring Forties than a motorway slipstream.

A lorry marshall loomed out of the dark: 'Is that the real *Gipsy Moth*?'

It was a question that would be repeated thousands of times over the coming months and years.

Negotiating the low bridge at Fareham, the low-loader had to mount the pavement. Half an hour later we were rolling into Camper & Nicholsons' yard at Gosport. 'Well, that's the first leg of her round-the-world voyage,' Terry said, breathing a sigh of relief.

A figure walked out of the dark... the night watchman, I wondered? It was Giorgio Bendoni, back from Greenwich. *Gipsy Moth*'s arrival was important enough for the boss to come and unlock the yard gates. She was safely home.

At the beginning of December I invited Nigel Irens, one of Britain's top naval architects, who designed Ellen MacArthur's trimaran

Graham Snook/Yachting Monthly

B&Q, to come to Camper & Nicholsons and see *Gipsy Moth IV*'s famous rudder – which had caused Chichester such grief. Chichester famously said he needed an elephant to move the tiller. Sailing has advanced to the far frontiers of science-fiction in the four decades since Chichester set off in *Gipsy Moth IV*. His record of 226 sailing days around the world was now down to 71 days, 14 hours 18 minutes and 33 seconds, thanks to Britain's 21st century heroine, Ellen MacArthur, then 26! Take a look at Mike Golding's new Open 60 spacecraft *Ecover 3* or Alex Thomson's carbon-black *Hugo Boss*. The question was: should *Gipsy Moth* be restored exactly as before, 'warts and all'? Or did we dare to make even the smallest improvement with new ideas and technology?

The unusual thing about *Gipsy Moth IV* was the keel and rudder configuration, which Chichester believed was the cause of his helm balance problems. During his single 'pit stop' in Australia it was modified by adding a keel extension aft, on the advice of naval architect Warwick Hood. Later, Chichester never ceased to be amazed by the improvement it made in directional stability.

Nigel's verdict was that since the addition in Sydney appeared to have had such a positive effect, it seemed logical to go one step further

and extend the rudder down to the 'new' heel while reducing its chord (width) to help diminish tiller loadings. 'I'm sure this would have been considered at the time in Australia, but perhaps they had run out of time?' He added, somewhat presciently: 'While this might sort out the upwind steering balance, the boat is unlikely to be a joy to steer downwind in a seaway.' *Gipsy Moth* was designed at the height of a difficult transition period when keels were getting shorter, but rudders, with some notable exceptions, had not found their rightful position further aft – where their ability to control a boat was much enhanced.

Chichester's book of his voyage was a litany of complaints about *Gipsy Moth*. Arriving in Sydney, he wrote in his log: 'I fear *Gipsy Moth IV* is about as unbalanced or unstable as a boat could be!' From the start of his circumnavigation, until his self-steering failed, a few thousands miles short of Australia, Chichester hadn't succeeded in balancing his 'cantankerous' boat which 'hobby-horsed.'

In his book, he describes how, on a toy manufacturer's model of *Gipsy Moth IV*, designed to race on a pond in Kensington Gardens, they had to increase the rudder and reduce mizzen and main to achieve balance! Chichester wryly observed: 'What a pity the designer didn't make such a model before the boat was built and save me from her vicious faults.'

The scale model of Gipsy Moth IV *made by Nauticalia in 2007*

Top naval architect Nigel Irens with UKSA project manager John Walsh and Paul Gelder

Graham Snook/Yachting Monthly

Gipsy Moth's hull stripped bare of paint for her 'under-the-skin' survey at C&N.

Graham Snook/Yachting Monthly

Camper & Nicholsons' shipwright Bill Shaw (left) and project manager Olly Cameron, a Scottish naval architect.

Graham Snook/Yachting Monthly

The stern post was rotten for its full length, along with much of the dead wood. 'You can push your finger into it,' said Bill Shaw.

Graham Snook/Yachting Monthly

Rotten wood cut away from Gipsy Moth's stern sections left a gaping hole and thousands of hours work to replace the solid and cold-moulded sections.

Graham Snook/Yachting Monthly

Graham Snook/Yachting Monthly

n the cockpit around the engine control panel gauges. A new engine d be needed, but the ketch's spars, paraffin heater, cooker and toilets d all be restored.

The entire cockpit had to be cut out and replaced. Gipsy Moth also needed to be re-wired, re-plumbed and re-painted for her second circumnavigation in 36 weeks' time!

David Green, the backbone of the project, standing alongside Gipsy Moth's *new backbone. The word 'no' was not in his volcabulary.*

Paul Gelder/Yachting Monthly

In fairness to designers Illingworth and Primrose, self-steering systems were primitive in those days. While the debate about the rudder continued, Broadblue Catamarans and the International Boatbuilding Training College (IBTC) in Lowestoft had offered to make a new one for *Gipsy Moth IV* free of charge.

On 10 December, 22 days after the Greenwich lift out, and following her major 'under-the-skin' survey, we all met at Camper & Nicholsons and were told it was 'viable to restore *Gipsy Moth IV* to sail around the world again.' But at an alarming cost.

'We don't see her getting afloat for less than £175,000,' said Scottish Project Manager Olly Cameron. From the first survey I had commissioned in 2004 (when 2,500 man hours' work were estimated), the hours had soared to a frightful 5,800 – 4,000 for the hull alone.

Taking the hull apart had revealed the full extent of the spreading rot. Lockers, which had been screwed shut for years, were opened. Chichester's empty Whitbread beer keg was retrieved from the bilges, together with a frying pan. The port side was the worst affected, because that was the side facing prevailing southwesterly winds as she sat in dry dock at Greenwich.

The 20-page survey report for 'Design No. 916 Illingworth and Primrose' showed the extent of work needed. Shipwright Bill Shaw reported 4ft of the stern was rotten from the top down – 'you can push your finger into it.'

The stern post was rotten for its full length and needed removing and renewing with a new stern tube log and boring. The hull external planking had been hammer and spike tested and areas of rot found: 1,800 hours' work alone. The forward galley bulkhead had fungus growing out of it and was rotten 2ft up from the bilge. And so it went on, for page after page. The chart space was the only area with a zero in the columns for hours' work and cost of materials. *Gipsy Moth* also needed to be re-wired, re-plumbed and re-painted. Preparation and new paintwork was 497 hours. A new engine was needed.

It was an impressive document: thorough and comprehensive from keel to masthead – and, of course, it bore the usual disclaimer at the bottom of every page: 'The estimate of hours is based on what C&N staff can observe of the yacht in its current state. These hours may be subject to change as areas are exposed further during restoration work.' In the end Bill Shaw's estimate proved remarkably accurate and John Walsh was able to produce preliminary costings of £295,000, including materials and VAT and a 10% contingency.

It was not for the faint-hearted. But David Green, I was discovering, was not a man daunted by bad news. He always saw the positive side of things. In fact, it wasn't easy to bring David negative news during the whole time of the project. He was a supremely confident PR man, something of a spin doctor. With his drive and enthusiasm he could sell sand to a desert Arab, let alone Corum watches. He could also talk the hind legs off a donkey.

He was part Alastair Campbell, part Billy Graham and part General Montgomery. Like Campbell, he liked to 'manage' or 'contain' the news'. Like Graham, he had a missionary zeal to convert people to his cause. He was delighted when I called him 'the Billy Graham of the boating world,' for his evangelical approach to the *Gipsy Moth* project. And like Montgomery, he mustered his troops with rallying speeches, drew up meticulous, military precision 'battle plans' for set-piece big occasions and was 'Supreme Allied Commander'.

The next big occasion, after Greenwich, was a party in four days 'to announce to the world' that the restoration was going ahead. Just as Chichester raced against the *Cutty Sark*, so we would race against the clock to get *Gipsy Moth IV* restored for her second circumnavigation in 36 weeks.

Gipsy Moth was to be restored as closely as possible to her original blueprint. 'If we can get old stuff working and reliable, we'll use it,' said Jon Ely, Green's deputy. This was to include the original spars, much deck gear, the Hasler self-steering, the Primus stove, the Blake's toilet and the original paraffin heater, described by shipwright Nick Gates as 'the biggest sock dryer I've seen!'

Equipment was to be selected on the basis of historical integrity, safety for the use of young crew and availability of spares. To meet public interest in the voyage, satellite equipment would be fitted to transmit pictures, video and stories. Another concession to new technology was that the hull would be sheathed 'to preserve the integrity of the yacht.' Dan Primrose, son of designer Angus, coincidentally, worked then for SP Systems Ltd, who had offered to donate materials. The keel would be restored to her post-Sydney status and a new propeller (the old one was an 'egg whisk') fitted lower in the water for safety reasons with young crew aboard. 'The prop on my model plane is bigger,' said John Walsh.

There would be no radar, no hot water, no showers and no roller furling foresails, but the yacht would have larger water tanks and a water-maker, as a concession to her crew of six. Chichester relied on an ingenious water catcher in the boom to augment supplies from rain off the sails. He nearly ran out of water at Cape Horn. The yacht's cockpit was rotten and would be cut out and replaced. The galley would be placed slightly further forward to allow access to a new engine replacing the old Perkins diesel.

The authentic 'Chichester experience' would begin on deck and continue as you stepped back 40 years in time through the companionway and into the cabin.

Camper & Nicholsons' workers restored the ketch as closely as possible to her original blueprint.

Paul Gelder/Yachting Monthly

Champagne corks popped at C&N as 100 people gathered on 14 December to celebrate the re-birth of a legend. *Gipsy Moth*'s hull had been stripped back to the wood. Guests and supporters ranged in age from Brian Chivers, 97, a former C&N worker, who fitted Chichester's beer barrel and tap in the saloon, to 37-year-old Tara Perris, a Cowes-based yachtswoman, who had volunteered to work at the UKSA three days a week for no pay. Murlo Primrose, widow of Angus, co-designer of the yacht, was there with her son, Dan: 'Angus would be over the moon,' she said. 'He was absolutely livid the boat was put in concrete and also very sad that by the end of his circumnavigation Francis wasn't talking to him.'

Colin Silvester, a draughtsman with Illingworth and Primrose, who had been closely involved in the detailed design work for *Gipsy Moth IV* said: 'When she went to Greenwich it was if she'd been put in a concrete coffin and was an embarrassment. By keeping her ashore, we were never able to take some of the ideas on to the next stage. The entombment of the boat put the seal of confirmation on what Chichester had said about her.'

*BELOW:
Naval architect
Colin Silvester
with Dan and
Murlo Primrose.
CENTRE:
Eric Goulding.
RIGHT:
Roy Berry and
Brian Chivers
(97) ex C&N
shipwrights*

The men behind the scenes who would mastermind all the work were C&N's project manager, Olly Cameron, 30, and the UKSA's project manager, John Walsh, 64, who, by coincidence, had assisted in Sir Francis Chichester's reception and knighting by the Queen at the Royal Naval College Greenwich in 1967. Coming from a Royal Navy background, he served in the Fleet Air Arm and as a frigate navigating officer and had an extensive sailing background.

Two former C&N joiners, Roy Berry, 83, and Eric Goulding, 64, who fitted the interior of the yacht 38 years ago had returned to see their handiwork. Eric fitted the famous gimballed chair in which Chichester sat in his velvet green smoking jacket on his 65th birthday as he crossed Biscay. The chair would be left back in the UK for the second circumnavigation. With six crew aboard it took up too much space.

Graham Snook/Yachting Monthly

At *Yachting Monthly*'s annual contributors' Christmas party, David Green, Jon Ely and Frank Fletcher brought along the first batch of *Gipsy Moth IV* branded sailing jackets from Henri-Lloyd, who had made Chichester's oilskins in the 1960s. Henri-Lloyd also produced polo shirts, baseball caps, navigation cases and oilskins to sell and help raise funds at January's London Boat Show.

By the time the boat show was finished, David was reporting that the *Gipsy Moth IV* fund stood at an amazing £250,000 in just two months. Some of money came from the marine industry in the form of donated goods: winches and deck gear (Lewmar); new electronic navigation equipment (Simrad/Brooks & Gatehouse, who also refurbished the original B&G instruments); paint, epoxies and anti-fouling (International Paints); a dinghy (Avon); charts and pilot books (Kelvin Hughes); fixtures and fittings (Sims Leopard); cabin table and interior work (Sweden Yachts); cordage (Marlow Ropes); liferaft and safety equipment (Ocean Safety); sunglasses (Sundog) and, prophetically, crisis management support (Oceanassist).

Chichester's stainless steel gimballed chair was at the boat show and visitors were invited to sit in it and drink a gin and tonic for a £5 donation. Robin Knox-Johnston and Pete Goss were among those who tried the 'gin sling'. Pete Goss said he'd prefer kneel in front of it rather than sit in it! Giles Chichester gave a fund-raising talk at the show, entitled 'My father's voyage around the world'.

A *Gipsy Moth* '1,000 Club' for supporters, with a £1,000 'joining' fee, signed up its first member, the Ocean Cruising Club's Commodore Alan Taylor, followed by Peter and Annette Seymour, from the Blue Water Rally, Tom Pindar, father of Andrew Pindar, whose printing company sponsors offshore racing, Fred Normandale, a Scarborough fisherman, Greenwich Yacht Club, Martyn Jennings, Tony and Heather Jackson and RD Sansom. Soon we had £10,000.

Giles Chichester tries the 'Gin Swing' at London Boat Show – with David Green, the author and Murlo Primrose, widow of Gipsy Moth's designer Angus.

Tom Cunliffe said: '*Gipsy Moth IV* looked wonderful. We always used to reckon the first thing to do when you bought a wooden boat was to burn her off and see what you'd really got. Well, they did, and doesn't she look inspiring!'

David announced that a target of £1 million had been set to secure the yacht's future for the next 20 years and to provide bursaries for young people to sail on her. We described the project as a 'milestone in Britain's maritime history'.

Yachting Monthly's next issue reported support from Crusader Sails in Poole, who were making sails worth £20,000 at no charge; Bainbridge International supplying the sailcloth; SP Systems offering £4,000 worth of resins and epoxy; and the British Marine Federation and National Boats Show giving free stand space at the London ExCel Boat Show.

Mark Pepper/PPL

Pete Goss said he'd rather kneel before Chichester's chair than sit in it!

Mark Pepper/PPL

Sir Francis Chichester meets Robin Knox-Johnston after Robin's solo non-stop circumnavigation in 1969.

In February Britain was on a maritime high with Ellen MacArthur's triumphant return as the fastest woman round the world in her trimaran *B&Q*. We had good news, too. £150,000 was being donated to the restoration fund by the South East England Development Agency (SEEDA) with the Isle of Wight Economic Partnership and Isle of Wight Council. A new maritime heritage centre was planned for East Cowes

and *Gipsy Moth IV* would be the centerpiece. Mike King, managing director of the Isle of Wight Economic Partnership said: 'This will not be a dusty static museum.'

The announcement was made at a second gathering at C&N sponsors and supporters could see progress on the restoration. Giles Chichester attended and said: 'It's a journey down memory lane. I remember seeing her here 40 years ago, being built upside down on a mould.' He also revealed that at one time the yacht's name was to be *New York Express* – 'because my father was very keen to get there first and fastest, after Frenchman Eric Tabarly won the second OSTAR!'

In April, Sir Robin Knox-Johnston was guest speaker at a black tie gala dinner and auction at the Royal London Yacht Club, Cowes, when £12,000 was raised for the cause. Sir Robin said 'The restoration of *Gipsy Moth IV* is, in sailing terms, as important as the restoration of Westminster Abbey.' Nick Bonham, who was to conduct more auctions for the UKSA, including one in Sydney, Australia, sold off more than 60 items, including *Gipsy Moth IV*'s original mizzen mast winch

Work stops on Gipsy Moth (in background) for a special announcement that she will be the star of a proposed Cowes Maritime Heritage Centre.

Graham Snook/Yachting Monthly

(£1,000), keel bolts (£350 each), and polished sections of her old keel mounted on plaques. An Admiral's Cup watch with a £3,795 price tag was donated by Corum, *Gipsy Moth*'s Official Timekeeper, and went under the hammer for £2,300. Corum's president Michael Wunderman had also donated £40,000 to the project and made a special limited edition *Gipsy Moth IV* wrist watch costing some £10,000, with a percentage going to the project. A watercolour painting of the ketch by Martyn Mackrill sold for £1,600.

Work at Camper & Nicholsons was going ahead at a fast pace. In the 1960s, the Maritime & Coastguard Agency (MCA) didn't exist and Chichester, a free spirit, would no doubt have disapproved of our 'Nanny State'. But sailing with young and old crew around the world, *Gipsy Moth* had to be 'coded' as a commercial vessel to meet modern fire safety and stability requirements. Her electrical and fuel systems, battery stowage and hatches all had to meet legal requirements. Skippers had to have medical fitness examinations and undergo sea survival courses and other crew members needed radio and first aid qualifications.

By now, C&N had a new project manager. Olly Cameron had left to take up a new job and Martyn Langford (62) joined as one of the most complex parts of the restoration began: the making of a new backbone for *Gipsy Moth*. A sculptural 16ft-long curved piece of wood (made up from 16 $\frac{1}{8}$in laminates of African mahogany glued together) replaced the rotten timber in the stern and wooden keel area. Peter Robertson, 24, and James Swanson, 22 were two young shipwrights who worked on this part of the refit. Martyn's contribution, as a professional engineer, was to prove fundamental to the timely completion of the project.

The restoration spanned generations: schoolboy Adam Vince, 15, spent two weeks sanding down locker doors and 97-year old Brian Chivers, an ex-C&N joiner, advised on how original fittings were made. *Gipsy Moth IV*'s main companionway hatch cover was being rebuilt in African mahogany by Eric Goulding (64), one her original joiners. The £10,000 of mahogany used in the refit was supplied by Sykes Timber, who also gave a £1,000 cash donation.

Martyn Langford took over as C&N's new Gipsy Moth Project Manager.

James Swanson and Peter Robertson (right), two young shipwrights who worked on the new backbone, being laminated (left).

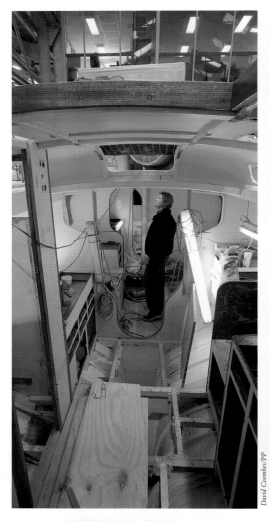

David Coombes/PP

Each time I visited Camper and Nicholsons' there was a new advance in Gipsy Moth IV's rapid renaissance.

Graham Snook/Yachting Monthly

Carpenters, painters, electricians, engineers and craftsmen worked in shifts in a race against the clock.

David Coombes/PP

Graham Snook/Yachting Monthly

Sails

Crusader Sails made 10 sails for *GMIV* worth £20,000. The wardrobe included: light working jib; working jib; staysail; two crusing chutes; mainsail; mizzen; mizzen staysail; storm jib; trysail. Crusader used 150 piston hanks, 18.5 m of plyester bolt rope, 1km of thread and 15m of acrylic for sail covers. Bainbridge International supplied 611m of their sail cloth, worth £4,500.

Masts

The original Proctor masts were painstakin[...] restored by the UKSA (mizzen pictured belo[...]

Pulpit

The original pulpit was restored.

Stanchions

All the stanchions were removed, rechromed and re-bedded.

Windlass

Restored – the windlass that Chichester used to deploy and recover the warps he streamed astern to steady the boat in Southern Ocean storms.

Bow

Rotten sections of the bow had to be cut away and replaced with new strips of laminate before a new bow roller was fitted.

Heads

The original Baby Blake heads was fully restored by craftsmen at Camper & Nicholsons.

Electronics

The facia of the original Marconi Kestrel radio transmitter/receiver is mounted on a dummy panel that lifts to reveal the latest Simrad/Brookes & Gatehouse electronics, including a chart plotter.

Stove

Southampton engineer Henry Pugh restored the original two-burner Primus stove. The paraffin heater was restored by Peter Hebard.

Cabin Hatch

Eric Goulding, a former Camper & Nicholsons joiner, made a new cabin hatch in his workshop at home.

Winches

Lewmar provided new self-tailing winches to replace the originals.

Self-steering

The self-stering gear, designed by Blondie Hasler, was restored by marine engineer Patrik Maude.

Compass

Compass adjustor Ron Robinson, who swung *Gipsy Moth's* steering compass back in 1966, restored the original compass.

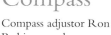

Topsides

The hull was sheathed in hi-tech epoxy resin by SP Systems and finished with 14 litres of International Paint's Mediterranean White topcoat.

Prop

Members of the Royal Sydney Yacht Squadron raised £1,500 to buy a Hydraline folding prop, which can drive *Gipsy Moth* at up 8.5 knots.

Engine

A new 56hp Yanmar 4JH4 donated by EP Barrus, replaced the original Perkins diesel.

Skipper's bunk

Chichester could monitor a set of repeater instruments from his quarterberth.

Rudder

A new rudder was designed by project director John Walsh and Bill Shaw, and drawn by naval architect Ian Darley. It was built by the International Boatbuilding Training College in Lowestoft.

New laminations clamped and glued in place in the cold-moulded coachroof.

Thousands of hours' work went into rebuilding Gipsy Moth's rotted stern sections.

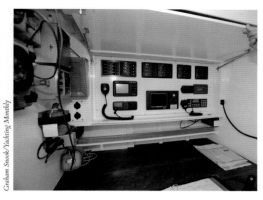

Graham Snook/Yachting Monthly

Graham Snook/Yachting Monthly

The finished Gipsy Moth emerges from C&N's shed. A false panel lifts to reveal a state-of-the-art navigation station behind the old Marconi-Kestrel radio.

Paul Gelder/Yachting Monthly

A proud moment for UKSA project director John Walsh, while (left) work goes on below decks and the saloon looks resplendent

Naval architect Ian Darley, designed a new rudder, 10% bigger than the original, finishing flush with the Sydney keel extension. The old rudder was rotten. Ian was also responsible for the MCA stability tests.

Simrad fitted the latest state-of-the-art electronic navigation kit from B&G, ingeniously concealed behind a false panel on which Chichester's original instruments, including his Marconi-Kestrel radio, were mounted. The electric windlass on deck was overhauled and back in service.

All sorts of people appeared 'out of the woodwork' to contribute to the re-making of a legend. Southampton engineer Henry Pugh, 54, repaired *Gipsy Moth IV*'s two-burner Primus stove and brewed up the first pot of coffee on it since it was last used in 1967! John Walsh had sought help from a web forum (www.spiritburner.com) to get the stove repaired and Henry volunteered.

Gipsy Moth's original Hasler self-steering gear was renovated by a marine engineer who turned up at Camper & Nicholsons and offered to help. Patrik Maude, 52, from Seaview, Isle of Wight, contacted the Amateur

Barry Pickthall/PPL

Yacht Research Society, which put him in touch with an engineer who worked with Blondie Hasler on the gear.

Compass adjustor Ron Robinson, of Hamble, who swung *Gipsy Moth*'s original steering compass back in 1966, restored it for her new voyage.

Lewmar's technical support manager, Dave Mellish, restored *Gipsy Moth IV*'s original genoa cars to pristine condition. Dave was from Emsworth, Hampshire, where *Gipsy Moth IV*'s designers Illingworth and Primrose, had their offices at 36 North Street. Lewmar also provided 10 new winches for the cockpit and mast, worth £7,000, plus other deck gear.

The original Baby Blake toilet was restored to re-chromed glory by C&N's Kevin Palmer, 42, a plumber by trade. The elegant galley hand-pumps and taps were re-chromed. A 54hp Yanmar 4JH4E diesel engine was delivered, courtesy of Tim Hart and EP Barrus and a watermaker donated by Peter Snare, MD of Seafresh, was installed.

By now solo round-the-world sailors Emma Richards, Pete Goss and Mike Golding had agreed to become patrons of the project.

Paul Gelder/Yachting Monthly

'The first time I saw *Gipsy Moth* in dry dock at Greenwich, I was a young lad full of dreams,' said Pete. 'She seemed to be crying tears of rust down her imprisoned hull. She'll carry a new message around the world to inspire a new generation of adventurers.'

Mike Golding was just four years old when Chichester made his epic voyage. 'He laid the foundations of solo circumnavigation,' said Mike. 'He paved the way for the next generation of pioneers – Chay Blyth and Robin Knox-Johnston – childhood heroes who inspired me.'

Shipwrights worked night and day to get *Gipsy Moth IV* ready for her re-launch on 20 June, seven months after she left Greenwich.

So the public could follow the restoration, Southsea photographer Stefan Venter created an online 'virtual tour' of the yacht with 360° images on deck and in the cabin.

Chichester's spirit may have been with us in more ways than one. Shipwright Bill Shaw was working alone on the boat one evening down below in the saloon when he felt 'a presence' …and the hairs on the back of his neck stood up.

Each time I visited Camper & Nicholsons there was some thrilling new advance in *Gipsy Moth*'s renaissance. I was amazed and humbled to see how from one small seed, planted during a Friday night chat in a wine bar, a forest of workers were beavering away to make my dream come true.

It was a nine month refit completed in five months, said Martyn Langford. A team of volunteers from the UKSA worked alongside C&N shipwrights sandpapering and varnishing. They reconditioned and polished the original masts to a silver sheen with advice from John Morris at Formula Spars Ltd, Lymington.

Her hull was baked at 35°C for a day and a half in an 'oven' of polythene sheeting to give her hi-tech epoxy sheathing maximum strength to protect the hull. At times up to 35 workers were engaged in the refit. By day, painters concentrated on the boat's exterior while joiners, electricians, and engineers

Graham Snook/Yachting Monthly

Martyn Langford and Bill Shaw lower the new Yanmar engine into place.

worked inside to re-wire, plumb in new Tek-tanks and fit the engine.

C&N's painting expert Bob Purnell, 53, used 14 litres of International Paints' topcoat to bring *Gipsy Moth IV*'s repaired hull back to full gloss perfection.

215 days since leaving Greenwich and an estimated 9,000 man hours later, *Gipsy Moth IV* would soon be sailing again. C&N's bill amounted to £303,000. Project director John Walsh said: 'The input of C&N craftsmen so enthusiastically given means she will be a much better boat than she was originally.'

Graham Snook/Yachting Monthly

Installing the new Tek-Tanks, donated by the manufacturer.

Afloat at Last

Solo sailor Emma Richards handed over a £1,000 cheque at the launch from her sponsor Pindar.

A launching party was 'something I don't approve of,' Chichester wrote. 'The time to celebrate is after a boat has done something, not before'.

When his wife Sheila launched *Gipsy Moth* with a bottle of champagne in 1966 the occasion was 'a terrible omen', and Chichester's heart sank. The bottle failed to break. On the second try it smashed perfectly, but the ketch stuck on the greased ways and wouldn't move. 'A cold despair of premonition' gripped Chichester, who jumped down and pushed with his own shoulder against the launching cradle. Slowly she floated off. But she floated high on her marks and he watched as two or three tiny ripples from a harbour ferry made folds on the glassy surface of the harbour and *Gipsy Moth IV* rocked fore and aft.

'My God, she's a rocker!' he exclaimed to Sheila.

For *Gipsy Moth*'s second launching party on 20 June 2005, there was no cradle to get stuck. *Gipsy Moth IV* was lowered as gently as a baby at a baptism into Portsmouth Harbour in the slings of a Travelhoist as three cheers resounded from a crowd of 500, including celebrated veteran Atlantic OSTAR sailor Mike Richey (88), a friend of Sir Francis Chichester.

A proud moment for David Green and Paul Gelder as Gipsy Moth *touches salt water for the first time in 38 years.*

As a representative of the newest generation of solo round the world sailors, Emma Richards handed over a £1,000 cheque from her sponsor, Pindar, to help youngsters sail on *Gipsy Moth*. Appropriately, three schoolchildren, plus Ginnie Chichester and Emma, performed the launch ceremony. Ginnie apologised that Giles was missing, because of his duties as an MEP. 'He missed the first launch, too, sitting university exams!' she said.

The three young crew were Robert McClaren, 16, from South London, Karen Smith, 17, from Newport, Isle of Wight and Peter Heggie, 17, from Plymouth.

By the time of the launch party the UKSA had acquired a massive mobile exhibition trailer, with plasma screen and an exhibition of Chichester memorabilia: his seaboots, cap, safety harness and other items. The UKSA *Gipsy Moth IV* Roadshow was a formidable, unstoppable vehicle and with David Green at the wheel he now awarded himself the omnipotent title of 'Global Project Manager'. Nothing, it seemed, was impossible. Miracles just take 215 days!

As the party ended, *Gipsy Moth* had just completed her first 'passage' in 38 years – 50 yards from the launching dock to a marina pontoon.

Graham Snook/Yachting Monthly

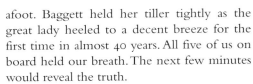

*Ginnie Chichester
at the launch
ceremony*

As fate would have it, she was to be one of the last yachts to emerge from the sheds of Camper & Nicholsons' illustrious boatyard. The next month it was announced that after 213 years the yard would close. The lease – taken out in 1792 for £42 per annum – was up for renewal in 2006 and C&N had decided not to renew it. One of the reasons cited was that it had proved difficult to get permission to bring the listed buildings up to date.

More than 50 shipwrights would be made redundant. The company – owned by Nautor's Swan since 2001 – was famous for building J-Class legends *Shamrock V*, *Endeavour* and *Velsheda* and a host of iconic yachts. The C&N brand would continue, but building powerboats. A special day out was arranged by the UKSA for the shipwrights, and everyone who had worked on *Gipsy Moth IV*, to meet the Duke of Edinburgh.

First sail trials

Gipsy Moth's first sail trials after 38 years were awaited with suspense. Chichester had begged Camper & Nicholsons to get his boat finished by the end of January 1966, but she was not launched until March. And from the moment she touched the water she was in his bad books.

Camper's men had told him she lay over with her toe rail under the water in a moderate puff of wind on her mooring. 'The thought of what she would do in the huge Southern Ocean seas put ice into my blood,' Chichester wrote.

Now, with her new rudder configuration, would she prove to be the cranky old dog Chichester claimed, or would she behave like the ocean greyhound her slim, elegant lines suggested? *Yachting Monthly*'s boat tester James Jermain went aboard with the UKSA's skipper Richard Baggett, John Walsh and Ray Nicholson to find out on a summer's day in June. 'Thunder clouds were gathering to the north and lightning flickered on the horizon,' reported James. 'If you believed in Norse gods you could be sure something portentous was

*Peter Heggie,
Robert McClaren
and Karen Smith
spoke at the
launch ceremony.
RIGHT: Murlo
Primrose joins the
sail trials*

afoot. Baggett held her tiller tightly as the great lady heeled to a decent breeze for the first time in almost 40 years. All five of us on board held our breath. The next few minutes would reveal the truth.

'The sails filled, she heeled as the apparent wind built in 12-14 knots breeze and she started to slice through the water. We had the full main, big off-wind genoa and mizzen set – ideal for power reaching. Water began to surge past her lee topsides. She stiffened up, accelerated and Richard's grip on the helm visibly relaxed. Brows unfurrowed; lips began to crease into broad grins. Richard found himself with just a thumb and forefinger on the shapely, curved tiller. Suddenly we were giggling like schoolboys as *Gipsy Moth IV* surged westward down the Solent at close to seven knots. "We've still got a lot of trimming and tuning to do,' said Richard, 'but this is a pretty good start."

'We tacked around and bore off again for the eastern Solent. I took the helm and confirmed what Richard had demonstrated. *Gipsy Moth IV* was running straight and true with the slightest hint of weather helm. A tiller line or pin rail would have kept her on course as long as the wind held. When she did deviate, it took a major heave to bring her back on course. Even the redesigned rudder couldn't

Graham Snook/Yachting Monthly

Smiles and deep satisfaction at the successful completion of the refit. Paul Gelder and David Green on sail trials. BELOW: Skipper Richard Baggett

disguise the fact that she has a keel like a barn door. She is long and slim, weighs over 11.5 tons and draws 7ft 6in (2.3m). She does not treat the inattentive helmsman kindly.

'We came on the wind, which built to 18 to 20 knots apparent. The full-cut genoa didn't allow us to sail as close to the wind as we might have liked but she tacked cleanly if

Graham Snook/Yachting Monthly

slowly through 100° and her displacement kept her footing through the eye of the wind. The log hovered around the six-knot mark – not particularly quick, but good, steady progress. We were well heeled – 25 or 30° – but the helm remained balanced and she more or less steered herself.

'As we played around with sail trim off Wootton Creek, Patrik Maude who restored the windvane connected it for the first time and it steered a very acceptable course up and across the wind. On a run it was, as one would expect, at a bit of a loss.

'The verdict on *Gipsy Moth*'s first trial sail was that in moderate conditions and sheltered water she had given an exciting yet undemanding sail and shown no particular handling vices. The sails had been easy to handle, the helm positive, the deck well laid out and safe. But she was both tender and under-canvassed. Chichester was right on this count. She was not the boat Chichester ordered or expected. He was originally promised a boat of 8 tons and 48ft (14.6m). This grew to 54ft (16.4m) – later cut back to 53ft (16m) – and the design weight increased to 9 then 9.5 tons. However, because Chichester insisted on sails of a certain maximum size so he could handle them, the sail plan could not be increased. When she was launched she was clearly grossly under ballasted and her final displacement soared to 11.5 tons driven by the sail plan for an 8-ton 48-footer.

'So Chichester had a boat that was overweight, under-canvassed yet still tender – and she still is, but not nearly to the extent a disillusioned and angry Chichester claimed. All

Gipsy Moth sails past HMS Endurance to take the royal salute by the Queen during the International Fleet Review.

I can say for now is that we had a rompingly good sail,' concluded James, who was looking forward to joining the crew for the Atlantic crossing in a few weeks.

Special guests on a later Solent sail trial were Murlo and Dan Primrose, widow and son of *Gipsy Moth*'s co-designer Angus Primrose. Poignantly, it would have been Angus's birthday on the day they sailed with *Yachting World*'s Matt Sheahan. Tragically, Angus died in 1981, aged 53, after being swept from his sinking 33ft yacht *Demon of Hamble* in heavy seas off the United States, having successfully competed in the 1980 OSTAR.

Murlo found memories flooding back from the late 1960s. She recalled 'the frisson' between Chichester and Angus. 'When Francis arrived in Sydney he sent Angus a telegram complaining about everything on the boat. Angus sent one back saying:"Don't worry she'll be all right when she's broken in!" I think that was the end of their relationship!' She recalled how Chichester would speak to Primrose when he had fallen out with Illingworth, and vice versa, during the boat's sail trials.

Murlo's son Dan added:'I know that my father and Sir Francis didn't see eye to eye and I think Angus was pretty happy when the whole thing was over.'

A week after her re-launch, *Gipsy Moth IV*'s first official outing was at the International Fleet Review, the biggest peacetime parade of naval ships from around the world, held on June 28 and organised to commemorate the 200th anniversary of the death of Nelson, at the Battle of Trafalgar.

Boarding *GMIV* at Cowes it was my turn, at last, to take the sweeping tiller for the first time. Her cockpit is very small and looking forward she's very narrow. Her 10ft 6in (3.20m) beam is the same as a Sigma 33. Heeling to the breeze, with her lee rail skimming the water, she felt a complete thoroughbred. It was a proud moment and thrilling to see crew from other yachts waving, cheering and shouting 'Well done!' She was a boat that inspired much affection.

UKSA

UKSA

We sailed off to join other veteran round-the-world yachts, *Suhaili*, with Sir Robin Knox-Johnston aboard, and *Lively Lady*, the ketch belonging to the late Sir Alec Rose. An armada of 167 ships from the Royal Navy and 35 nations lined the Solent from Portsmouth to Southampton Water as the Queen took the salute aboard the Arctic patrol vessel and ice-breaker HMS *Endurance*, accompanied by The Duke of Edinburgh.

As they watched *Gipsy Moth IV* storming past under reefed canvas, memories must have flooded back of the last time they saw her afloat: in July 1967, when they went aboard her at Greenwich after Sir Francis was knighted with the sword Queen Elizabeth I used to knight Sir Francis Drake. As *Gipsy Moth* and *Suhaili* sailed passed HMS *Endurance*, Sir Robin fired his own salute from a polished brass canon on the foredeck of his 33ft ketch.

In the evening a *son-et-lumière* mock sea battle with 17 Tall Ships blazing canon-fire, was followed by a massive firework display.

Two days later, *Gipsy Moth*'s next royal engagement was at Portsmouth International Festival of the Sea. One of the first visitors aboard was Princess Anne, who

Graham Snook/*Yachting Monthly*

expressed astonishment at *Gipsy Moth IV*'s speedy restoration and unveiled a plaque to commemorate her visit. Others who signed the VIP guestbook that day were Olympic gold medallist Shirley Roberston and former America's Cup contender Peter Harrison.

Gipsy Moth shared the Number 2 dock with Ellen MacArthur's giant trimaran, *B&Q/Castorama*, which Ellen had sailed around the world solo in 71 days, four months earlier, plus *Lively Lady* and Clare Francis' *Robertson's Golly*, an Ohlsson 38, in which she became the first woman to finish the OSTAR (solo transatlantic race) in 1976.

Next on *Gipsy Moth*'s list of high profile outings was opening Skandia Cowes Week, with Ellen MacArthur and Giles Chichester at the helm. It was Giles Chichester's first sail on the boat for 38 years. 'It's wonderful to see her given a new lease of life,' he said as he took the helm off Osborne Bay.

A De Havilland Gipsy Moth biplane swooped overhead as Ellen helmed the boat that inspired her to take up sailing. 'I haven't seen *Gipsy Moth* since I went to Greenwich with my mum when I was about eight,' she told me. It's very special to see her back on the water.' With Ellen were Adam Vincent, 16, and Jessica Morris, 17, from the Ellen MacArthur Trust.

Princess Anne visits Gipsy Moth *at the Festival of the Sea. David Green introduces the team (left to right): John Walsh, Paul Gelder, Martyn Langford, Ray Nicholson and Richard Baggett.*

Barry Pickhall/PPL

Nigel Reid with the restored Gipsy Moth bi-plane, which his father flew to greet Chichester home in 1967.

The bi-plane, call-sign G-AAWO, was the same plane that welcomed *Gipsy Moth* home to Plymouth in 1967. At the controls was Nigel Reid, whose father John was the original pilot. His brother Ian was sitting in the bi-plane's rear cockpit. This was the same model that Chichester flew to Australia in 1929-30 as an intrepid 28-year-old aviation pioneer, spending 180 hours alone in the cockpit. Nigel and Ian have both caught their father's flying bug and are commercial airline pilots as well as sailors.

As *Gipsy Moth* berthed at West Cowes Marina, Ellen and Giles stepped off the yacht to applause from crowds of spectators and David Green presented Ellen with one of the yacht's original keel bolts on a plaque. At the end of Cowes Week, skipper Richard Baggett said: 'I've been totally gobsmacked by the number of people who've told me they were inspired by Chichester and *Gipsy Moth* to go sailing.'

Ellen MacArthur and Giles Chichester sailed Gipsy Moth IV to open Skania Cowes Week 2005.

Barry Pickthall/PPL

Nigel and Ian Reid in their father's Gipsy Moth bi-plane fly past the ketch at the opening of Cowes Week. The brothers are former RAF Harrier pilots and keen sailors.

Barry Pickthall/PPL

Two days later *Gipsy Moth IV* was in the limelight again when the Duke of Edinburgh visited the UKSA to meet the project team and the Camper & Nicholsons workers. He was interested to hear that more than 80% of the yacht had been saved. The last time he was aboard was with the Queen, following Chichester's knighthood ceremony at Greenwich. In the cabin, Chichester's friend Erroll Bruce produced a bottle of champagne and as he struggled to open it, Prince Philip, warned him: 'Watch out Erroll, you'll squirt champagne at Her Majesty!'

It was fitting that redundant workers from C&N had their moment of royal recognition. Later, local vicar Richard Emblin blessed the yacht for her round-the-world voyage.

In August a special encounter took place between three world-girdling pioneers on a perfect summer's day in the Solent. For the first time ever, *Gipsy Moth IV*, *Suhaili*, Sir Robin Knox-Johnston's 33ft ketch, and *Lively Lady*, Sir Alec Rose's 36ft yawl, sailed together, side by side. Well, almost!

Scores of yachtsmen out for a day sail could hardly believe their binoculars as three iconic yachts sailed into view. Beken's photographer was out to capture the rare encounter for posterity.

Two friendly round-the-cans races were organised by the UKSA. The handicap, using each boat's average day's run during their historic circumnavigations, was protested from the start by Sir Robin. One wit at the prizegiving suggested: 'How about dividing each yacht's waterline length by the skipper's height and multiplying it by his inside leg measurement!'

After rounding the first mark off the Royal Yacht Squadron, *GMIV* was in the lead, skippered by John Walsh with tactician Paul Lees, proprietor of Crusader Sails, who made *GMIV*'s sail wardrobe. Paul was using Chichester's original Sestrel hand-bearing compass to take bearings on the race course marks. *Suhaili*, flying a spinnaker, chased *GMIV* under cruising chute. *Lively Lady* sported no downwind canvas but was surprisingly sprightly.

As the breeze strengthened, *GMIV* came into her own, skimming over the south side of the Bramble Bank before reaching back to the finish line in one hour and 49 minutes. *Lively Lady*, skippered by Alan Priddy, crossed 21 minutes later, winning the race on corrected time. *Suhaili*, skippered by Sir Robin Knox Johnston, retired.

The Duke of Edinburgh meets Camper & Nicholson workers and visits Gipsy Moth.

BELOW: The Duke with Richard Baggett and David Green.

Barry Pickthall/PPL

Mark Lamble

*A unique Solent sail past by Suhaili,
Lively Lady and Gipsy Moth IV.*

Paul Gelder/Yachting Monthly

ABOVE:
*Paul Lees from
Crusader Sails
with Chichester's
original hand-
bearing compass.*

RIGHT:
*John Walsh at
the helm of
Gipsy Moth
overhauls Suhaili.*

Paul Gelder/Yachting Monthly

*A Gipsy Moth
watch from
Corum, the
project's official
timekeeper.*

In the second race *Suhaili*, under spinnaker, slowly overhauled *Gipsy Moth* and held the lead downwind for a while. At the prizegiving, Alan Priddy's crew won the token prize bottle of Plymouth gin which they sportingly donated to *Suhaili*'s crew who were last! Soon, *Lively Lady* would also be sailing around the world a second time, with a crew of youngsters, to commemorate Alec Rose's achievement.

Nine months after *Gipsy Moth IV* left Greenwich on a low-loader she sailed up the River Thames for a royal re-dedication by Princess Anne on 7 September. A cheer went up from more than 1,000 people lining the waterfront as the ketch rounded a bend in the river, skippered by Richard Baggett. On board were Ellen MacArthur, Shirley Robertson, two-time Olympic sailing gold medalist, Ginnie Chichester, the UKSA's Frank Fletcher and myself, plus two youngsters from the Ellen MacArthur Trust: David Williams, 16, from

the Isle of Wight and Dean Welton, 15, from Uxbridge, Middlesex.

We berthed alongside Greenwich Pier, close by the *Cutty Sark* and Ellen jumped ashore with the bow line. Princess Anne met the crew as well as youngsters who would be sailing *Gipsy Moth*.

These included Amie Mayers, a 16-year-old Peckham schoolgirl, who was to sail on a Caribbean passage to Barbados, plus other teenagers training to sail aboard: Martin Dalby, 18, from Scarborough; Peter Heggie, 17, from Plymouth; Kaloyan Palatov, 17, from South London; Philip Holman, 17, from Dulwich; Josh Clarke, 14, from Scarborough; and Hamza Noor, 15, from Peckham.

Parked in front of *Cutty Sark*'s bowsprit was the original red Gipsy Moth bi-plane which flew above Sir Francis Chichester in 1967. Her pilot then, John Reid, now aged 75, was there to meet Princess Anne with his family, including son Nigel.

The Dean of Chichester, The Rev Nicholas Frayling, blessed the yacht before handing over *Gipsy Moth IV*'s original Royal Yacht Squadron pennant which went round the world in 1996-67 and had been on display in Chichester Cathedral's Sailors' Chapel and loaned for the second circumnavigation.

Michael Wunderman, president of Corum Watches, official timekeepers to the *Gipsy Moth IV* project, presented a £4,000 chronograph watch for her second circumnavigation.

'This watch will be at the heart of our circumnavigation,' said Green. 'We are using a sextant, the stars and paper charts, just as Chichester did, so your gift will help keep us off the rocks.' Alas, neither the Dean's blessing nor Green's remark would prove infallible in the South Pacific in eight months' time.

Next day, Tower Bridge was raised and *Gipsy Moth IV* sailed into the Pool of London, with Jon Ely at the helm, for a sponsors' and supporters' dinner on HMS *Belfast*. Here Lord Montague of Beaulieu pledged to reinstate the freedom of his privately-owned river for *Gipsy Moth IV*, which he had given Chichester in 1967.

Gipsy Moth's final duty as the undoubted sailing star of the summer of 2005 was to officially open the 37th Southampton Boat Show.

The yacht still had no communication system or a manual that would tell future skippers how the complex equipment worked. Dewi Thomas, Global Voyage Coordinator, with whom I would be sailing on the first leg across Biscay in a few days, had been given four months to organise a safety policy, risk assessments, operating procedures and a yacht equipment manual. 'It's fair to say we had not appreciated what we had taken on' he said. 'And we were fortunate to have the support of Peter Seymour and the Blue Water Rally.'

Dewi had agreed to be mate on the first leg from Plymouth to Gibraltar, so he could finish writing the manual and resolve any oversights for subsequent legs.

'The voyage was always about the young people and the ethos of the project was simple,' said Dewi. 'The problem with young people is that they don't think. Our role was to give them the chance to think about what they want from life. If they could see what Chichester had achieved at 65, they'd see their dreams and aspirations were within reach.'

His remit was to select three deserving young people for each leg, and it proved difficult to bury the term disadvantaged. Affluence was not a barrier and if young people had a strong enough desire they were given a chance to sail. Crew were chosen from schools, charities and organisations involved with the project via sponsors, the UKSA or a direct approach. Some crew were selected on the strength of personal letters describing why they wanted a berth. 'Many were very humbling stories,' said Dewi.

On the eve of *Gipsy Moth*'s departure on her round-the-world cruise a dinner was held at the Royal Western Yacht Club where Giles Chichester made a farewell speech recalling this was the 10th eve of departure of a *Gipsy Moth* from Plymouth he'd attended.

Gipsy Moth *heads up the Thames to her old home in Greenwich, with Shirley Robertson, Ginnie Chichester and Ellen MacArthur.*

'The first was in 1960, for the first-ever single-handed transatlantic race, when I attended a particularly merry dinner at Pedro's Restaurant in the Octagon,' he said. 'Afterwards I followed my father and Mike Richey as these two great navigators weaved their way across the Hoe pretending to make observations of the moon, or possibly street lamps while obviously enjoying the spirit of the occasion. The yacht was *Gipsy Moth III* and she and my father won that solo race to New York.

'My father would be flattered that his achievements are being celebrated anew on this latest blue water voyage,' he said. 'I wish *Gipsy Moth*'s new crew fair winds, a safe passage and great success.'

OVERLEAF: Gipsy Moth *opens Southampton Boat Show. Inset: sailing to a dinner on HMS Belfast in the Pool of London; the UKSA/Corum stand at the boat show; Princess Anne meets young crew at Greenwich.*

Plymouth to Gibraltar

Big Brother Goes to Sea

Leg 1

Distance:
1,100 miles

Skipper:
Richard Baggett,
UKSA (34)

Mate:
Dewi Thomas

Crew Leader:
Paul Gelder (58)

Crew:
Elaine Caldwell
(23), Peter
Heggie (17) and
Matthew Pakes
(16)

Leg sponsor:
UKSA and Isle
of Wight

Sailing into the teeth of a Force 7 in the Bay of Biscay on *Gipsy Moth IV*'s maiden voyage, I wasn't expecting to feel like an extra in TV's Big Brother. The skipper, Richard Baggett, might as well have shouted 'Lights! Camera! Action!' instead of calling 'All hands on deck!'

For when we finally cast off from Queen Anne's Battery, Plymouth, on Sunday 25 September, to begin *GMIV*'s long-awaited second circumnavigation, we were in the media spotlight – escorted by an armada of 100-plus vessels packed with supporters, well-wishers and camera crews.

Then, beyond the horizon and heading towards the Eddystone Lighthouse, we were at last alone – well almost, if you didn't count our

Barry Pickthall/PPL

bleeping satellite communications dome on the mizzen mast, plus the CCTV cameras. We were in Oceania, George Orwell's fictitious country from *Nineteen Eighty-Four*. They say Britain is the most spied-upon nation and at sea there was no escape. On deck we were 'spied' on by two remote-controlled webcams located on the main and mizzen masts. Two more webcams were down below, in the galley and saloon, plus a portable video camera on deck. Which of the six crew would be first to get voted overboard by our internet audience? The young crew had been given 'camera training' by Conrad Humphreys, the winning skipper of the 2000-01 BT Global Challenge Race and another enthusiastic supporter of the *GMIV* Project.

The irascible Sir Francis would never have tolerated such an intrusion. To him any form of media was a plague and nuisance. He once famously berated a *Sunday Times* reporter who radioed him on his solo voyage from Sydney to ask what his first meal was after Cape Horn: 'Strongly urge you to stop questioning and interviewing me which poisons the romantic attraction of this voyage...' he snapped back her. I knew how he felt.

But Richard and the First Mate, Dewi Thomas, accepted no excuses. It was our duty to send a daily video report back to www. gipsymoth.org. While Chichester was harassed by poor radio communications, our 'curse' was to have state-of-the-art satcoms, plus a website and '*GMIV* TV' hungry for daily stories.

Gipsy Moth's crew was skipper Richard, Mate Dewi (the Global Voyage Co-ordinator), myself and our three young crew: Elaine Caldwell, from the Isle of Skye, Peter Heggie, from Plymouth, and Matt Pakes, from the Isle of Wight. None of the youngsters had spent a night at sea on a yacht before and Matt had never been away from home on his own. We were bound across Biscay for Gibraltar with an ominous forecast of strong winds and heavy seas in the Western Channel to temper youthful excitement with apprehension.

It was a rugged first night on deck in Force 5/6 winds. Thirty-nine years ago this night, also a Sunday, Chichester ended his fourth week at sea after 3,887 miles and crossed the equator. He wrote in the logbook, *Gipsy Moth* 'was bucking to shake my teeth loose'. Down below things were no different for us. Pete was thrown out of his forepeak bunk and came on watch at 0400 with a bruise above his eye. By dawn the navy blue spray dodgers were carrot coloured. Most of the young crew had been seasick. Was my beef stew that bad? Cooking for six on *GMIV*'s restored two-burner Primus stove was a challenge, but at least the fish enjoyed it.

It was thrilling to sense *Gipsy Moth IV* coming alive, spreading her wings under the half moon and stars. No longer was she a static museum exhibit becalmed forever in concrete. Her spars and rigging creaked, the sound of water rushed past the 7/8th inch mahogany hull and the rattle of saucepans and cans in lockers added to a seagoing symphony. In the eerie red glow of the B&G cockpit instruments, skipper Richard, shrouded in his oilskin hood, took on the ghostly mantle of Sir Francis.

DAY 2 At daybreak on Monday after an exhilarating night with Force 7 gusts we had light winds and were rolling in a big swell. We were due to rendezvous with an RAF Nimrod aeroplane taking aerial photos but the French authorities declined to give permission since we were in their territorial waters, just inside the 12-mile limit. At noon, Richard and Dewi showed the young crew how to take a noon sight using the Freiberger sextant, donated by the Maritime Trust and the snazzy Corum *GMIV* watch, a prized item on the skipper's wrist which cost nearly £1,000. Bling comes to sea!

The start of Gipsy Moth's second great adventure – sailing past Plymouth Hoe with a bi-plane escort.

Barry Pickthall/PPL

By that afternoon we were motor-sailing down the Chenal de Four to put into the port of Brest, so Elaine, Pete and Matt could find their sea legs more gradually. We notched up a record (so far) 9 knots running down the Rade de Brest, surfing waves with a glorious sunset astern. Berthing at Le Moulin Blanc marina in strong winds, teamwork demonstrated how quickly our young crew were literally learning the ropes. This was *GMIV*'s first foreign port of call since Sydney, 38 years ago and she attracted plenty of attention. Paul Shearwood, British skipper of a Nicholson 35, took our lines and welcomed us in with astonishment. He was the first of many sailors in ports all over the world who had been inspired by Chichester's derring-do and was delighted to see her back in the water. We gave him a tour of *GMIV*.

DAY 3 After a day spent going over shipboard routines and systems, we topped up water and fuel tanks and cast off at dusk. Under the eagle eye of Dewi, aka 'Stephen Spielberg', Richard filmed six 'takes' for the daily internet diary of the crew busy preparing for departure. Elaine and Pete had been hoisted up the masts in a bosun's chair to clean salt off the webcam lenses. The young crew soon entered into spirit of recording their emotions and sharing their thoughts with the audience back home via the internet video diaries.

No longer becalmed in a sea of concrete, Gipsy Moth *shows her tendancy to acute angles of heel – but she looks a complete thoroughbred.*

Graham Snook/Yachting Monthly

A forecast of Force 5 NW winds made it desirable to head across the Continental Shelf into deep waters, avoiding the rough waves where the seabed suddenly rises from two miles to hundreds of metres.

Our next waypoint was Cabo Finisterre, western-most point of Europe. That night Elaine spotted her first dolphins – a pod of 10 swimming alongside. 'In 10,00 miles of sailing I had not seen a single fish in the water… only flying fish in the air,' Chichester wrote in his log book in 1966.

With the backdrop of a wild and windy night, Force 6 gusts and dramatic white wave crests breaking up the black seascape, Elaine confessed it was 'daunting' to helm the 53ft ketch. When a rogue wave hit the long, deep keel, the whole boat shuddered and lockers sprung open, spilling their contents on the floor. Chichester described the cacophony in his book as like 'a country fair in full swing'. In his forepeak bunk, Matt battled tiredness and seasickness. He probably felt like Chichester in the Roaring Forties, who recorded: 'The rolling was frightful and I felt as feeble as a half-dead mouse.'

Matt might have taken comfort from Giles Chichester's departure speech in Plymouth when he said: 'There are a few people who do not suffer seasickness and I have to say their air of superiority and disdain for the rest of us who do is frankly rather insensitive. I was tempted to say nauseating but I thought that might be over-egging the point! I have always suffered seasickness but long passages have showed me how to get over it and to enjoy life at sea. The secret is patience, plus keeping warm, dry and hydrated and when you do emerge from the misery you feel more alive, more in tune with nature than ever and I think it is worth a little suffering on the way to get that feeling.'

DAY 4 A third of the way across Biscay, we headed towards a point on the chart marked 'Biscay Abyssal Plain'. Elaine declared: 'It's like infinity… a void… the sea and sky just go on and on. I feel I'm in prison and I want to escape to anywhere there's a surface that doesn't move.'

*Dewis Thomas,
Global Voyage
Coordinator, takes
a noon sight.*

*RIGHT: Peter
Heggie, for whom
the voyage opened
a new chapter.*

At night, hurtling along in the blackness, it felt like being on the edge of an abyss. Bracing yourself in the cockpit at 45° was exhilarating and uncomfortable. Like driving a car with no headlights or shock absorbers over a ploughed field. No seatbelt, brakes, or windscreen wipers either – imagine the car is a convertible and it's raining salt water!

We all got well and truly soaked by the odd 'souser', as Chichester called them, a wave slapping *GMIV*'s beam.

There was a mini-glossary of Chichester terms:

Strikers: 'waves that slam into the yacht viciously.'

Souser wave: 'the bit that came through the hatch and emptied straight into my trousers.'

Underfugs: Long winter woollies worn with a wool shirt. 'With oilies keeping all air out, I was parboiled on the foredeck…'

Shemozzle: a nautical uproar, kerfuffle or 'to-do' – usually on deck in a rising wind.

Tight as a coot: 'I don't know how a coot could be tight. It was very good rum though.'

We had at least one luxury item Sir Francis never enjoyed – a sprayhood to shelter the helmsman from wind and spray – but it didn't always work! Trying to live at the acute angle of heel, with occasional violent swings to 40°, was like the ultimate aerobics class. I lost 5 lb in five days.

Getting togged up in boots, oilskins, lifejacket and harness to go on watch was like being an aquanaut heading into a watery orbit. And going to the heads was akin to being a Grand National jockey battling to stay in the saddle at Beecher's Brook with trousers round ankles. *GMIV*'s tendency to try and throw her 'riders' or hurl them across the saloon as she lurches ('like a whip cracking' said Chichester), means there are a trio of 'bum straps' – at the chart table, galley cooker and 'video media-editing suite'. A 'bum strap' is a padded sling that goes round your bottom and hooks onto the table, or cooker, so you can brace yourself against the forces of gravity. We needed a fourth for the sink when washing up!

DAY 5 After the rough we relished the smooth – motor-sailing under a starlit sky on a silken sea ruffled by the ocean swell. Astern off the port quarter, a sliver of moon rose on the horizon. To port Orion's Belt sparkled and Mars glowed pink. I wondered which stars Sir Francis sighted as he sailed past Spain.

Off the bow, the lights of Spain's city of La Coruña were reflected in a faint glow in the sky. We looked in vain for the loom of the world's oldest lighthouse, the Torre de Hércules, built by the Romans to mark Coruña's natural harbour. It's Land Ho!… well almost.

There's a magic about night sailing as exhilarating as it's enchanting. Seeing the stars shine so brightly in an infinity of velvet blackness is a sailors' privilege. There was no big city light pollution to dim our private show.

'Nights like this make the rough bits worth the suffering,' said Elaine. Before dawn, Dewi got the sextant out of its box to get some star sights. Meanwhile, another light show was going on beneath us – in the ocean. Still in deep water, just off soundings, *Gipsy Moth IV* left a comet trail of 'sparks' astern … 'bio-luminescence' from plankton in the water. It was another world beneath our keel and Elaine was fascinated. She wanted to catch a marine 'Tinkerbell' to take home!

By day, the ocean in these parts was some two miles deep and a beautiful dark shade of cobalt blue. In last three days we'd seen Biscay in all her moods… except real anger. It was as if she'd been toying with us.

At noon we hove-to to carry out the thrice daily MetOcean environmental measurement. Weather permitting they are carried out at 0600, noon and 1800, measuring water clarity and the state of our oceans around the globe. The data is emailed back via satellite with latitude and longitude.

Dewi Thomas

The tests were arranged by Dr Andrew Eccleston, a lecturer in Nautical Studies at Plymouth University's School of Earth, Ocean & Environmental Sciences. Andrew, a keen *GMIV* supporter as well as a sailor, was also our official meteorologist around the world.

Mid-morning we spoke to a passing cargo ship by VHF radio. It turned out to be a Belgian-owned cargo ship with a Russian skipper taking quartz rocks to Norway!

With the sun blazing, it was time to peel off the oilies and put on shorts and T-shirts. 'Can we go swimming out here?' asked Matt. We could, but there was no time to stop.

DAY 6 At night the sweet scent of earth was carried on the wind 30 miles out to sea from the Spanish coast. Or was it the smell of the skipper's deck shoes which had been banished to the lazarette (the furthest aft locker) two days out of Brest?

As a smudge of land – the mountains of Galicia and Cape Finisterre – hove into view around lunchtime, a pod of 30 or 40 bottlenose dolphins streaked up both sides of *GMIV*, as if to escort us into Spanish waters. Matt, who was asleep, suffering for many days from debilitating seasickness, shot through the forehatch like a Polaris missile, clutching the camera he'd worked overtime to buy as a waiter in his local Isle of Wight pub. The magic encounter with this aquabatics team performing barrel-rolls and sychronised swimming cured his malady.

With light winds and practically every stitch of canvas flying, not to mention some crew laundry drying, the cockpit was a snakepit of ropes. As we rolled on downwind even Richard admitted poling out the headsail was 'a bit of a work up!' We called it 'pole dancing' but we all marvelled at how 65 year old Sir Francis coped with it singlehanded. The spinnaker poles and Proctor masts and spars were all Chichester's original, restored to shining silver by Jacob, part of the maintenance team at the UKSA.

With Richard amidships on the sat-phone to the UKSA and me in the bow, listening to my iPod, Dewi was showing the young crew

In three days we saw Biscay in all her moods… except real anger. Was she toying with us?

Dewi Thomas

Elaine tries her hand at rope work. 'I feel I'm in prison,' she said of Biscay's limitless void.

how to take a noon sight, using the Freiberger sextant. When Peter later tried his hand at 'shooting the sun' his sights placed us within four miles of our GPS position.

When night came we could hardly see where the navy blue dodgers ended and the night sky began. Sailing south to Bayona, a necklace of twinkling lights marked the Spanish coast abeam. With no detailed charts for our landfall, we dropped the foresails and reefed the main to slow *GMIV* down for a daylight arrival.

DAY 7 Time becomes irrelevant on passage. Spanish time? Greenwich Mean Time? We'll get there at dawn. For the fourth time we had a dolphin escort. From midnight to dawn they were our 'outriders', streaking like luminous torpedoes and criss-crossing our bow wave. Every now and then they'd disappear off somewhere, like a dog off the leash, returning to 'sniff' around *GMIV* and make sure we were okay. It was as if the dolphins were welcoming *Gipsy Moth IV* back to the sea after her solitary confinement in dry dock. Her long, deep keel scattered a trillion sparkling diamonds in her wake as if in celebration.

As the sun rose over the rugged mountains of Galicia, the tiller was pushed to starboard and *Gipsy Moth IV* headed towards the lights of the bustling fishing town of Bayona. Nothing beats a dawn landfall after a decent passage and this one was spectacular.

Scores of tiny fishing boats were out for the early morning catch and waved at us. Tying up to a pontoon berth at the Monte Real Club de Yates, Elaine, Pete and Matt finally jumped ashore four days and five nights since leaving France. '*Terra firma…* less terror, more firmer!' someone joked.

'Having your sea legs obviously means losing your land ones!' joked Pete as he swayed and wobbled off for a hot shower. Chichester, too, confided he felt 'a bit wonky' when he stepped ashore in Sydney – but that was after 14,100 miles and 107 days!

Later, in one of Bayona's picturesque seafood restaurants we tucked into a celebration paella lunch. For Elaine, Pete and Matt, sailing from 50°N to 42°N, had been more than an adventure – it had been a baptism of fire and a rite of passage rolled into one. They'd learned how on a boat you trust your life to your shipmates and how they depend on you. They'd used the sun and planets to find our position on the globe by sextant – just as Chichester had done before the days of GPS sat-nav. Together we'd sailed 510 nautical miles in just over five days. But we'd covered a distance beyond measuring by mere calculator.

Reluctantly, it was time for me to leave *GMIV* and return to the office, while the crew spent a couple of days resting in Bayona, before coast-hopping down the Portugese coast to Gibraltar, via Lagos, Vilamoura, Cadiz and Puerto de Santa Maria.

One crewman short, they tried out Blondie Hasler's windvane self-steering gear. Sir Francis complained that the windvane had great difficulty keeping *GMIV* on course. With a breeze on the beam, Richard tried for an hour and eventually threw his hands in the air with a cry of, 'What are crew for?'

In Vilamoura they picked up new crew leader Tom Buggie, from UKSA. With the Portuguese Trade Wind *(Nortada)* and a southerly current to accelerate progress down the Portuguese coast, they had the running headsail poled out on the starboard side when a wave and a gust ambushed the yacht, skewed her to starboard and the pole buckled and folded in half. It was a distressing moment.

'We felt we'd broken a piece of our national treasure,' said Dewi. But Sir Francis also broke a running pole, although not quite so early on in his voyage.

The final leg round Cape Trafalgar tested boat and crew with a full gale gusting 40-45 knots. A big roller broke on the foredeck swamping the boat and stopping her dead in her tracks. Richard fired up the Yanmar engine, which pushed *GMIV* along at 5 knots. At the start of the Straits of Gibraltar they had a steady three-knot tide in their favour.

On arrival in Gibraltar, Richard had the easiest customs clearance he'd ever experienced. The customs officer read the name *Gipsy Moth IV* on the ship's documents and couldn't believe the famous ketch was back at sea.

Gipsy Moth IV had come through her 'shakedown' cruise with flying colours. Since her launch on 20 June, she'd clocked up a mere 884 miles on Solent sail trials and her passages to Greenwich and Plymouth. This had been a shake, rattle and roll cruise, since the Moth loves to roll downwind and sail on her ear upwind.

Yes, she had a few leaks – the forehatch and two skylights above the saloon, plus the chainplates. But Chichester said he 'needed a tent pitched in the cabin to stay dry!' Dewi wore his oilskins in his bunk. 'Welcome to the authentic *GMIV* experience!' said skipper Richard. Yet, after one of the fastest maritime restoration projects in recent history, she had performed all we could have asked of her. Three cheers were well deserved for Camper & Nicholsons' shipwrights... not forgetting Richard.

He's an instinctive seafarer who was probably born at an angle of 45° – ideal for skippering *GMIV*. He sails by the worn seat of his patched pants, defying gravity and sticking to the decks like a magnet. What Richard doesn't know about sailing you could write on the sharp end of a marlin spike.

He inspires confidence in his young crew, teaching life as well as sailing skills to those who might not otherwise get a chance to sail. His reward is to see them cast aside fear and uncertainty and discover self-reliance and confidence.

The verdicts from the young crew said it all.

'Sailing *GMIV* was tough... like being inside a pinball machine. But the rewards were amazing... some things I'll keep in my heart and treasure forever,' said Elaine. Her comment that *GMIV* was like a seed, growing out into a tree with her branches reaching out to everyone, even brought a lump to the throat of old sea dogs.

'*Gipsy Moth* and Sir Francis have taught me that you can do anything if you put your mind to it,' said Matthew.

'How on earth did Chichester do it at 65?' asked Peter. 'The voyage opened a new chapter for me... I never knew about Chichester before. He was an amazing man. I've never liked giving up and letting something beat me... I've learned if you can always bring a positive to a negative it makes life much happier.'

Wise words from *GMIV*'s new young salts – and a wonderful start to her second voyage round the world giving a new lease of life to a new generation of adventurers.

Matt Pakes, like many young crew who followed in his wake, suffered days of debilitating seasickness.

Rally start at Gibraltar

When Ray Nicholson and his wife Antonia, both 33, joined *Gipsy Moth IV* as skipper and mate in Gibraltar, it was the first time the 53ft ketch had enjoyed a husband-and-wife crew in command since Francis and Sheila Chichester sailed her in 1967. Ray and Antonia both took great pride in the boat's appearance and already *Gipsy Moth IV* was turning heads and creating interest.

While Antonia briefed the new crew of schoolboys, Ray was busy sanding a damaged patch of paint on the bow following a minor clunk with driftwood. He and Antonia had spent many hours sanding, varnishing and painting *Gipsy Moth IV* during her restoration at Camper & Nicholsons. Antonia gave the three young crew a tour of their home for the

Leg 2

Skipper:
Ray Nicholson
(33), UKSA

Mate:
Antonia
Nicholson (33)
UKSA

Crew Leader:
Mike King,
Isle of Wight
Economic
Partnership

Crew:
Kaloyan Palator,
Philip Holman,
both from
Bacon's College,
Peckham,
Shaun Kerslake,
from Plymouth
Watersports

Antonia Nicholson

next seven days and showed them how the notorious Primus stove was fired up and how a marine toilet worked! All the food lockers were checked and they made a menu plan for the week and a shopping list.

Crew leader Mike King, from the Isle of Wight Economic Partnership, one of the major sponsors of the project, had already given two very special brothers a tour of the yacht. They told him how 39 years ago they had travelled from Yorkshire to Plymouth, especially to see Chichester's triumphant arrival from Australia. One of them, a soldier, had gone AWOL to witness the historic occasion.

Unluckily for them, lack of wind meant Chichester was late arriving, so they decided to go to the cinema to kill time. But by the time the film was over and they got to the quayside it was packed with spectators and they couldn't see a thing. Spotting a BBC TV outside broadcast unit truck, they grabbed

Peter Seymour

Graham Snook/Yachting Monthly

LEFT: *The Blue Water Rally Team with Peter and Annette Seymour, Richard Bolt and Tony Diment.*

RIGHT: *Ray Nicholson.*

BELOW: *Class of 2005-07, with rally skippers and crew.*

Peter Seymour

a length of electrical cable and, posing as technicians, shoved their way through the crowd and got to the quayside just as Chichester stepped ashore.

'It seems everyone has a tale to tell about this amazing boat,' said Mike.

Later, the crew set sail for Cadiz, 60 miles from Gibraltar. They were turned away from their first port of call, Puerto America. Having motored into the basin they found there was no room, so they went across the bay to Puerto Sherry, arriving at 0400. But here the swell was too much and *Gipsy Moth IV* was lurching back and forth. They tried the fuel berth, but even here the fenders and lines would not have survived for long. Eventually, they motored around to Puerto Santa Maria, where they were spotted by a yachtsman who had last seen *Gipsy Moth IV* in Sydney, Australia. He couldn't believe she was the same boat! This was a scenario that was to be repeated around the world – so famous was *Gipsy Moth IV*. The marina office asked them to move again, because they didn't want two yachts rafted on a hammerhead berth together. They cast off for

a berth in Puerto Rota. At least the crew were getting familiar with the mooring technique! Finally, they tied up, nearly ten hours since their arrival in the bay and cleared customs, paid the fees and plugged into shore power. 'I'd berthed *Gipsy Moth IV* more times in one day than Sir Francis did during his two-year voyage!' lamented Ray.

Next day Ray spent the morning dismantling the Primus stove because only one burner worked. The cleaning needle had seized in its housing. 'I wonder how many times Sir Francis would have had to do this on his voyage,' thought Ray.

Gipsy Moth IV went on to sail across the Straits of Gibraltar to visit Tarifa and Ceuta, the Spanish enclave in North Africa, before going on to Morocco and returning to Gibraltar to change crew after a week. 'The crew joined the boat as three individuals and will be departing as a team,' said Ray.

Two days later, *Gipsy Moth IV* joined a fleet of Oyster yachts to celebrate the 200th anniversary of the Battle of Trafalgar off Cape Trafalgar. Some 20 to 30 yachts took part and

Gipsy Moth *heads across the Straits of Gibraltar on her first visit to North Africa.*

Tony Diment

the Tall Ship *Lord Nelson* took the place of HMS *Victory*. *Gipsy Moth IV* received a warm welcome and became an honorary Oyster for the occasion. It was an emotional occasion. There were readings – including Nelson's prayer 'England Expects…' made via VHF radio. 'We were emotionally touched at the sight of wreaths and flowers cast on the water,' said Ray, who was joined by John Jeffery, appointed by the UKSA to train new crew back in the Solent. Little did John know that in seven months he would be assisting *Gipsy Moth IV*'s rescue from shipwreck on a Pacific reef. He and Richard Baggett were to become the two sailors who clocked up the most miles round the world on *Gipsy Moth IV*.

Next day *Gipsy Moth IV* joined a group of Blue Water Rally yachts for a cruise across the straits to Smir, Morocco, accompanied by rally co-director Tony Diment and his wife Christine. 'It was exciting to feel a part of the beginning of a round the world adventure,' said Ray as 17 rally yachts fanned out astern.

They left Gibraltar in the dark, with the backdrop of a fantastic sunset. Next morning the wind came up with the sun and they set the main, mizzen, staysail and the running sail and spotted three or four dolphins.

In Morocco they visited the city of Tetuan, with its market of carpet sellers, spice sellers, a tannery, wood working shops and blacksmiths. 'It was a time warp,' said Ray. They ate kebabs and cous cous and drank mint tea before sailing back to Gibraltar to join the fleet next day. 'The sense of community on the rally is building into something very special,' said Ray. 'I'll be sorry to leave, but pleased I'll be rejoining the yacht with Antonia on the other side of the Atlantic Ocean.'

The Governor of Gibraltar and his wife made an informal visit to *Gipsy Moth IV* and Antonia and Ray also took the Commodore of Gibraltar's Royal Navy for a sail with his wife and son, assisted by three 15-year-old sailors from the Royal Gibraltar Yacht Club.

'Everyone appreciated what a hard and monumental task it was for Sir Francis when he went around the world singlehanded,' said Ray.

Tony Diment

Christine Diment, from the Blue Water Rally, took Gipsy Moth's helm on a cruise to Smir Morocco.

Gibraltar to Tenerife

By Dick Durham

Well heeled!

Leg 3

Distance:
740 miles

Skipper:
Steve Rouse
(50) *UKSA*

Mate:
Antonia
Nicholson (33)
UKSA

Crew Leader:
Dick Durham
Yachting Monthly

Crew:
Myles Grant-
Butler (16),
Rahim
Kheraj (17)
and Martin
Dalby (18)

Leg sponsor:
Corum

Take a 53ft boat, toss it into the North Atlantic during a full gale at night in a downpour. Add unmarked 'motorways' of giant ships blundering past, indifferent to your pathetic attempts to get out of their way at walking pace. This is no place in which to be ill!

On our first night at sea, four of the ship's company suffered *mal de mer*. Our bunks became heaving, twisting, tumbling surfaces to be gripped, let go of and braced against. In time, I felt, I'd develop a washboard stomach.

Just a few hours earlier, a mournful foghorn on Gibraltar's Europa Point and starbursts of rockets marked our departure with 20 other yachts at the start of the 2005–07 Blue Water Round the World Rally. We'd all recovered from a Mount Gay farewell party, hosted for the rally at the Royal Gibraltar Yacht

Club, by *Gipsy Moth IV*. It was such a success, some crew (not ours!) woke up on the other side of the border in Spain.

Crossing the Strait we saw pilot whales and dolphins as we ate cold lamb sandwiches for lunch. Skipper, Steve Rouse, has a policy of throwing absolutely nothing over the side. Asked what to do with the lamb bones he said: 'How would you like it if a dolphin came into your front room and chucked rubbish all over the place?' A fine sentiment, which was soon ignored by Dulwich College student Myles Grant-Butler, who was obliged to return his lunch to the sea. He was followed by Yorkshire catering student Martin Dalby

Paul Gelder/Yachting Monthly

as nightfall brought rain and 40 knots of apparent wind from the south-west.

I steered between one ship's stern and a trawler's array of lights which signalled something I'd forgotten from my RYA Yachtmaster theory. As I eased the mainsheet, the boom end dragged through the sea and Steve and Antonia clawed to get the sail down. The pitiful, arcane, roller-reefing gear was taking an age to make its effect felt and Steve agreed that for the sake of safety we needed a makeshift slab-reefing system. In the end we dropped the whole damned sail, lashed it into a spray and rain-sodden pulp and ran off under headsails alone – north. The wrong way! To get her to come about we put the helm over and backed the sheets. First time she refused, throwing spray back over us. Next time we got her about and sat exhausted, soaked and with the rest of the night in front of us.

The third student, Rahim Kherag, also from Dulwich College, helped manfully in the cockpit even though his first night on a boat offshore was proving a challenge. He later wrote: 'I spent much of the night on deck terrified, holding on for my life, cold, wet, and scared sick as Steve and Antonia fought with sails and Dick wrestled with the tiller. Where I could I tugged and yelled, but I felt helpless before nature... the sea can be kind but also evil. It is a night I will remember for a long time.'

On hearing of our wild night in the Strait of Gibraltar, the UKSA HQ in Cowes asked that next time we were fighting wind and wave we should activate the satellite-linked video cameras rigged so our misery could be shared worldwide!

Gibraltar was now just a memory: a comfortable hotel bedroom, sweet-smelling leather coat shops and too-early Christmas trees.

David Green

Gipsy Moth sails past Europa Point at the start of the Blue Water Round the World Rally

Paul Gelder/Yachting Monthly

More than 30 yachts would join the 2005-07 Blue Water Round the World Rally – some joining in the Caribbean.

Steve, wearing a T-shirt with the legend 'Control Freak' in several languages, was worried about Myles dehydrating. A rugby prop for London's Dulwich College, Myles had been in a permanent one-man 'scrum' on the aft deck since Gibraltar.

'If you don't eat and drink I'll adminster a saline drip because you'll become a liability instead of an asset, Steve warned him. The threat worked and Myles started chewing on a slice of bread and later ate three apples.

To add insult to injury, we all carried the infuriating image of Chichester who endured all this alone and at an age when most of us are happy to circumnavigate our home town on a free bus pass.

The quiet hero of the trio was turning out to be Rahim, who was first in line to tend sheets, hand sails, re-stow leaky diesel jerry-cans, make tea, steer and take charge of the oceanographic experiments.

Next day the wind eased and a strange plateau-like surface appeared over the sea in the Atlantic swell as we crossed the 200m contour into the 600m contour. Dolphins came leaping towards us: 'The only things we get like this in Thirsk are battered and they come with chips!' said Martin. 'They're like kippers, only bigger.' The voyage was already giving Myles a new perspective on life aquatic. We discovered

our first night's heavy weather had swept the boathook over the side and contaminated one of the spare diesel jerry cans with salt water.

The following night the loom of Casablanca was the only evidence of land, partly obscured by a rolling black Atlantic swell. It was hard to imagine that the dirty yellow glow of this exotic African city contained the gin joint where Humphrey Bogart met Ingrid Bergman and Sam played 'You must remember this...' – again.

Aside from Hollywood stars, Martin was counting shooting stars: 'I'm up to 15, That's more than most people see in a lifetime,' he said, 'and I bet there's more going on behind me.'

It's said that every shooting star is the soul of a sailor outward bound for the last time. St Peter must have been busy for dissolving fireballs were melting against the earth's protective shield all night. We all saw them. A couple actually even lit up the mainsail.

Just 24 hours earlier, the same Martin had described his normal vicarious world of second-hand experiences from television, internet sites and videos. His naturally enquiring mind and scientific bent had been stretched by nothing more than characters in Red Dwarf discussing black holes. Now he can't wait to share the experience of his 'spooky' night watches with girlfriend Lisa.

The seventh crew member aboard is Blackbeard, the ship's mascot. You may remember Chichester writing about needing a chimpanzee crew with long arms to work the ship. Our monkey spends all his time lying in a net hammock guarding the bananas.

At dusk in the 'twilight zone' Steve helped Antonia catch some 'falling' stars on the sextant to determine our position. All good sailors respect this noble art, even though they rely almost totally on GPS. You ignore it at your peril: those who consider the sextant obsolete are heretics and may as well make a headdress of albatross feathers and await providence to act with a power systems failure. The satellites are apparently pock-marked from flying 'rubble' in outer space, so even they are not infallible.

Dick Durham/Yachting Monthly

While the bulkhead over the chart table glowed reassuringly with our satellite-determined location, Steve and Antonia braced themselves in the cockpit to pull stars down to the horizon and measure their distance and angles to get us a fix. It can only be done at dusk or dawn, when there is enough light to see a horizon, but not so much that you can't see the stars.

Antonia's duties included transmitting daytime video clips via the sat comms station

at night. Here, the daily log for the website is typed on a laptop PC set in what looks like an old school desk with a lid. The keyboard is four inches below the lip of the desk making it tricky to type even on the level.

On our fourth night out, Antonia became aware of a presence beside her. The position she works at was once the site of Sir Francis Chichester's famous gimballed chair. 'I thought it was you or Steve,' she said, 'but when I turned to look nobody was there.' Perhaps the old man was watching over us to see *Gipsy Moth IV* safely round the world again?

Three days from Tenerife in an ugly cross sea and up to 40 knots of wind, we dropped the mainsail and large jib which was overpowering her narrow hull and sailed under staysail alone. We tried to re-set the mizzen, which on most ketch-rigged craft should have produced a good heavy weather sail plan, but this caused her to stall. So the miniscule staysail dragged her towards the Canaries at an acceptable 4–5 knots. Meanwhile she rolled, rolled, rolled.

The motion sent Martin, sick, back to his bunk, and hurled Rahim bodily onto the chart table where he sat like a mystic in a kasbah coffee shop. Myles was thrown off

Skipper Steve Rouse, from the UKSA, was a former sergeant major in the Royal Anglian Regiment.

Dick Durham/Yachting Monthly

Rough weather, two days out from Tenerife. Myles is on the helm with Steve Rouse behind him and Antonia Nicholson on the right.

the helm onto the cockpit floor. The locker drawers opened as she rolled to port then shut as she rolled to starboard. Locker doors waved at us from head to galley as though in some abandoned house. When Antonia started making supper she opened the one locker which hadn't already opened itself and was showered with jars of jam, Lea & Perrins sauce bottles, plastic tubs of peanut butter and narrowly missed being brained by a heavy duty jar of Marmite.

'★!★@!★ this,' cursed skipper Steve, 'those ★!★@!★ing bottles are going over the side. This is like the first day on the Somme.' Not that Steve was there, but he is a former Company Sergeant Major from the Royal Anglian Regiment who served in Northern Ireland.

Just making a cup of tea was a major offensive in the lurching bedlam of the Mad Hatter's kitchen. Firing up the Primus stove meant liberally hosing down the stove with methylated spirit, followed by the conflagration from the too-cold paraffin jets. It was like trying to cook a three-minute egg with napalm.

A satellite phone call came in from the UKSA's Simon Hay. 'Could you stay at sea for another day? We're arranging a civic reception.'

An exhausted skipper replied unequivocally on behalf of his knackered crew: 'No!'

During our last night at sea a breaking wave pooped *GMIV*: her cockpit was filled to the top of the side-benches and even came over the lower wash-board to soak me in the quarter berth before draining into the bilge.

Eight days out of Gibraltar, *Gipsy Moth IV* romped downwind under jib and staysail making up to 12 knots in the surfing waves. Tenerife was 40 miles away but we still couldn't see the snow-capped Teide volcano which, at 3,718m, is the highest mountain in Spain. Scanning the horizon with his binoculars, Steve said that if Doomsday comes it could start here, when tectonic plates buckle and part of Tenerife slides into the sea, causing a tsunami which would drown Manhattan.

On the starboard bow after sundown, Steve saw a stab of light above a giant swell – there could be no doubt this was the northern end of Tenerife, 21 miles away.

As our 740-mile passage neared its end, Rahim became reflective. It had been tough: *Gipsy Moth IV* is not an easy boat to sail with her cranky traditional ways. 'I think Chichester was a stubborn old man and he would have been suited to his stubborn old boat,' he said.

We entered Santa Cruz harbour at 0130 on 6 November. David and Jean Lennon of *Fai Tira*, a Bruce Roberts sloop and one of the Blue Water Rally yachts, not only took our lines, but graciously gave us a case of beer.

The rally sailors have been amazed at *Gipsy Moth IV*'s cramped interior, compared to modern boats of 53ft. They were also surprised at how basic she is, with no shower, hot water or proper oven. Their boats have luxuries like fridges, freezers, even washing machines and flat screen TVs, on which they watch DVDs.

Gipsy Moth IV is unique in the rally because most of the other yacht crews stay onboard for the whole circumnavigation while our skipper and crew change at the end of each leg. The pressure is on for the departing skipper to hand over the boat in the best possible condition and, as any sailor will testify, the 'to do' list mounts up at an alarming rate, even on a new boat, never mind a vintage restored wooden one.

Skipper Steve used his army parade ground tactics to get us scrubbing and cleaning the boat for visitors. 'Remember, this is like a floating stately home, but one we have to live in!' he barked.

Yachting Monthly's Dick Durham takes Gipsy Moth's helm on his first ocean passage.

Steve Rouse

Dick Durham/Yachting Monthly

The Blue Water Rally flotilla leave Gibraltar astern.

The great thing about being part of a rally is that there is always someone to talk to or an event to attend. Antonia joined Rob and Amanda from *Riff Raff* and John and Jenny from *Tzigane* for some tapas and they swapped stories and discussed routes for the Atlantic crossing to come.

There's an air of apprehension and excitement for what will be almost everyone's first ocean crossing. Gibraltar to Tenerife was certainly my longest passage to date. I've cruised to Norway and France and the West Country, but this kind of sailing was on another level. I learned a lot about seamanship from Steve who had an extraordinary ability to raise morale when the second gale arrives at dusk, the dinner plates are unwashed and your sleeves and trouser bottoms are damp. It is the mark of a true leader – after all, who raises HIS morale?

While we were berthed in Santa Cruz, children from Tenerife's English Education Centre visited the yacht and donated 200 Euros (their ice cream money) to help other children sail on *Gipsy Moth IV*. It was enough to make a grown man cry.

Carole May, 69, appeared on the dockside with a dog-eared copy of *Gipsy Moth Circles The World* to be signed. Her late husband Ronald had died four years ago and she was determined to sail back to Niue Island in the Pacific in their 52 ft catamaran to return the book to the immigration officer who gave it to her husband in the first place. *GMIV* makes the world go round!

Thirty-nine years ago *Gipsy Moth IV* sat abandoned by the sea, promenaded, paid-off and prematurely retired. Her skipper had closed the circle, written the book and signed the tea-cloths. He had no further need for the 'rocker' and unsentimentally moved on to the fifth and last of his record-chasing mistresses. Now all that is history. But as we sat rocking gently more than 2,000 miles from Greenwich, a woman passed by on the pontoon. She did a double-take and asked. 'Chichester's boat?'

'Yes,' I said.

'Bravo!' she called.

Tenerife to Antigua

By James Jermain

Joining *Gipsy Moth IV* in Santa Cruz a day later than the rest of the crew, my first contact with them was after midnight, when all I could see was the tops of heads sticking out of sleeping bags. Next day we were at that awkward stage when nobody knows anyone else and everyone tiptoes around each other: 'Who's that old fart?' 'Who's that young whipper snapper?'

We had two days to prepare the boat for sea and were all on a steep learning curve. Skipper Richard was a man of consummate competence and unlimited patience. The three youngsters, Kirsty Gibbons, Kimberley Morris and Anthony Palmer were all from the Pompey Study Centre, an organisation sponsored by Portsmouth Football Club, which provides after-school facilities for pupils wanting to catch up on schoolwork. Clare Martin, who was their guardian for the crossing, managed the centre and also taught there. She is also

very competent yachtswoman with several long passages to her credit.

We had expected our preparations would be tricky enough, but then we discovered the Blue Water Rally fleet had already cleared the shelves of the nearest supermarket by the time we arrived. There was no tinned meat but 60 varieties of tuna!

Leg 4

Distance:
2,700 miles

Skipper:
Richard
Baggett (34)
UKSA

Mate:
James Jermain
(58) *Yachting Monthly*

Crew Leader:
Clare
Martin (40)

Crew:
Anthony Palmer
(15)
Kimberley
Morris (15)
and Kirsty
Gibbons (15)
all from Pompey
Study Centre,
Portsmouth

Leg sponsor: BT

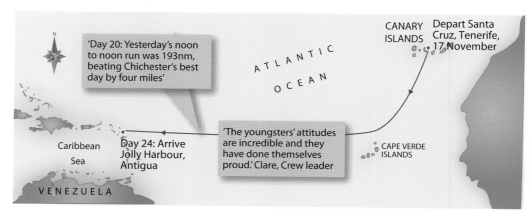

'Day 20: Yesterday's noon to noon run was 193nm, beating Chichester's best day by four miles'

CANARY ISLANDS   Depart Santa Cruz, Tenerife, 17 November

ATLANTIC OCEAN

Day 24: Arrive Jolly Harbour, Antigua

Caribbean Sea

'The youngsters' attitudes are incredible and they have done themselves proud.' Clare, Crew leader

CAPE VERDE ISLANDS

VENEZUELA

Gipsy Moth
*had the honour of
leading the rally's
parade of sail
exactly a year to
the day that she
was lifted from
her concrete tomb
in Greenwich.*

By departure day, 17 November, *Gipsy Moth IV* was as ready as she could be and we had the honour of leading the rally's parade of sail. Incredibly, it was exactly a year ago to the day that she was lifted out of her concrete tomb in Greenwich. What an incredible amount was been achieved in just 12 months.

As the fleet headed over the horizon for Antigua, we turned back to the marina... in the maelstrom of preparations, Richard had not had time to give the crew a full safety briefing. It was a seamanlike decision. We finally cast off that evening and drifted slowly into the twilight on our 2,680-mile passage. *Gipsy Moth IV* carried only a limited amount of diesel, and we were reluctant to use the engine in the early stages. Others in the fleet motored off in search of the Trade Winds, reputed to be developing close to the Cape Verde Islands.

The first three days were very quiet as we inched along in light, mainly northerly winds. These were ideal conditions for a young and inexperienced crew to acclimatise to the ocean cruising lifestyle. We settled into watch-keeping duties and learned about the 'extra' duties required by our masters, the UKSA, and sponsors. Chief among these was the need to keep a regular video diary and written record of the voyage, transmitted by satellite each day to a world waiting for news. Where Chichester had his gimballed chair there was a computer and communications station. Three times a day we also had to carry out oceanographic research for Plymouth University. One task was to measure water clarity, which involved heaving-to and lowering a white disc on a measured rope. It was still visible at more than 32 metres!

On day three we had our first minor disaster. One of the burners on Chichester's original primus stove was out of action. Richard restored calm and banished fears of cold food for 20 days by setting off a controlled 'explosion', following which the reassuring roar and smell of burning paraffin re-established itself under our cottage pie.

About this time we also crossed the track of the great Chichester himself, who was in the same waters on 8 September 1966. Chichester was headed south for the Cape of Good Hope and the Roaring Forties on a 14,000-mile sail to Sydney. We, lucky people, were headed west for the Caribbean for Christmas. Chichester had experienced severe weather and a 'super-schemozzle' while passing Madeira. His account of the Canaries passage suggests he was in a foul mood. He had nearly lost a sail under the boat, his damaged leg ached and he was convinced *Gipsy Moth IV* was too big for him. He wrote in his book: 'There was a time when I thought sailing would be no good to me because it provided no physical effort and exercise! At that moment, that seemed a pretty good joke... The sea here gave a curious impression of being like a desert, a Sahara, lifeless and empty, instead of teeming with fish and bird life, as I believed it to be. The water was pale blue-black like diluted blue-black ink'. He had a brandy to cheer himself up. One thing I missed was Chichester's plumbed-in beer barrel and well-stocked cellar!

Gipsy Moth photographed from an RAF Nimrod plane on day four of her Atlantic crossing.

RAF

On the daily roll-call with the Blue Water Rally fleet, we discovered that some successful fishing was taking place. Top angler was *Fleur de Me*r with one dorado, one large tuna and an unidentified one metre-long-something. We'd had no luck.

On day four, we had our first taste of a proper wind with a series of squally showers which produced little rain, but established a Force 4 to 5 southwesterly. Meanwhile, the computer weather maps showed signs of serious trouble ahead: a wide area of calms with a wall of unseasonable and very strong south-west winds. We didn't know it yet, but this was the first indication of a very late rogue tropical storm which, uniquely, doubled back on itself and travelled east to cause serious damage in the Canaries.

The strong winds induced the first signs of seasickness as we adjusted to *Gipsy Moth IV*'s habitual heel angle of 30° to 35°. But no one missed a watch. As the winds eased a bit Richard struggled with, and eventually won a battle with the self-steering gear. We never found this piece of original kit designed by Blondie Hasler to be reliable, but in the right conditions it worked well enough and made the jobs of the watch on deck a lot easier. The 'right' conditions were quite narrow – a moderate wind just free and blowing at a steady speed. Once the wind was much abaft the beam or if it was light or fluky, the gear could not hold a steady course.

Day four also bought one of the most memorable events of the crossing. At around noon an RAF Nimrod flew over us for nearly an hour filming and photographing. We had our sponsors' cruising chute flying proudly – which was no easy task as the wind was very light. We all entered into the spirit off things and waved madly – all except Clare who had her hands full trying to keep the chute full. The Nimrod made a dozen or so passes, some so low we ducked instinctively and sheepishly. On the final pass they ignited the afterburners and soared away to the north-east rattling every rivet and fastener that held *Gipsy Moth IV* together.

During one of Richard's regular 'clean and maintain' sessions a baby jellyfish appeared in the cabin sole via a bucket of cabin washing water. It was despatched with much shrieking with a pair of spoons.

These interludes took our minds off the increasingly dire weather situation. There was no prospect of finding Trade Winds for at least seven days and the current calms meant most of the Blue Water Rally fleet was burning precious fuel to make progress. We had to restrict our engine use to battery charging and were falling further and further behind our companions. But we ran it in gear which gave around five knots.

For the time being we bowled along in a steady southerly. It was one of those days at sea when you trundle along and the wind is constant so there's no need to trim sails. The windvane was doing the work and the crew were all chilling out (an odd phrase in 28°C). We scanned the horizon, wondered why there were no dolphins, took video footage for transmission home, snapped a few pictures and ate concoctions you wouldn't have given cooker room in a Dickensian workhouse.

Later that night we were fighting squally thundershowers and torrential rain. The wind was southeasterly Force 5 and rising. *Gipsy Moth IV* was reaching at up to eight knots. Lightning flickered around the horizon like poorly wired Christmas lights. But an hour after a change of watch the squalls struck with a vengeance. At one time Richard had himself, Kirsty and Anthony all in the bows handing and reefing sails while the windvane steered the boat. After an hour of this I looked out into the streaming, lightening-lit cockpit to see a set of oilskins steering the boat. A handless sleeve was draped over the tiller and long, floppy legs trailed on the sole. The hood drawstring was pulled up tight and I could see no face except a pair of big, white eyes. 'Are you frightened of thunder?' I asked. 'Yes' Kirsty replied.

By morning the wind had eased and the rain stopped, but the massed army of squalls still patrolled the horizon. Clare, Kimberly and

James Jernam/Yachting Monthly

I played bold and put the big running sail up but an approaching black wall made me heed Clare's advice and we replaced it with the small working jib. The wall promptly collapsed and we were left rolling around in a complete calm. And boy, can *Gipsy Moth IV* roll. It was when a 12in knife flew out of the sink and buried itself, quivering, in the heads door that her rolling became a serious concern.

She adopts a permanent angle of heel of 30°, occasionally dipping towards 40°, then lifts and, finding nothing under her, flops over on her side. Another lurch follows adding a further 5° of discomfort before jerking upright, like a guard caught asleep at his post. Chichester reported a 90° swing from one side to the other.

All this weather was the outrider of the approaching storm, now slow moving in the middle of the Atlantic. We tacked to get as far south as we could before it reached us and this seemed to work. We had plenty of wind, mostly on the nose, but never anything like a storm.

The worst aspect of life on board, apart from living at an angle of 30° or more, was the humidity. Everything had a film of damp on it. Even clean clothes felt clammy. Our fresh fruit and veg, hanging in hammocks by the forward

Becalmed in mid-Atlantic – earlier on Gipsy Moth *crossed tracks with her 1976 route south to the Cape of Good Hope.*

saloon bulkhead began to develop mould. Our three young crew, however, were coming along in leaps and bounds. They were now quite at home on the foredeck tackling headsail changes on night watches. Watching young Anthony skip about on deck with the sure-footedness of a mountain goat made me wistful of days long gone by! I could see why Chichester said *Gipsy Moth IV* needed a chimpanzee with extra long arms to get around the boat – above or below decks. One night we had a great example of the young crew's high state of morale. My watch was woken by an infestation of ghosts hell-bent on scaring Clare out of her skin. While Kirsty and Kimberly swooped around covered in white sheets, Anthony filmed it on the video camera.

When flying fish landed on deck, Richard gutted and filleted them ready for breakfast. This is what Chichester enjoyed for his morning victuals, so how could we argue with that! In the end, with some hilarity, we all tasted the delicacy and had to agree it was quite delicious.

The passage of Tropical Storm Delta to the north of us left confused seas and fickle winds for a few days. Several rally yachts sought shelter in the Cape Verde Islands in the face of dire forecasts, but in our part of the Atlantic it was never as bad as all that and our decision to carry on proved the right one.

With the wind and seas on the beam, *Gipsy Moth IV*'s motion was surprisingly comfortable, but the cockpit was cramped and uncomfortable – but then it wasn't designed for six! I am ashamed to confess that all 16 stone and 6ft 2in of me broke Chichester's compass off its mountings when I was picked up by a large wave and thrown across the cockpit: I was undamaged, but the compass was left minus two replaceable split pins. From a sailing point of view it was not much of a disaster because we hardly used it. It's mounted aft of the helm on the mizzen mast. Instead, we used a Plastimo hand-bearing compass with integral night light mounted on the cockpit bulkhead. It worked very well.

On day 12 we crossed track with the Jubilee Sailing Trust's sail training barquentine *Tenacious*. Despite looking stunning under full sail in a light breeze, the sunlight reflecting off her snow-white canvas, she was struggling to make to windward. She must have been one of the few vessels on the Atlantic crossing that year that was slower and less weatherly than *Gipsy Moth IV*. We later saw them again motoring for all they were worth to keep an appointment in Barbados.

A day of light wind, low humidity and warm sunshine encouraged us to open all the hatches, haul bedding on deck and do some serious washing of selves and clothes. A check of stores revealed food for 30 days, though chocolate was running out. Richard observed that if the youngsters were left to their own devices the chocolate and crisps would have gone already and they'd be in bed with dehydration and malnutrition. He sympathised with Jamie Oliver's school meals campaign!

The good news was that a second tropical depression was heading north well clear of us so we were able to tack back to the west and, for the first time, head straight for Antigua. Two days later we had a bit of an incident when a blood blister on my knee turned septic. Richard, already *Gipsy Moth IV*'s cook, cleaner, rigger, sail-maker, engineer, plumber, electrician, navigator, child psychologist, dad, mum, video production manager and nutritionist now turned doctor! 'This trip really is turning out to be one of life's challenges,' he said.

After referring to the Ship Captain's Medical Guide and taking advice, via the NERA sat phone, from FirstCall International Centre for Maritime Medicine, based at Aberdeen Royal Infirmary, it was decided the blood blister needed to be drained of puss. *Gipsy Moth IV* carried two huge MCA medical supplies bags. The operation was a great success and after a shot of penicillin, followed by penicillin tablets, I was confined to my bunk for 24 hours.

Richard had other problems to cope with. A fluky tailwind was making *Gipsy Moth IV* difficult to steer and lack of concentration by our younger helms often led to a spinnaker wrap. This finally happened once to often and for the first and only time we saw the sterner side of Captain Baggett. There is no doubt now that the whole crew finally grasped the importance of concentration on the helm especially in these conditions!

On day 15 we had a live telephone conference with BT in London, as well as parents and friends in the Pompey Study Centre. Kirsty began the proceedings, talking to David Green of UKSA and Jeremy Thompson of BT like a real pro.

On day 16, we passed the halfway mark. We celebrated with a party and opened goody-bags sent with us by loving friends and relations back home. They mostly contained sweets. It was an emotional but joyous moment accompanied by coke and cake and loud rock music on the CD player.

The wind, too, began to play ball and our daily runs started to creep up. By day 18, our distance to run dropped below 1,000 miles and the computer was estimating we had just six days to go. I wrote in my daily log: '*Gipsy Moth IV* is being a bit of a star at the moment. She really loves this beam to broad reaching stuff with all sail set – it gives her the power she needs without the heeling forces. In the 24 hours to midday today, without effort or undue sail trimming we covered 170 miles. Good sailing.'

During this period we were also crossing tracks with the rival ARC rally and were passing or being passed by a steady stream of yachts. One passed close just before dusk but she didn't respond to VHF calls. As darkness fell, she didn't put on her navigation lights, either, so we spent some uneasy hours overnight close to a yacht we couldn't see with no more than a feeble new moon to illuminate the sea. There was no real danger – they could, we hoped, at least, see us – but it was unsettling.

On day 19 with 765 miles to run, we had another 'shemozzle', one of which Sir Francis Chichester would have been proud. Shemozzle was his favourite word and referred to any cock-up, catastrophe or accident that caused him more than passing grief.

The incident was typical of the frustrations the fickle weather was forcing on us. It happened at around 0630, towards the end of Richard's watch, when a squall approached from astern. The cruising chute and mizzen staysail had to come down quickly to be replaced by the running sail – a big, full-cut jib – and staysail. It was something we'd done often before but not for a while and certain things had been forgotten – like which is the halyard and which is the sheet. Sails flew off in all directions, taking, among other things, Anthony's cap. By the time it had all been sorted out, a 15-minute job had taken an hour and, by now, the squall was long gone. At this point the watch changed and I immediately started complaining that *Gipsy Moth IV* was

Anthony Palmer skipped about the deck with the sure-footedness of a mountain goat.

under-canvassed. Richard obligingly came back on deck to rig the running pole and set the running sail wing and wing. No simple undertaking. The pole is controlled by no less than six lines. How Chichester set it on his own I cannot imagine. Having played around with this for 20 minutes, the only difference was that we rolled a bit more! So, Richard agreed we should put the cruising chute and mizzen staysail back up. This went smoothly but it was past 1100 when all was squared away and Richard could get back to his bunk.

24 hours later we were celebrating a record day's run, 193 miles, comfortably beating Chichester's own record of 189 miles, which in 1967 was the furthest anyone had sailed solo in 24 hours. The odd thing was that we achieved it in comparatively moderate conditions in which, I am sure, Chichester would have been driving the boat equally hard. We weren't conscious of anything particularly remarkable happening but we were assisted by a strong North Equatorial Current.

On the down side we were still being buffeted by squally showers so hatches had to be kept closed, making it impossibly hot and dank below decks. The squalls moved with unnerving unpredictability and we never knew which one was going to get us. It wasn't so much the wind, but the torrential rain. Chichester would have activated his special in-boom water catcher and diverted gallons of fresh water to his depleted tanks. We had our efficient and, so far, reliable Seafresh water-maker. Another piece of kit that was been worth its weight in gold was been the Ampair towed generator. At the start of our voyage, when winds were light, we relied entirely on the engine to charge the batteries and had it going for up to two hours every watch. But with the winds filling in, the Ampair was permanently deployed and engine running was cut to an hour every other watch. While the generator slowed our speed by up to half a knot, the fuel saving on a long passage was invaluable, as was the peace and quiet with no engine noise.

One of Chichester's original pieces of equipment that proved its worth was a curiously Heath Robinson-looking device called the oven box. After 20 days we ran out of bread. Clare broke out the ready-mix and set to with the kneading. Once risen, it was popped into the box, which sits on the Primus. Twenty minutes later delicious smells wafted through the boat and two gorgeous loaves appeared.

With less than 400 miles to go we were in the final phase of our crossing, but it was by no means the most comfortable. The wind had settled into the east and was blowing Force 5 to 6, occasionally 7 to 8. *Gipsy Moth IV* was running under much reduced canvas, at a pedestrian six knots, rolling like a pig, often through as much as 60°. The 3 to 4m rollers made her extremely difficult and heavy to handle. These waves could spin her round so fast you wondered whether she had a keel at all, let alone one that had been twice reshaped and, anyway, was the size of a cathedral door. When you tried to pull her back on course you felt every inch of the laminated, cold-moulded length. Waves frequently swept the cockpit and Richard issued the 'harnesses at all times on deck' command as part of standing orders. Chichester referred in his book to dressing in 'full war paint – shorts, lifeline, harness and cap!'

As the distance to go reduced, the winds settled to a gentle northeaster, which wafted us comfortably westward. We were now looking forward to fresh food – or at least three adults were. The teenagers dreamt of Big Macs, Burger Kings and Kentucky Fried Chicken. What we'd do when we first got ashore was the subject of much debate. Clare wanted to kiss grass. Richard and I would head for a cool beer or rum punch.

By midday on 9 December, our 23rd day at sea, we were less than 50 miles from Antigua. But the gods had one last trick up their sleeves. A short spell of headwinds as we approached the island delayed our arrival until after dark. We anchored in a bay, The Cove, just half a mile from our final destination of Jolly Harbour, to wait for daylight before making our grand entrance. Sleep came quickly and, anchor watch set, we retired for the first night's rest on an even keel for 24 days. Bliss!

At dawn there were squeals of delight from on deck as Kirsty, Kim and Anthony saw the Caribbean for the first time: 'Look at the water – it's well blue!' 'Wow! Palm trees!' It wasn't long before we were all in the water.

Once again, Richard had to call us to order. It was time to make our formal entry into Jolly Harbour and face customs and immigration. While Richard coped with officialdom, we began the laborious task of mucking out *Gipsy Moth IV*. Every locker had to be emptied, cleaned and disinfected. Strangely quivering eggs were lured from their hiding places, socks marched off to the launderette, rigging washed, decks scrubbed, bedding doused and aired. She smelled and looked a new boat and we were ready to invite guests.

We had two days to enjoy the delights of Antigua, before heading home. Blue Water Rally parties, plus the famous steel band 'jump up' on Shirley Heights, merged with jet skiing, riding, swimming and karaoke (for the young crew).

We learned that only eight Blue Water Rally yachts had so far made it to Antigua. Some put in to the Cape Verdes to avoid bad weather. We also learned that only a few days after we left Tenerife, the island was struck by the Tropical Storm Delta, which sank three boats in the marina and dismasted an 80ft Oyster, belonging to the boss of Oyster Marine, Richard Matthews, on passage between Tenerife and the Cape Verde islands. We'd been lucky.

We'd also been very lucky to have a skipper of Richard's calibre. He is quite capable of taking *Gipsy Moth IV* round the world singlehanded and would probably relish the prospect. I've met very few people in 50 years sailing who are more naturally at home on a boat. Watching him work was a real joy – fast, accurate, multi-talented, tireless. He is a fine role model for any youngster with a genuine interest in learning big boat sailing and Anthony was a more than willing pupil.

James Jermain/Yachting Monthly

Tropical swimmers: Kirsty, Kimberley and Anthony enjoy a Caribbean baptism.

Kirsty and Kim tackled a difficult passage with extraordinary good humour and fortitude and came through with flying colours. Clare, despite her chronic sickness, was a tower of strength. She also curbed the teenagers' wilder excesses while gently urging them on when the going got tough.

It also turned out that her seasickness was morning sickness! The medical kit required for ocean passage-making is extensive, but who would have thought it included a pregnancy test kit? And who'd have thought we'd use it aboard? Clare was *Gipsy Moth IV*'s first and only pregnant crew leader carrying, perhaps, the youngest ever transatlantic voyager.

It had also been *Gipsy Moth IV*'s longest passage since Chichester sailed her home from Sydney to Plymouth: 15,517 miles in 119 days. It was certainly a milestone for me. My first ocean crossing. Not always comfortable or easy. There were some seriously wobbly moments. But friends, relatives and, ultimately, grandchildren will be bored to tears by my stories for years to come. Even Richard admitted: 'Although *Gipsy Moth IV* got us here safely, it was probably one of the most uncomfortable crossings I've ever done!'

I had always admired Chichester's skill and stamina but after *Gipsy Moth IV*'s latest passage I had a special reason to hold him in complete awe.

Antigua to Barbados

From Peckham to Paradise

Leg 5

Distance:
300 miles

Skipper:
Antonia
Nicholson (33)
UKSA

Mate:
Ray
Nicholson (33)
UKSA

Crew Leader:
Claire Frew (25)

Yachting Monthly

Crew: Karen
Clampey (46),
Jamie
Hallett (16),
Highshore
School, Peckham
and Amie
Mayers (16)
Peckham
Academy.

Leg sponsor: BT

For the first time *Gipsy Moth IV* had a woman skipper, Antonia Nicholson, a full-time sailing instructor from the UKSA who sailed as mate with skipper (and husband) Ray Nicholson on legs 2 and 3 from Gibraltar. From Antigua to Barbados their roles were reversed.

'The idea of a female skipper is not as surprising as, perhaps, it was a few years ago, when I first skippered a yacht in the Caribbean – thanks to Ellen MacArthur, Emma Richards and Tracy Edwards!' said Antonia.

It was also the first time in nearly 40 years that *Gipsy Moth IV* was cruising as a 'family boat', since Francis, Sheila and Giles Chichester had sailed her together after her epic solo voyage. They were joined by crew leader Claire Frew from *Yachting Monthly*, Karen Clampey, 46, a Special Teaching Assistant from Peckham and two lucky teenagers.

One of them, 16-year-old Amie Mayers, had been plucked from the mean streets of South London, a world away from the blue seas of the Caribbean, and was one of scores of disadvantaged youngsters given a unique chance to escape inner-city privation through the *Gipsy Moth IV* Project.

Amie was looking forward to meeting her grandmother, aunt and several cousins when they sailed to Barbados, her mother's birthplace, for Christmas.

Before she left England to join the yacht, *Yachting Monthly's* Dick Durham spent a day with her in South London. Home for Amie is a council flat in a grim-looking tower block down the road from the Elephant & Castle.

Graham Snook/Yachting Monthly

Bradenham House had been condemned as unfit for human habitation and was soon to be demolished. Some front doors were boarded up, but on the tenth floor one stood out, gleaming from a fresh coat of black paint and sporting a shiny brass knocker. On the threshold someone had painted a sign: 'Shoes off'. Amie's 43-year-old mum, Hyacinth, invited Dick in with photographer Graham Snook.

The warmth of their reception belied the reality of life on an inner city estate where gangs of teenagers roam the streets selling drugs, mugging people and stealing cars. Amie had learned karate to defend herself from 'the bad people on the streets'.

'But some things have improved,' said Hyacinth, who worked as a cook at Westminster fire station. 'They used to throw TVs and beds onto the street from the upper storeys... now it's only bottles that get thrown on cars!' Two floors below Hyacinth's £83-a-week, two-bedroom flat, where Amie shares a room with her 17-year-old brother, Sean, a friend of the family was recently murdered.

It's a short walk to The Academy, Peckham, Amie's school, but she gets the bus because of the 'riff-raff' on the streets. 'It's got worse since many of the youth clubs have been closed,' she said. 'There are the 'Brickies' (from Brixton), the Peckham Boys and other 'crews' (gangs) who cause problems. 'They are full of "What you doin' in my area?"' said Amie. 'They fight a lot and when you meet them you don't look them in the eyes.'

Amie escaped from her bleak surroundings by playing the saxophone and writing and performing her own rap music with two friends in her group, the 2 Two'z.

After breakfast, Dick and Graham joined Amie on the bus to school, where she proudly gave them a guided tour. The school had 1,000 pupils and offered vocational training for girls in a full-sized hairdressing salon, with a garage workshop for pupils who want to learn motor mechanics.

Later they joined Amie on a visit to the London Boat Show at ExCel in Docklands, where, for the second time, Amie was introduced to Princess Anne, a patron of the UKSA, and a strong supporter of the *Gipsy Moth IV* Project.

On the way Amie described to school friends what it was like doing her sail training on *Gipsy Moth IV*. 'Downstairs it was well rocky and the others were sick, but I loved it! Except that everything is pump. You use the loo, you pump... you want water, you pump... you wash a dish, you pump. Pump, pump, pump!'

When Amie finished school she had a cadetship course awaiting her at the UKSA's Cowes base. She wants to make a career in sailing: 'I'll start off in a low position. I'll do anything as I love it,' she said.

'Going on this voyage means so much to me,' said Amie. 'It's a one-in-a-million chance. I never thought something like this could happen to me, a young girl who grew up in a tough part of town.'

Amie Mayers' view from her tower block home in Peckham, South London, and from Gipsy Moth's cockpit in the Caribbean.

RIGHT: Amie meets long-lost relatives Grace-Ann and Jamel.

BELOW: Crew leader Claire Frew.

A tropical squall descends on the lush green Caribbean islands 'like a scene from Jurassic Park,' said Jamie.

The other teenager aboard *Gipsy Moth IV* for the 330-mile leg to Barbados was Jamie, 15, also from Peckham, and accompanied by Karen, a Special Teaching Assistant from his school.

After a couple of days working on the boat and exploring the island, it was time to leave. Somebody once said that if God created the Caribbean, he must have been a sailor. How otherwise could he have aligned the broad crescent of islands – from the Grenadines to the French West Indies and British Virgin Islands – which run north to south so perfectly with a trade wind that blows from the east most days of the year? Combined with a reliable tropical sun and just enough rain to keep things lush, these islands are a paradise for the cruising yachtsman.

Before leaving their berth at Antigua Yacht Club, in Falmouth Harbour, the club presented Antonia with $400 EC (East Caribbean dollars), a donation towards the cost of *Gipsy Moth IV's* adventure from race fees and bar proceeds.

Departure, however, was not plain sailing. With the engine running and all ropes cast off, *Gipsy Moth IV* wouldn't budge. The tide had dropped and she'd made a hole for herself in the muddy seabed and was firmly aground. They left on the next high water.

In Amie's words, the first day's sailing 'didn't go too good with my stomach! I never knew vomit could fly so high. Next time remind me NOT to eat chicken and potato roti before sailing.' Jamie and Karen also suffered

seasickness. Amie had been given sail training at the UKSA and proved a natural at the helm. Sailing at night was breathtaking, she thought. 'Ray showed me all types of stars... Orion's belt, the Milky Way, Venus and Mars – it beat TV any day as we sailed past several beautiful islands, like Montserrat, Dominica, Guadeloupe and Martinique.'

Since this leg was sponsored by BT, a bonus came on the 20 December when Amie, Jamie and Karen took part in a satellite telephone conference with friends and teachers from their schools. Amie told her friends: 'It's a great opportunity to be here and you've got to grab it with both hands. I'm surrounded by blue water and all we have in Peckham are puddles of mud outside Pitzys Chip Shop!'

Claire's three night watches with Ray were the wettest with the shiftiest wind angles. 'Each time we returned to our bunks with our clothes soggy. It seemed the boat would never settle for long and when she did the wind died and we were forced to use the engine.'

It was a warm moonlit night as they passed Guadeloupe and they could clearly see all the street and houses lit up. By the time the sun came up they had their first glimpse of Dominica, with Martinique a grey shadow in the distance. The islands were luscious, green and mountainous and Jamie said it was like a scene from Jurassic Park, with little towns and villages nestled in the valleys.

They finally arrived off Rodney Bay, St Lucia, after nightfall, salty, shattered and hungry, dropping anchor with the sound of West Indian music drifting across the water from the town. Apart from skipper and mate, they'd all completed their first offshore passage: 34 hours at sea and 160 miles.

Next day they moved into Rodney Bay marina and went on an island tour, visiting the market at the bustling capital, Castries, plus Sulphur Springs, the only active volcano on the island, with its neighbouring town, Soufriere, named after the French translation of sulphur-in-the-air, and Marigot Bay, a beautiful secluded, palm-fringed bay anchorage.

Reeds Nautical Almanac cautions: 'Few sailors will make the rough trip against the trade winds to reach Barbados from the rest of the Antilles.' As *Gipsy Moth IV* motored away from St Lucia on 23 December bound for Barbados the crew sang Christmas carols. Beating to windward in 20-plus knots, they were forced to motorsail all the way. Each time the deck was awash, a torrent of water leaked through onto Karen's bunk, but she still thought it was one of the best experiences of her life. She remembered as a child waving to Sir Francis Chichester with a union jack flag and visiting *Gipsy Moth IV* in her Greenwich dry dock, never thinking one day she'd sail her.

0100 on the morning of Christmas Eve they could see the loom of lights from Barbados on the starboard bow. 'From five miles off we could smell the rum from the distilleries. A great incentive for Ray!' Claire wrote in the logbook.

At dawn Amie was woken by Antonia: 'Amie, Amie, we're here, in Barbados! Wake up!' As Amie recalled: 'A smile suddenly sprang to my face with happiness and relief. I made a "BR-AP!" sound (local teen celebration gesture) and jumped out of my casket (bunk) to see the view of my mother's birthplace. I was overwhelmed.'

She couldn't wait to get on to dry land. Some 22 hours after leaving St Lucia, they tied up at Bridgetown Docks at 0650, surrounded

Amie enjoys watermelon: a totally tropical taste!

by huge cruise liners. After clearing customs, Amie called her cousin, Grace-Anne, to say she'd arrived and by lunchtime they'd anchored in Carlisle Bay. After flipping the dinghy and 'drowning' the outboard engine in the surf on a provisioning trip to town, the crew were invited for Christmas Eve drinks aboard a beautiful neighbouring Oyster 62, *Wishanger II*. Jaws dropped at the stunning accommodation and luxury.

Gipsy Moth IV did, at least, have a 'chimney' – for the paraffin stove – but the crew didn't think Santa would be able to get down it! Christmas Day in the tropics next morning didn't stop them decorating the saloon with snowflakes and paper chains while Ray served a breakfast of scrambled eggs with sparkling wine and strawberries on deck. Later Amie was collected by her family to stay with them for Christmas day and night. On Boxing Day Amie's auntie returned to take the crew on an island tour.

By day 13 of the adventure it was time for the crew to go home. Antonia and Ray celebrated New Year's Eve alone aboard *Gipsy Moth*. 'We couldn't leave her. What a year it's been!' said Antonia. 'I've been involved with the project all year and Ray since spring 2005, so there's no better place to see in 2006.' Mount Gay from Barbados and some Caribbean rum cake did the trick.

Skipper Antonia gets into the Christmas spirit.

Barbados to ABC Islands

Leg 6

Distance:

500 miles

Skipper:

Antonia
Nicholson (33)

Mate:

Ray
Nicholson (33)

Crew Leader:

Kelle McQuade

Crew:

Ben
Johnson (23),
Simon
Blackman (21)
and James
Grace (18)
all from
The Prince's
Trust

Leg sponsor:

The Prince's
Trust and the
Peter Harrison
Foundation

Three of the crew for leg six were selected through The Prince's Trust, a UK charity set up by the Prince of Wales in 1976, to help people aged 14-30 transform their lives and fulfil their potential. The Trust focuses on those who've struggled at school, been in care, in trouble with the law, or long-term unemployed.

James had endured a tough life. His mother had committed suicide and his father was an alcoholic. He became involved with The Prince's Trust through their mentoring scheme. Ben used to do voluntary work with special needs kids, but began abusing alcohol and drugs and got involved in crime. On release from a prison sentence, penniless and homeless, he approached The Prince's Trust for help. They recommended a 'get into maritime' course at the UKSA, which selected him for the *Gipsy Moth IV* voyage. Ben's ambition was to become a watersports instructor.

Simon had also been through some difficult times. He was sent to prison at 18 and after his release the Trust put him touch with the UKSA. Now he, too, was hoping to make a career in watersports. His ultimate aim was to become a dinghy instructor, teaching disabled youngsters. The trio's team leader from The Prince's Trust was Kelle McQuade. Simon and James had some sailing experience, but it was new to Ben and Kelle.

Antonia got the charts out and showed them their route from Barbados to Aruba, in the Dutch West Indies, via Grenada. A voyage of some 700 miles and quite a challenge for neophytes. Aruba is the first of the ABC islands (Aruba, Bonaire and Curacao) and lies 12 miles north of the equator and 18 miles off the coast of Venezuela.

Before leaving Barbados, the crew attended a Mount Gay party and toured the distillery. Peter Marshall, Marketing Director, made a speech welcoming *Gipsy Moth* and presented two miniature barrels of specially blended rum to travel around the world with the ketch. There was also a live telephone link to the London Boat Show, where David Green hosted a 'chat show' from the *Yachting Monthly* stage. Later, Ben talked to Simon Hay, the project's Global Communications Manager, and Antonia spoke to Peter Seymour from the Blue Water Rally. It was a testament to Antonia's persistence with the satcoms that the link worked. She spent many hours talking to engineers trying to sort out glitches in the satcom equipment.

A new spinnaker pole, flown to Barbados, to replace the one broken on leg one, arrived just in time for the downwind sailing. Finally on their way to Aruba, Antonia and Kelle took the first watch, but Kelle soon succumbed to seasickness, though she fought valiantly on, using a bucket, emptying it and then taking the tiller back. 'If only everyone could be like that!' Antonia thought. They sailed 'dead downwind' for some 140 miles, rolling heavily all the way to Grenada. 'How can you cope with this? I feel awful!' James shouted down at Ray. But James still had a grin on his face. The question asked most often was: 'How far have we got to go and when will we be there?'

They sailed into Grenada's Prickly Bay in darkness and anchored at 0500. This first ocean foray may have had some of the crew agreeing with Dr. Samuel Johnson, the great essayist and compiler of the first English dictionary, who didn't like seagoing. He wrote: 'No man should be a sailor who has enough contrivance to get himself into jail. For being at sea is like being in jail, with the added possibility of being drowned.'

The sight of wrecks scattered along the shores of Grenada's bays, following Ivan, the strongest hurricane of the 2004 season, was not a reassuring sight for landlubbers either. But at least this was post-hurricane season.

The crew's reward was sunshine, blue water and a lush green landscape with pretty houses. They moved the boat to Mount Hardman Bay and a small 'marina' that was once The Moorings Secret Harbour base.

Antonia Nicholson

Straightaway there was work to do. The watermaker unit had lost its securing bolts. Another problem was the lack of a bimini. There was little shade on deck and Antonia was concerned. 'Most of the crew have fair skin and the temporary awning we made in St Lucia flaps madly without a frame and gets in the way.'

The crew had a quick tour around the southern half of the island, a similar size to the Isle of Wight with a population of 98,000. Its main exports are nutmeg, mace and cocoa. It was *GMIV*'s lushest landfall so far.

The thought of four more days on the ocean provoked apprehension among the crew. From Grenada it was around 550 miles to Aruba – more downwind rolling. Antonia generously cracked sheets on a course 15° to the north to ease the rolling and keep pressure on the sails.

On passage, Ray decided to shave his hair off. He hadn't expected to spend most of the British winter in the Caribbean and it was hot! The crew's verdict on his radical 'haircut' was: 'You can see the top of his head from a mile away!'

For Antonia and Ray the best part of the technology aboard was the sat-phone. 'It's

Bridgetown, Barbados, the departure point for Gipsy Moth *on leg six.*

amazing. You can get so much advice from so many people.' On Chichester's epic ocean passages, he had a cranky Marconi-Kestrel radio to call his reports into the *Times* and *Guardian* newspapers twice weekly. 'I wonder what Sir Francis would have made of The Oceans weather package and GRIB files we can download?' asked Ray. 'He only had the clouds, sky, sea, skill and intuition to guide him.'

Gipsy Moth IV's electronic charts were fantastic for making passage plans. 'The Simrad GPS and B&G Deckman, plus C-map charts, takes a lot of the work out of navigation. But we do use the paper charts all the time. It's the seaman-like thing to do!'

Engine problems caused a scare when smoke leaked from the engine hatch. Ray discovered exhaust fumes and water pouring out of the water trap and silencer. Minus the engine, they deployed the Aquair 100 tow generator. By this time they had sailed past Bonaire, the most easterly of the ABC islands and expected to be in Aruba before midnight. But it was Friday the 13th and they hoped Sir Francis was watching over them.

Thirteen days later another Blue Water Rally yacht was also bound for the ABC islands. Jacques Demarty (62) was en-route to Bonaire in his beautiful Bowman 40, *Fleur de Mer*, with his wife, Catherine, and four crew.

They had made a detour to explore the Los Roques archipelago, off the Venezuelan coast, famous among the cruising community.

Their late-running schedule meant they were navigating in dangerous waters as darkness fell and it was difficult to appreciate distances in such conditions. They also had a known error of three-quarters of a mile on their chartplotter. Sailing downwind, the sound of rolling breakers and the noise of the sea crashing on the reef wasn't heard even 40 metres away.

The wind was Force 5 to 6 and they sailed with one reef in the mainsail. Suddenly Jacques heard a horrible grinding noise and *Fleur de Mer* heeled over at 30°. 'We'd hit the coral reef that extends south-east of the island,' he later said. The yacht had sailed into a fatal trap and big, breaking rollers continually lifted the hull and punched it down onto the reef.

Even though the general structure of their strongly built yacht was still intact, huge fractures began to appear. Water poured inside and soon the crew had to abandon her. They launched the liferaft but it was punctured on the coral. The crew all swam safely to shore and spent a night on the beach in a state of shock. Another Blue Water Rallier Norwegian Niels Jahren and his Bavaria 48 *Blackbird*, helped the stricken crew next morning and salvaged some of their personal effects from the wreck.

Jacques had sailed 100,000 miles offshore. 'But you can never afford to be complacent,' he said. His insurer, Pantaenius, paid the full claim for the total loss of *Fleur de Mer*. Undeterred, Jacques bought a new yacht and signed up for the 2007-09 Blue Water Rally.

It was a salutary story with many valuable lessons to learn. And who could have guessed that less than four months later, in the middle of the Pacific, Antonia and *Gipsy Moth IV* would be at the centre of the world's headlines when they were the second shipwreck on the Blue Water Rally.

The wreck of Blue Water Rally yacht Fleur de Mer, *a Bowman 40, skippered by Frenchman Jacques Demarty. All the crew escaped unhurt when she struck a reef in Los Roques.*

Barbados to ABC Islands

Antonia Nicholson

Ray Nicholson

Skipper Antonia takes the helm on the way to the ABC islands.

LEFT: Ray checks the weather on the laptop PC

On this Friday the 13th, luck was with Antonia, almost, as she sailed right up to the fairway buoy of Orangestaad harbour. But the moment she started the engine as the sails were lowered it suddenly fizzled out. In the moonlight she sailed *Gipsy Moth IV* between the reefs, passing a massive cruise liner, *Carnival Destiny*. 'There were flashes from passenger's cameras but I don't think they would have seen it was *Gipsy Moth IV*, just a beautiful yacht.' said Antonia. They decided to anchor just outside the harbour to await daylight for a safe entry.

Next morning, the crew had their first experience of windward sailing as they headed, engineless, for commercial dock. Close by, they dropped the sails and had lines and fenders ready on the port side. 'It was my most nerve-wracking moment with *Gipsy Moth* so far. The dock was concrete and we all know how she handles!' said Antonia.

Steve Rouse had likened it to pushing a supermarket trolley on ice. Others said she had the handling characteristics of a supertanker, due to her interesting rudder and folding prop configuration. Antonia heaved a huge sigh of relief, as the bow line was secured ashore by Ray. Later they were towed to Renaissance Marina.

The crew were later grinning from ear to ear after a visit to the hotel's private island, with its flamingos, parrots and turtles. They had discovered the beach and pool. After their

686-mile voyage, Antonia had to admit the crew had found the experience stressful at times. 'Being in a confined space that rocked and rolled and getting knocked and bruised, as well as being away from girlfriends, wasn't easy. They couldn't sleep for more than six hours and had to wake up at odd hours for watches. Not being able to get off the boat or have any privacy was also tough. But they learnt to deal with it themselves,' she said. 'I hope they'll treasure some of those special moments and next time they face a challenge will look back at what they've achieved. Most of all I hope they'll see there are opportunities out there waiting to be grasped.'

Leg six had been another amazing experience. The crew had visited three islands in two weeks, swam with turtles, seen dolphins, sailed the Caribbean sea, seen shooting stars, roaming iguanas and flamingos.

For Antonia, the burden of being skipper wasn't always easy. 'A bad day on the water is always better than a good day in the office,' she wrote in the log. 'But the constant motion of the boat, the responsibility of six lives, including my own, and the planning and preparation of a passage and organising other people, takes a toll on the human battery. Ray and I have been on *Gipsy Moth* for nearly five weeks, with just one-and-a-half-days off in Barbados. We've decided to take a whole day off tomorrow!'

ABC Islands to Portobello

Leg 7

Distance:
550 miles

Skipper:
Antonia
Nicholson (33),
UKSA

Mate:
Ray
Nicholson (33),
UKSA

Crew Leader:
David Wilding
(62)

Crew:
Melanie
Pudney (19),
Edward
Oliver (20) and
Luke O'Shea (16)

Leg sponsor:
RYA Sailability
and Peter
Harrison
Foundation

Leg seven was another challenge for Antonia and Ray, with a crew hand-picked by RYA Sailability, which helps people with a disability to go boating. Antonia had never skippered a special needs crew – or, as she discovered, a crew with such courage and good-natured patience. Under the guidance of crew leader David Wilding, Eastern region organiser for RYA Sailability, Melanie Pudney, Edward Oliver and Luke O'Shea often reduced the skipper and mate to tears with their displays of sheer pluck and determination.

When they arrived, two of the crew were travelling light – their bags still somewhere in Miami airport. Antonia hoped they'd arrive next day because they included spare parts for the engine they desperately needed.

Getting onto the boat in the marina was the first challenge for Ed and Melanie, as *Gipsy Moth IV* was moored bow-to at Renaissance Marina. The greenhorn crew were thrown in

at the deep end, with a shakedown sail into 25 knots of wind, before their voyage to the Panama Canal, via the San Blas islands.

'The thought of five continuous days at sea wasn't easy for them to comprehend,' said Ray. 'And we didn't want them to set off on a 500-mile voyage with no idea of what to expect.'

First they were briefed on the 1001 jobs there always seems to be to get the boat ready for a passage. This was also one of the last opportunities to work on the boat before Panama and the long Pacific crossing, when marinas and spare parts would be harder to come by.

The crew's first outing in a fairly powerful sea gave Antonia and Ray plenty to think about before the long haul to the San Blas islands. Luke hit his eye on the boom crutch and later stubbed his toe, which had to be strapped with tape. 'He did say he was accident prone, but I didn't expect two injuries in less than six hours!' said Ray.

The crew were all seasick – 'we'll be sending out for a bulk delivery of Stugeron' – but they worked well and supported each other. Despite spinal difficulties, lack of balance and feeling cold and tired, Mel coped well. 'But night watches could be interesting,' observed Ray.

Luke's endless energy and determination to prove himself was combined with a compassionate nature, as he took care of both Mel and Ed when they needed help. Ed was the crew comedian and could diffuse situations with humour. He also proved a brilliant rower of the inflatable dinghy. When he was born, it was not known if Ed would be able to walk or talk. He can, of course, but his speech is often indistinct. Having led a sheltered life, he relished the freedom and independence aboard *Gipsy Moth IV*.

Mel had her first swim off the boat, and was hoisted back aboard using the bosun's chair, since the boarding ladder was not a feasible option.

The first delay in *Gipsy Moth IV*'s departure from Aruba was when David plugged the handheld VHF radio into the inverter and it blew a fuse. Then the computer turned itself off and the satellite phone stopped working. Ray went to buy fuses and the marina office declared: 'We have some on order, but they won't arrive for another three weeks!' The problem was eventually traced to a malfunction in the 12/24 volt power converter and the UKSA arranged for a new one to be sent.

While they waited for the spare part to arrive by express airmail, there was plenty of time for the crew to build their confidence, though Antonia was concerned time was running out. They needed to be in Portobello in time for the crew's return flight home.

Finally, several days later, they cast off. The first day's run was an astonishing 183 miles, which then dropped to an average of 150 miles. The first three days at sea were challenging, with seas two to three metres high. Luke thought it was great to go to bed after a three-hour watch. Ed found the night watches hard with just a small compass to steer by and Mel proved a good helmswoman, enjoying the stars and watching dolphins escort them in the moonlight. When the wind dropped to less than eight knots, they spent 30 hours motoring. Finally *Gipsy Moth IV* negotiated the reef-riddled San Blas islands off Panama, always a major highlight of the Blue Water Rally. The islands are inhabited by pygmy Indians who live on tiny remote coral atolls off the north Panama coast. The only way to get here is by small plane or boat. It's a journey back 500 years in time.

Just 25 years ago, an intrepid *Yachting Monthly* cruising correspondent, John Campbell, reported: 'Visitors are welcome to the San Blas islands by day, but any white person found ashore after dark is ceremoniously put to death.'

Fortunately, it was daylight when *Gipsy Moth IV* arrived on the shores of this Robinson

Paul Gelder/Yachting Monthly

Antonia Nicholson

Ray and Antonia with colourful Kuna indian women at Sapibenega in the San Blas islands.

LEFT: A Blue Water Rally yacht at anchor.

Antonia and Ray: skipper and mate and wife and husband.

Francis Chichester would surely have approved of the air transport – an ancient 1970s De Havilland Twin Otter propeller plane with 20 seats. The passengers are mostly an exotic assortment of native Kuna Indians – men and woman wearing multi-coloured ankle bracelets, bangles, perhaps a bone through the nose – returning home to the islands after a visit to the Big City selling their crafts.

Much to the relief of Tony, none seemed to be carrying a large missionary-sized cooking pot. The Kuna's are the second smallest race of people in the world after African pygmies. When the plane finally rattled down the runway it was like something out of the James Stewart movie, *Flight of the Phoenix*. Minutes later, it was skimming the dense Darien jungle that separates North and South America.

The notion that you are flying on a wing and a prayer is reinforced as passengers break into spontaneous applause as the plane lands on a horribly short airstrip at the first island, Corazon de Jesus. The Americans laid these tiny airstrips in the jungle during the Second World War so air patrols could protect the Panama Canal from German U-boats.

Crusoe world, perhaps one of her strangest, most exotic landfalls so far.

Blue Water Rally director Tony Diment had made the marathon 22-hour journey from the UK to meet rally yachts. From Gatwick Airport he changed planes in New York for a flight to Panama City. After few hours sleep in a hotel beside the Panama Canal, he took a taxi at dawn to the city's domestic airport. You know this is going to be no ordinary journey when the check-in desk clerk asks your body weight, as well as weighing your luggage.

The journey for rally crew joining in the San Blas islands begins in Panama City and ends by dugout canoe from a jungle airstrip.

Paul Gelder/Yachting Monthly

A second bumpy landing at Playon Chico was almost the final stage of Tony's journey to the rally rendezvous. Next he boarded a *cayuco* (dugout canoe) with a native in Levi jeans rather than loin cloth and a 15hp outboard engine instead of a paddle.

Antonia was concerned not to see any other Blue Water Rally yachts as *Gipsy Moth IV* approached the island of Sapibenega. Then out of the blue she heard Tony calling on the VHF radio. 'You've missed the party!' They'd arrived in the nick of time – the last day of the stopover before Tony made the return trip to civilization. The other 23 rally yachts were already on their way to Portobello.

Sapibenega (meaning 'life' in Kuna language) is no bigger than two football pitches and as *Gipsy Moth*'s crew came ashore in the tender and stepped on *terra firma* after 200 hours at sea they might well have greeted Tony by saying: 'Dr Livingstone, I presume?' Two Kuna Indian ladies held a tray of drinks.

The San Blas archipelago is not much bigger than the Solent, with an island for almost every day of the year. It's a blue water sailors' dream. A land where the sun shines on coconut trees growing on white sand beaches with safe anchorages and friendly natives.

The Kuna Indians have been here since 400 BC and their simple, sustainable lifestyle means they can live on the fish they catch, crops they grow on the mainland, plus the *molas* (embroidered cloths) they sell to passing sailors.

That night *Gipsy Moth IV*'s crew enjoyed supper in the thatched Kuna Lodge on Sapibenega with Tony and his wife, Christine. Next morning they all visited Playon Chico, with its population of 3,000, of which 2,000 are children, crammed onto an island no bigger than a square acre. The natives were full of smiles and keen to sell bead necklaces, *molas*, or polished shells. Despite their violent history, the Kunas are quite shy. Some will only be photographed if you brandish dollars, but the kids will follow you everywhere. If you have a camera, you'll feel like the pied piper.

Paul Gelder/Yachting Monthly

Antonia wrote: 'This was a real eye-opener into how some people live. The women were dressed in beautiful handsewn blouses and skirts, some had bones through their noses and beads wrapped around their legs. Some had rouge on their cheeks and nose tattoos.'

That afternoon, *Gipsy Moth IV* sailed to Porvenir to clear customs, before the final hop to Portobello, the jumping off point for the Panama Canal. Here the crew said their final farewells. Antonia and Ray had been impressed at how well the youngsters had managed the challenging conditions. They'd pushed themselves beyond their comfort zones and daily routine back home – cooking for six, washing up on a rocking boat, eating different foods, being away from parents and not being able to phone home – and, of course, sailing an historic maritime treasure. Their 'taxi' from Portobello to the town of Colon to begin the long journey home was a pick-up truck... almost as bumpy as *Gipsy Moth IV*.

A visit by dugout canoe to a Kuna indian burial ground near Sapibenega.

Portobello to Balboa

Leg 8

Distance:
200 miles

Skipper:
Steve
Rouse (50)

Mate:
Simon Hay,
UKSA

Crew Leader:
Stephen
Crowe (46),
a teacher at
Longcause
Special School
in Plymouth.

Crew:
Daniel
Brimacombe (15),
one of Stephen's
pupils, plus
Jason Firth (17)
and Dan Ford
(17), selected by
the Hampton
Trust, Isle of
Wight.

Leg sponsor:

Corum

Portobello, formerly Puerto Bello, is one of the last ports of call for yachts heading through the Panama Canal to the Pacific. It's a sleepy town with a deep natural harbour and a population of less than 5,000. But 500 years ago it was one of the ports for the Spanish treasure fleets. When *Gipsy Moth IV* dropped anchor here she crossed paths with history. For Francis Drake – who was knighted with the sword that was also used to knight Francis Chichester – was buried at sea here in a lead coffin after he died of dysentery in 1596. The town was captured and plundered by the famous buccaneer Captain Henry Morgan in 1668. Today, its ruined fortifications are a World Heritage Site.

Gipsy Moth's new skipper was Steve Rouse, who sailed with Antonia Nicholson as mate on leg 3 from Gibraltar to Tenerife. His

mate for leg 8 was Simon Hay, normally back at the UKSA HQ monitoring the boat's systems. Now he was the on-the-spot Mr Fixit, trying to solve the satellite communications problems, so that video films, photos and emails could be sent back to the UK and uploaded onto the *Gipsy Moth* website.

New crew members Steve and Dan ventured to the local village to complete shopping for food. In these latitudes you eat what you can find and the choices in UK supermarkets are a fond memory. With fresh crew from the UK, a few days acclimatisation was essential. 'The tanned bodies go back to UK and the pink ones arrive,' said Steve, who organised an afternoon's sail training.

Next morning they slipped out of Portobello, heading the 20 miles or so for Cristobal and the famous Flats anchorage, gateway to the Panama Canal. Tony Diment from the Blue Water Rally found *Gipsy Moth* a berth for the night at Panama Yacht Club in Colon. The club is a crossroads for world-girdling sailing gypsies of all nations. Simon made an excursion into town and returned looking a little disturbed. Colon has a notorious reputation for crime, which is why the yacht club is surrounded by barbed wire. Forty years ago, famous cruising sailor Eric Hiscock got 'mugged' when his wallet was cut from his pocket with a razor blade. Today is no different. Tourists are told: 'Take off you wrist watch, hide your camera and lock your car windows.'

Soon, port officials were aboard to measure *Gipsy Moth* for her canal transit. Yachtsmen face a mass of form filling, inspections and measuring, but the rally organisers take care of most of this. Each yacht must have four line-handlers to cope with the four 125ft lines to steady the yacht in the giant locks. The 50-mile canal offers a short-cut through the heart of central America, saving a 5,000-mile round trip around Cape Horn. It was hacked out of swamp-infested jungle with a death toll of 25,000 workers struck down by yellow fever, malaria and cholera. Hundreds of canal workers also died in landslides helping build this eighth wonder of the world. The famous French painter Gaugin worked here on his way to Tahiti. The canal opened in 1914, completed by the Americans 33 years after the French had started.

There are a total of six locks and it takes 11-hours from the mangrove swamp on the Atlantic side through Gatun Locks (an 85ft rise) and across the 23-mile artificially created Gatun Lake, beneath which lie 24 Panamanian villages. Then the route goes through Galliard Cut, an eight-mile channel carved and exploded through rock and shale, to Pedro Miguel Locks and Miraflores Locks, before dropping back down to sea level.

Gipsy Moth's young crew had a trial run through the Panama Canal on another rally yacht.

BELOW: Rally yachts (Gipsy Moth in the third row) dwarfed by a tanker in Miraflores Locks.

Peter Seymour

Gipsy Moth *in a raft of three yachts, with* Bibi *and* Anouk, *heads through the canal's giant locks.*

Peter Seymour

Portobello, where Sir Francis Drake was buried at sea in a lead coffin.

Peter Seymour

Gipsy Moth's crew were soon recruited as line handlers on *Freewheel*, another Blue Water Rally yacht transiting the canal. Steve, Daniel and Jason joined Anne and Julian, onboard *Freewheel*. This would be a valuable dress rehearsal for *Gipsy Moth*'s transit to follow. Steve was 'staggered by the awesome engineering achievement of the canal's six gigantic locks'.

When *Gipsy Moth*'s turn came their transit advisor (pilot) came aboard at 0345 in the darkness of a busy harbour with ships moving around and rally boats peeling off the anchorage 'like a flight of Spitfires in the battle of Britain, all heading for the first set of locks at Gatun, lit up like a small city in the desert of darkness.'

Yachts transit the canal in rafts of three, and *Gipsy Moth*'s 'buddy boats' were *Anouk*, a Swan 57DS, with Ekrem and Ann, and *Bibi*, a Hallberg-Rassy 48, with Eduard and his family, including one of the youngest circumnavigators in the fleet, a four-month-old baby boy. It takes a steady hand and a cool nerve to control a raft of three expensive yachts and accidents do sometimes happen in the locks. There have been several cases of yachts being crushed in the swirling waters, including the Whitbread racer *Flyer*, which filed a claim for $1 million damages. But the Blue Water Rally has seen nearly 200 boats through the canal without accidents. For yachts up to 50ft the cost of the transit is around £300, with a £400 returnable 'bond' to cover any fines or damage.

Steve had goose bumps and was 'in a state of euphoria' as he thought of the enormity of delivering such a precious piece of Britain's maritime history safely from one ocean to another. *Gipsy Moth* passed through the canal without incident and champagne corks popped and cheers rang out on rally boats as the flotilla sailed under the Bridge of the Americas, linking Central and South America, with the wide blue Pacific lying ahead. Panama City, with its skyscrapers, shopping malls and the old quarter, a mixture of Havana and Miami, was a taxi ride away.

Gipsy Moth's berth for the next few days was at Flamenco Marina, where company president, Miguel Lopez Pineiro, had granted a free berth to the famous yacht. She was also visited by Mrs. Penny Walsh, Vice Consul of the British Embassy in Panama, who was presented with a plaque from the Isle of Wight Council for the ambassador's residence.

Simon, meanwhile, was tearing his hair out trying to solve problems with *Gipsy Moth*'s communications system, mainly related to the humidity and corrosion. He checked the cabling that runs through the bowels of the boat and 'looked like a sea of boiled spaghetti gone mad.' Forty years ago Chichester faced his own gremlins with his HF Marconi–Kestrel radio. But he didn't have to cope with additional computer software glitches in the satellite comms.

The crew had a day off in downtown Panama City, while Steve and Simon took a taxi to buy more anchor chain and charts and visit the port captain's office to get clearance to sail to the nearby Las Perlas islands. As a reward for the crew's maintenance work on *Gipsy Moth*, they sailed in company with other Blue water rally yachts to explore the nearby 'lost paradise' of the Las Perlas archipelago, including Isla Contadora and Isla Viveros.

The local natives, the Embera and the Wounaan Indians, live along the rivers in thatched huts on stilts. The interiors of the huts are dark with smoke from cooking fires and hide treasures. The women shyly show baskets woven in beautiful shapes and adorned with exquisite traditional patterns. The men pull out a piece of old rag wrapped around delicate wood carvings of animals.

'Sitting at anchor in these islands is like being in a David Attenborough wildlife programme with a 360° screen – and it's all happening literally just feet away,' said Steve. 'The aerial displays by birds would make a Top Gun pilot proud: pelicans fly past in perfect V-formation, right under our bow, just inches off the water, and dive bomb for fish. Just when you are about to go below decks, a shout from one of the crew, "Look at this!" brings everyone rushing on deck to see some new amazing sight.'

Back on the dock in Flamenco Marina, waiting to take *Gipsy Moth*'s lines, were her new skipper and mate for the next leg to the Galapagos, Sam Connelly and Jon Curtis. Soon the electronic engineers were back aboard installing a new black box. 'Why does everything depend on a black box these days?' wondered outgoing skipper Steve Rouse.

Blue Water Rally crews visited Embera Indian settlements.

Local Panama native Indian children were entranced by the magic of 'instant' digital photography.

Annette Seymour

Balboa to Galapagos

The three girls aged 17-20 from Northern Ireland who stepped aboard *Gipsy Moth IV* at Flamenco Marina, in Amador, on the Pacific side of the Panama Canal, had all been offered places on the voyage by the Ellen MacArthur Trust which takes children suffering from cancer, leukaemia and other serious illnesses sailing – usually for four day periods. But this was to be a voyage of more than 1,000 miles.

In the summer of 2000, before the start of the Vendée Globe round-the-world race, Ellen MacArthur went sailing in France with a group of children suffering from cancer and leukaemia. The trips were organised by the French charity *'A Chacun son Cap'* (loosely translated as 'Everyone has a Goal'). 'We

'The girls had shown a particular aptitude for sailing and they had all been through a hell of a lot'
Frank Fletcher, Ellen MacArthur Trust

Leg 9

Distance:
950 miles

Skipper:
Sam Connelly (31)
UKSA

Mate:
Jon Curtis (37)
UKSA

Crew Leader:
Peter
Topping (36)

Crew:
Maria Turner (18)
Laura Walsh (20)
and Barbara
Kennedy (17)
all from
Northern Ireland

Leg sponsor:
The Ellen
MacArthur Trust

laughed so much we had tears in our eyes and the kids were just incredible,' said Ellen, who described it as one of her best day's sailing. Two years later she launched the Trust.

Twenty-year-old Laura Walsh's battle against Hodgkinson's disease had begun three years ago in the cancer ward of a Belfast hospital, before she found herself on the trip of a lifetime sailing to the Galapagos Islands.

Laura, from Glengormley, was a 17-year-old catering student when the rash she kept scratching produced a lump on the left side of her neck. A biopsy at Belfast's Royal Hospital produced the dreaded diagnosis. Her life was put on hold and she underwent chemotherapy via an intravenous drip every

two weeks for five months. Her energy levels plummeted and she vomited for weeks. She watched her friends carry on with their lives: going to university, getting jobs and going out with boyfriends as she fought the enemy within. But she eventually beat off the disease and was approached by Peter Topping, youth programme manager for the Northern Ireland Cancer Fund for Children, who was looking for crew to fill 10 places being offered by the Ellen MacArthur Trust to go sailing.

'At first I didn't want to go,' said Laura. 'Sailing was something I'd never done before.' But she signed up for five days' sail training at the UKSA in Cowes with two other youngsters from Northern Ireland: Maria Turner, 18, from Saintfield, just outside Belfast, who had beaten off leukaemia, and Barbara Kennedy, 17, from Dungannon, 40 miles from Belfast, whose brother Robert, 15, had died from the disease.

'We all became firm friends at Cowes. The weather was freezing and we all kept each other's spirits up.'

Later, when the UKSA was looking for crew to sail aboard *Gipsy Moth IV*, Laura, Barbara and Maria, were chosen. 'They showed a particular aptitude and they'd all been through a hell of a lot,' said Frank Fletcher, Chief Executive of the Ellen MacArthur Trust.

The trio flew out to Panama, in Central America – a 33-hour journey that was particularly gruelling for Barbara, who had never flown before. Their crew leader was Peter Topping. 'The problem all these youngsters suffer is that they feel people don't understand them and what they've been through. It's because their contemporaries move on, while they stand still and have to deal with their condition before they themselves can move on. It undermines their confidence and self-esteem.'

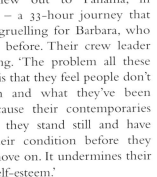

The sailors' ancient Crossing the Line (equator) ceremony was a chance for a fancy dress competition.

But sailing aboard *GMIV* put paid to all that. The fact that Francis Chichester had also battled against suspected cancer at the age of 58 and then sailed solo round the world at 65 was an added inspiration for the trio.

'The Ellen MacArthur Trust crew are certainly the life and soul of the party. And if there isn't a party, they start one!' said skipper Sam Connelly.

The girls spent some spent nine days at Flamenco Marina, Balboa, while problems with *Gipsy Moth IV*'s satellite communications were solved. While Simon Hay, mate on the last leg from Portobello, was still a 'stowaway' aboard trying to fix the Nera Fleet 55 sat-com unit, the girls toured the Gamboa rainforest and the canal.

Eventually, sat-com spares were flown from the maker in Norway and *Gipsy Moth IV* cast off with most of her systems working, so video film and reports could be sent back for the website.

One of the first messages from mate Jon Curtis was: 'I'd rather clean the bilges with my own toothbrush than be put through another four hours of bending over this flat screen monitor! Chichester once said the best place for *Gipsy Moth* was in a block of concrete in Greenwich! I think he would agree with shoving this flipping computer in a block of concrete and bunging it in the ocean!'

Laura, meanwhile, was bewitched by the sailing: 'My night watches were amazing. I saw electrical storms and thousands of stars,' she enthused. While the nearest beach was 500 miles away, the weather was sometimes calm enough for them to stop and go swimming in the 3,000 metre deep ocean.

Forty years ago Chichester was diving towards 55° south as *Gipsy Moth IV* headed for Cape Horn. Now just 6° north of the equator, skipper Sam had a cloudless sky and the wind had dropped from 20 knots to just four knots. Sam was asking if Chichester's gimballed (self-leveling) chair, which had been removed to make way for the hi-tech communications station, could be swapped back. 'Could we also have the beer tap and the gin back on board?' was his plaintive appeal.

Before they left Panama, the girls had bought some colourful material to make costumes for the ancient and traditional sailors' ceremony of Crossing the Line (equator). Maria's costume was pink, Barbara's was red and Laura's was yellow. Sam, as King Neptune, wore orange. The girls were dressed as sea creatures, with Laura a starfish, Barbara a sea horse and Maria a dolphin. Mate Jon wore a sexy fluorescent green wig.

Just east of the Galapagos islands, in very hot and windless conditions, Neptune baptised them with a ghastly brew of mustard, rice and curry and threw flour over his 'slaves'. Alas, Sam slipped on his own yucky concoction and went head-first over the side of the boat as the crew burst out laughing.

'Maria did us all proud with a wonderful costume collection. Look out Stella McCartney!' was Peter Topping's verdict.

The crew got to know Flamenco Marina very well – Gipsy Moth spent nine days there while sat-com problems and electrical problems were sorted.

Gipsy Moth IV's landfall in the Galapagos was at Puerto Ayora, on Santa Cruz island, near the centre of the archipelago. This is the centre for tourism in these 'enchanted islands', part of Ecuador's national park system, which includes the Charles Darwin Research Station.

Maria learned to swim for the first time in the Pacific, with sealions for company, while the girls also toured the lava caves, saw giant tortoises and swam with turtles, sting rays, 'funky fish' and a white tipped shark.

'The *Gipsy Moth* experience is truly character building and I can confirm that the three girls I brought away are not the same three girls going back,' said Peter. 'The smiles are wider, the laughter louder and, above all, the personal confidence is radiant.'

Back home in Northern Ireland, Laura was soon saving money to set off travelling again and wanted to do her RYA Day Skipper course. Barbara joined a sailing club in Northern Ireland and hoped to get a bursary to study her RYA Yachtmaster exam. Both Barbara and Maria were in Scotland in August 2007, with Peter Topping, working to achieve their Gold Duke of Edinburgh awards.

After returning home from the Galapagos, the girls helped other young cancer sufferers through an organisation called TACT (Teenagers Against Cancer Together). Later, in the summer of 2006, they were invited to a royal reception at Buckingham Palace to speak at a fund-raising reception for the *Gipsy Moth* Project, hosted by HRH Princess Anne. This was followed by a fund-raising dinner and auction at the Royal Thames Yacht Club in Knightsbridge, sub-titled 'The show must go on...' following *Gipsy Moth IV*'s shipwreck on leg 11.

The last word goes to Ellen MacArthur, who said: 'I face challenges out on the water, but these are challenges that I choose to do. Teenagers like Barbara, Laura and Maria battle against something harder than many of us could ever imagine – and they do it with the biggest smiles on their faces. To me they are truly inspirational and if we can help them in their battle in any way that's a fantastic achievement.'

Alberto Mariotti/PPL

The enchanting, exotic Galapagos Islands, where Maria learned to swim.

Galapagos to the Marquesas

Classic passage

By Alastair Buchan

Leg 10

Distance:

3,400 miles

Skipper:

Ray
Nicholson (33)
UKSA

Mate:

Alastair
Buchan (62)
Yachting Monthly

Crew Leader:

Hutch
Wright, (52)

Crew: Sue
Ballentine (48)
Lucy Scales (22)

Leg sponsor:

UKSA and the
Isle of Wight

Galapagos to the Marquesas is one of the great ocean passages of the world – 3,400 miles and about as far as you can sail on a trade wind route around the globe without stopping. Given the prevailing winds and currents, once you start there are no second thoughts. It's finish or else, for we were about to undertake the longest sail *Gipsy Moth IV* has made since Sir Francis Chichester was at the helm, non-stop from Sydney to Plymouth in 1967.

Five crew gathered in the Galapagos capital, Puerto Ayora, two days before we had to set off on our voyage. There were no teenagers on this leg because it was felt to be too arduous and long for the inexperienced, though Lucy Scales (22) had never sailed before. As Hutch remarked: 'Imagine the very first time you ever set a foot on a yacht is to sail across the Pacific on *Gipsy Moth IV* …how cool is that?'

The previous crew had arranged a fuel delivery but more was needed. It proved to be a time-consuming task as Puerto Ayora had no alongside facilities, except a jetty for water taxis. Finding fuel fell to me and Hutch, while Lucy and Sue scoured the markets for provisions – a task made difficult by earlier forays by other Blue Water Rally boats.

After lunch on the third day we sailed. It's doubtful that we were truly 'in all respects ready for sea' but timetables and cruise programmes wait for nobody, not even *Gipsy Moth IV*. It was fortunate that before the real sailing began we had to find the south–east Trades. These live below 5° south and to reach them we motored through the fluky winds and calms of the Doldrums. This gave us the opportunity to brush up our sailing skills. Our early attempts at sail handling were pitiful, but Neptune turned a blind eye and arranged kind winds and seas. We did improve and after 3,000 miles we could put on a convincing performance.

On any long cruise you must stay on top of maintenance: running repairs are done at sea while time is found in harbour for the rest. *Gipsy Moths IV's* frequent crew changes destroy the continuity that makes this possible. Each skipper has his own priorities and repairs at sea are of the 'get you in' variety. There's a danger that keeping to a schedule can encourage hurried handovers and only the most serious of defects, such as the sat-com failure in Panama, justifies delays. Minor defects are missed, dismissed or ignored until they insist on attention. We began to expect the daily defect.

Skipper Ray earned his WC (and bar) for diving into the heads to clear its blocked innards but after the third occasion he declared: 'SOMEONE else could clear the next time'. There were no more blockages.

The masthead block for the cruising chute halyard broke and luckily, as the wind was light, the chute came down into the sea like a grand old lady. Repairs meant a trip up the mast and small halyard winches do not make this easy. As racing yachtsman Hutch Wright wound Ray skywards he was in danger of a heart attack.

From day one, Chichester's original two-burner paraffin stove had only one burner and there was no replacement on board. Cooking for five for a month on a single burner was a challenge that Sue not just rose to but vaulted over, producing gourmet meals long after any normal cook would have been reduced to a menu of hard tack and salt beef.

A botched repair involving a stainless steel nut and a brass rod on the pump used to pressurise the stove disintegrated and we had no spares on board. A brass nut, of sorts, was cannibalised from Chichester's original paraffin heater. It sort of matched with the remaining threads on the brass rod and a dollop of epoxy cemented their union. Mercifully, it lasted the rest of the voyage.

Next our single burner died. Ray declared that he had seen the spares on board to fix it but despite a search so detailed it would have sent Customs officers into raptures they were never found. Happily, after a day of effort, the burner was coaxed back into life. The list of defects and deficiencies grew. None were serious but disasters come from the insignificant and we were always wondering. 'What next?'

Finally Hutch cried, 'I came to sail this boat, not rebuild her!'

Meeting other ships and wildlife were rare events. One night we came upon an unusual collection of approaching lights. They resembled nothing from any sailing manual

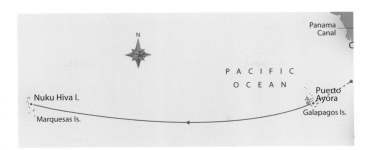

and the 'aircraft carrier' glimpsed through the binos turned out to be a Dutch pipe-laying barge. A few nights later we ran into a tuna fishing fleet that completely ignored us until Spanish-speaking Lucy took over the VHF. The fishermen had been at sea for two months and this was too much. They would not let go and we sailed over the horizon to their plaintive calls of 'Goodbye, girlfriend goodbye...'

Lucy recovered from her seasickness of the first few days and wrote in the log: 'I am beginning to understand Chantelle's

Lucy writes the daily blog for the Gipsy Moth IV website.

RIGHT:
Lucy and Hutch
on watch.
FAR RIGHT:
Lessons in
ropework from
skipper Ray for
Lucy and Sue.

predicament when she entered the Celebrity Big Brother house. She was the only non-celebrity there, desperately trying to act like one. Similarly, I am the only non-sailor on-board a yacht full of yachties. Sailing is a foreign language. With the help of my three sailing instructors ("the three wise men"), I have recently discovered that I already possess one of the most important sailing skills ... the ability to talk rubbish for many hours during day and night. Since everyone on board also seems to possess this ability, things are going extremely well as our mammoth journey gets under way.'

We briefly met up with another Blue Water Rally boat, *Jenard of Mersey*, a Hallberg-Rassy 43 sailed by British yachtsman David Pratt. They appeared as a masthead light just before dawn, crossed our bows and disappeared after a short chat. We saw no more ships.

Wildlife was just as scarce. Freddie the Frigate bird squatted on the mizzen mast and left his mark on the awning. Other occasional and unidentified birds were sometimes seen along with squadrons of flying fish and dolphins.

Once, when we stopped for a swim, a pod of whales passed without giving us a second glance. This suited us. These waters are famous for whales taking their revenge. This is hardly surprising. The early whalers called the Galapagos a whale nursery for they found nothing but cows, calves and easy slaughter.

When that was done the whalers moved west to the 'offshore ground' and it was here in November 1820 that the *Essex* was sunk by a whale and became the model for Moby Dick's *Pequod*. In the 1970s Maurice and Maralyn Bailey spent 117 days adrift (the title of their book on liferaft survival) after their yacht was sunk by a whale in these waters. Later, Dougal Robertson's family yacht *Lucette* was sunk by whales and he wrote a bestseller, *Survive the Savage Sea*. Whales obviously have long memories and take their vengeance cold.

On more than one day, when we were in calms we had a quick dip in the ocean to cool off after many hours of motoring. It was still rather difficult to comprehend swimming in three-mile deep water in mid-Pacific.

On day four there was a tale of two voyages. Two log entries 39 years apart contrasted *Gipsy Moth IV*'s two circumnavigations.

20 March 1967 Southern Ocean:

Latitude 56 degrees 03 S Longitude 67 degrees 19 W

Weather: wind west 50-plus knots; visibility moderate; sea state very rough: 50 metre seas. Chichester rounding Cape Horn aboard *Gipsy Moth IV*.

'As I was finishing the deckwork a big wave took *Gipsy Moth* and slewed her round broadside on; in other words she broached to. It was lucky I was on deck to free the self-steering gear and bring her round on to course again. I stood on the cockpit seat to do this...

I looked round and there was the Horn, quite plain to see. It stood up out of the sea like a black ice-cream cone.'

20 March 2006 Tropical Pacific:

Latitude 3 degrees 58 S Longitude 93 degrees 52 W

Weather: wind ENE 8 knots, visibility good, sea state slight: one metre swell.

Ray and crew en-route for French Polynesia.

'For days, it seems like forever, we have been buoying our hopes up with the promise of favourable winds. We are now more or less pointing towards the Marquesas and if the GPS speaks true we have around 2,500 nautical miles to go. It has remained overcast all day with a long procession of rain squalls marching over us. Each brought its own short-lived wind, leaving *Gipsy Moth IV* rolling in the swell flogging the sails to death. No wonder crews on square riggers went mad in the Doldrums.'

One week out, on 24 March, *Gipsy Moth* clocked up her 10,000th nautical mile – not a bad distance 9 months after her relaunch!

Lucy and Ray on watch: one week out from Galapagos, Gipsy Moth notched up her 10,000th mile since dry dock.

A few days later she made a 24-hour run of 177 miles. So far the day's runs had been good, averaging 150 miles.

We put on several 'shows' a day. There was our morning spot on the Blue Water Rally radio net. SSB radios are wonderful when they work and expensive ballast otherwise. Much of 'net time' was a poor remake of Hancock's Radio Ham, with disjointed voices fading in and out of the static.

The masthead block for the cruising chute broke, which meant a trip up the mast for Ray.

Ray makes an intricate rope bracelet for Sue.

Three times daily we analysed water samples for Plymouth University, until the batteries powering the gismo gave out. There were no spare batteries on board, not even for the steering compass or torches.

Ray wanted astro-sights for the website. This encouraged him to discover the mysteries of the sextant and sight reduction tables. Between times he explored the workings of the chart plotter. There were two handheld GPS sets aboard to resolve the confusion.

Each day we took photos, shot video clips and wrote the log for the internet and those following our adventures back home. It may not sound much, but it took six or seven hours a day and was intended to convey the everyday life of seafaring folk. What it could not do was convey the ups and downs of our morale and the mood swings that followed. Rightly, what it never did was record our rare sharp words, for despite huge differences in age, background and experience we rubbed along amazingly well and that in itself was remarkable given uncomfortable living conditions, long hours of hard work and broken sleep testing everyone's patience.

Take five strangers of very different backgrounds, ages and experience, stick them in a confined space for a few weeks, disturb their normal sleep patterns and it's perfectly natural to take bets on who will wear the pink leotard. Nicknames had been given – always a

good sign. So far we have Salty (me), Oily Rag (Hutch), Captain Bluto from Popeye (Ray) and Mum (Sue). Hutch was also later dubbed 'Lord High Cholesterol'.

Discomfort with five on a boat built for one was continuous. Provided they remained absolutely still, four could sit in the cockpit, but when sail handling it became a scene where crew, sheets, winches and tiller fought for supremacy to a barbershop chorus of curses and contradictory commands.

Ray, in a contemplative mood, wrote in the log: 'I often find myself thinking of my wife, Antonia, who is 300 miles ahead of us sailing on a French Blue Water catamaran, *Paulina III*, with Bernard Rocquemont and crew. Sometimes I find myself on the helm with only my own company and plenty of time to reflect. This is the true beauty of the open sea. It's not the waves, the fantastic sunrises and sunsets or the wildlife out here, but the time to contemplate and reflect. In this hectic day and age people don't make time to stop and evaluate what's happening in their lives. This kind of sailing opens up the doors to our inner minds. It gives us time to plan and appreciate what's good in our lives. This may drive some people mad. But I feel this is where the singlehanded sailor comes into his own. Nobody to blame for mistakes. Being completely self-sufficient is a rarity these days. This is perhaps what drives the single-handed and single-minded sailors, like Sir Francis, on and on.'

The bunks were based on 'some fiendishly medieval torture machine,' said Alastair. Younger crew called them coffins and caskets.

Rain or shine we hand-steered 24-hours a day. The windvane shaft of Chichester's original self-steering was bent in Aruba and was on permanent sick leave. Everyone put in at least five hours on the helm, often more, each day. It didn't help that *Gipsy Moth* had her own ideas where we should go and sometimes sloped off in any direction that took her fancy. There was no sleeping on this helm. The heat was fearsome but the awning could only be used if the mizzen was down, so we cooked.

Ray experimented with three or four different watch systems, none of which were helped by the state of the cabin, which was not a refuge of cool, calm and comfort. Instead, it resembled a hell ship. Chichester's original five berths had been raised to six by giving a narrow (17in) settee a lee cloth and everyone rated their berth the most uncomfortable and wettest ever. The general opinion was that they were based on some fiendishly cruel medieval torture machine, though seeing their occupants laid out, arms crossed over chest, the image that came to mind was of a coffin. On other legs I see crew referred to them as 'caskets'!

There was no personal stowage on board, so seabags occupied empty bunks or the cabin sole. In rain or heavy seas the hatches must be closed. Then temperatures climbed to over 100°F, creating a cramped, fetid, unbearable sweatbox. With hatches open we had a 90°F sauna.

In your bunk there was no way of shutting out the lights and sounds of shipboard life or the incessant chattering of lines and blocks. Only the heads gave us solitude.

Meals were eaten with doggy bowls in one hand, fork in the other and braced against the constant, unpredictable movement. 'We are all losing weight, which is good – apart from Lucy who, has a figure to die for!' wrote Sue in the log.

Throw in the stink from the bilge (Porton Down might want samples!), plus the cockroaches and weevils and any flint-hearted 19th century ship-owner would reckon his legacy lived on. And we had easy downhill

sailing, in warm waters and light winds. Imagine going upwind in heavy weather, water everywhere, everything wet, drawers crashing open, lockers ejecting their contents, a violent motion producing a rich crop of what Ray called '*Gipsy Moth* love bites' as you ricochet from one sharp edge to another and you have a scene from the seventh circle of hell – but one Chichester endured and survived alone. And previous crew on upwind legs, too!

After three weeks at sea, Lucy recorded in the log: 'We are all getting fairly tired of the night watches and I have started having strange dreams. Last night, Madonna was telling me that this journey was just a practice run.'

Hutch, meanwhile, was conducting a survey of 'Things the crew miss most'. So far it listed curry or a Thai meal, accompanied by a cold beer; ice for the gin or rum; a flat, dry bed; dry clothes; a walk in the green grass; watching rugby and cricket; my dogs; ice cream; Top Gear; gossip and a long hot bath.

Then there was the list of 'The things we didn't miss': TV, especially reality TV, quiz shows and soaps; traffic jams; visiting the bank; boring dinner parties; forms; bills; newspapers; queues and political correctness.

Running downwind under poled out headsails. The windvane self-steering was broken, so rain or shine, the crew hand-steered 24-hours a day across the Pacific.

And finally, what we'd miss when we left *Gipsy Moth IV*: The stars; the climate; the crew banter; losing all this weight (without trying); the achievement and the anticipation of arriving; Sue doing everyone's laundry; Sue's cooking.

He also had time to compile a useless statistic – our ages: 22, 32, 52 and 62. What else do you do on a long voyage?

At one point Oily Rag and his French Polynesian-style wind dances seem to be having some effect. We were trundling along at around 5 knots and hoped to be arriving in about five days.

A log entry appeared: 'The End As We Know It... By the Famous Five: As we sit in the cockpit enjoying our last tin of Pringles, we wait in anticipation for that long-awaited sight of land. Mixed feelings are beginning to emerge. Do we want the dream to ever end? Yes, we do. Do we want to return to the monotony and drudgery of our previous lives? This must be the eternal question of all intrepid adventurers.'

Finally, Te Henva Enana (The Land of Men), as the Polynesians call the Marquesas, appeared on our 24th day at sea. The Galapagos is remote. It took us six time zones, three aircraft, two taxis and a ferry to reach Puerto Ayora, but for the Marquesas we then sailed south to the middle of nowhere and turned right. They are truly one of the world's remotest, inhabited places.

The first European to see the islands was Alvaro de Mendaña in 1595. He renamed them Las Marquesas de Mendoza after his sponsor and the first part stuck, in various spellings because few ships came. In 1813 the USA briefly claimed ownership before they drifted into French control and they were claimed by France in 1842. Nuku Hiva, our destination, is the most northerly island in the group and the capital.

On our last night at sea, Neptune and his mates, the gods of fire, rain and wind, reminded us how kindly they had treated us. Ray and Sue had the deck with

Gipsy Moth IV under cruising chute and a 10-knot wind. Ten minutes later Sue reported a black, squally cloud coming up astern and all hell broke loose. The wind rose instantly to 25 knots. *Gipsy Moth IV* broached. Ray, emulating Chichester, went to lower the chute singlehanded. It dropped into the water and wrapped round the bows. It took all hands and a windy few moments to haul it inboard.

The rest of the night was a show of squalls, rain and lightning, sometimes all at once. At some point Neptune took the inflatable danbuoy, a lifebelt light and one of Chichester's original Lewmar genoa cars. Morning saw us shaken and stirred, motor-

sailing towards Nuku Hiva in a comfortable, quartering Force 3-4.

Gipsy Moth IV slid into Taiohae Bay and glided to a stop. The anchor rattled down and the crew posed for their last photos, shot a final video clip, wrote the last web log and took their bows. After 3,400 miles we had arrived, but as always, *Gipsy Moth* was the star.

Footnote: Lucy, the neophyte sailor among us, went on to sail across the Pacific to Tahiti, Tonga and Fiji in three Blue Water Rally yachts, *Bibi*, *Festina Lente* and *Blackbird*. 'The look on Lucy's face when she found out the yacht had a washing machine was absolutely priceless,' said Ray.

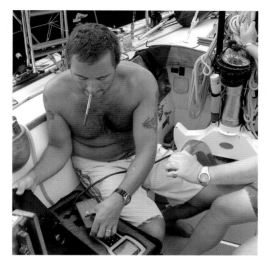

Ray gets ready to perform the thrice daily MetOcean environmental experiments.

Gipsy Moth IV at anchor. The 3,400-mile Pacific crossing from the Galapagos was the longest leg on her round the world voyage.

Marquesas to Tahiti

Shipwreck in Rangiroa

After four weeks sailing on the brand new, spacious French 45ft aluminium catamaran, *Paulina III*, another Blue Water Rally yacht, skippered by Bernard Rocquemont with his wife Dominique, Antonia admitted it was 'quite a shock to the system' to be back on the cramped and spartan *Gipsy Moth*, taking over as skipper from her husband Ray. With just three aboard *Paulina*, Antonia had enjoyed a hull to herself, with her own private head and shower.

Her new crew for leg 11 were three 16-year-olds: Charlie, from Cowes, Isle of Wight, who had won his place on the voyage through a competition in the local newspaper, *The Country Press*, plus Emmanuel and Kim, both from Manchester, who had been selected by the Brightside Trust, a charity which helps young people gain confidence and skills to overcome social disadvantage. The first mate

Leg 11

Distance:
640 miles

Skipper:
Antonia
Nicholson (33),
UKSA

Mate:
Chris
Bruce (24),
UKSA

Crew Leader:
Linda
Crew-Gee (48)

Crew:
Charlie
Riley (16),
Kimberley
Maudsley (16)
and Emmanuel
Oladipo (16)

Leg sponsor:
Brightside Trust
and Isle of Wight

'Site where Gipsy Moth IV struck a coral reef'

Avatoru Pass · Tiputa Pass · Avatoru · Tiputa · Motu Paio · Blue Lagoon · Ile aux Recifs · Rangiroa Lagoon · RANGIROA · Sables Roses

MARQUESAS
Hiva Oa

TUAMOTUS, FRENCH POLYNESIA
Manihi
Rangiroa

Moorea · Papeete · Tahiti
SOCIETY ISLANDS

'Gipsy Moth IV was towed by tug to Tahiti and then taken by ship to Auckland'

Antonia Nicholson

was Christopher (Brucey) Bruce, from the UKSA, with Linda Crew-Gee as crew leader, reporting for *Yachting Monthly*.

After a few days exploring magical Nuku Hiva, they weighed anchor to sail to Ua-Pou, another island in the Marquesas, some 30 miles away, an ideal distance to introduce the new crew to *Gipsy Moth IV*.

Gipsy Moth IV flew along with 20 knots of wind on the beam, showing off her full glory and taking the Pacific waves in her stride. It was exhilarating sailing and Linda was thrilled to be on *Gipsy Moth*'s helm for the first time.

They arrived in Ua-Pou in the early afternoon, much earlier than expected, and dropped anchor. They pumped up the dinghy and headed for the shore. But the swell was too high to land safely on the beach so they retreated back to the boat.

Next morning they set off for Makemo, the fourth largest atoll of the Tuamotus chain of French Polynesia, a passage of more than 400 miles. It would also be the crew's first night passage. The South Pacific may be a sailors' paradise, boasting some of the world's most exotic, enchanting waters, but lurking under her cobalt blue waters there are treacherous, low-lying coral reefs waiting to test the skills of the most experienced yachtsman.

The Tuamotus, east of Tahiti, were dubbed 'the Dangerous Archipelago' by French explorer Lois-Antoine de Bougainville as far back as 250 years ago. Comprising 78 coral reef atolls, they span an area of the Pacific Ocean roughly the size of Western Europe.

Atolls are low-lying islands, essentially high sand bars formed on coral reefs that encircled volcanoes which sank into the oceans millions of years ago. *The Pacific Crossing Guide* warns: '…the atolls are only as high as the tallest palm tree whose roots are only feet above sea level.'

Bird's-eye view from the mast as Gipsy Moth *leaves the Marquesas.*

It was here that Thor Heyerdahl's famous *Kon-Tiki* expedition came to grief when his balsa raft smashed into the reef at Raroia in 1947. The area is littered with wrecks and Robert Louis Stevenson and Jack London are just two of the writers who have used the region as a backdrop for some of their darker stories.

The Tuamotus region is especially dangerous to yachts because of its navigational challenges. Apart from submerged reefs and erratic winds, there are strong, shifting currents which can sweep sailors off course. The passes into the lagoons have strong currents going in or out, depending on the phases of the moon or how much water is in the lagoon. The waters are also shark-infested and typhoons have been known to sweep entire villages out to sea. In the 19th century, many Tuamotuans were cannibals and in the 20th century some islands of the group were used for French nuclear experiments. Leaving aside such perils, the Tuamotus are a paradise for cautious sailors. But given climate change and the rising seas these atolls may not exist in 100 years' time.

Linda Crew-Lee

Linda Crew-Gee on the helm: note the compass, behind the helm, mounted on the mizzen mast.

It would take three or so days to get to Makemo and Antonia wanted to make sure they arrived in daylight at their first atoll. The golden rule in the Pacific is never sail near the reefs at night or with the sun ahead of you. That night Linda stepped into the cockpit to be greeted by millions of bright distant stars above and phosphorescence twinkling on every wave crest 'like magic had been sprinkled everywhere.' Charlie and Kim couldn't wait to share the stories from their first night watch.

On the second night the crew were enjoying the sunset and looking forward to supper when they noticed the cruising chute was wrapped around *Gipsy Moth*'s twin forestays. Chris went up the mast to sort out the tangle and was swung around like a rag doll. After a long battle to drop the chute, he had to admit defeat and secured it round the forestay with a halyard to stop it billowing out. Next day, it was Linda's turn, as the lightest crew member, to go up the mast in the bosun's chair to retrieve the halyard. With the problem solved, the three teenagers then each had a turn in the bosun's chair.

Linda Crew-Gee

Linda Crew-Gee

Emmanuel drinks from a fresh coconut given to the crew in Manahi by native woman, Loana.

Later that evening, as the sun was dipping below the horizon, Linda was on the helm when sky and sea merged into one as curtain of rain came across the ocean. In seconds the wind rose from five knots to 30. It was her first experience of a squall and she held onto the tiller as if her life depended on it. 'It suddenly got dark and when Chris went to the aft-deck I thought, "Will I ever see him again... how could we recover a man overboard in this wind?" Would the boat capsize, be dismasted, or rolled over? I thought I was going to die with *Gipsy Moth* ending up at the bottom of the Pacific, 5,000 meters below us,' she wrote in her log.

In fact, Chris was just taking advantage of the opportunity to have a rainwater shower on the aft deck!

Meanwhile Linda, couldn't read the compass, which had a dim light and a tiny card. It was Chichester's original compass, fitted to the mizzen mast, so that it's actually behind the helmsman – not ideal for those unfamiliar with steering a compass course. 'Eventually, I found the course to steer (240°) only for Chris to tell me I was steering 340°!'

Down below in the cabin, Antonia was cooking dinner and asked Linda which sauce she'd like with her pasta. 'I felt I was in a Theatre of the Absurd play,' said Linda. 'But I was also reassured that perhaps things weren't as bad as they seemed!'

The whole ordeal lasted for about an hour. Linda was shivering and totally drenched, but 'happy to be part of the adventure – and survive!' Chris and Antonia later told her it was just a tiny squall.

Linda now fully understood the concept of 'mate' on a yacht. 'Chris was my angel saviour, putting me at ease and knowing what to do!' said Linda.

With light winds and slow progress, Antonia altered our course from Makemo atoll to Manihi, one of the northernmost of the Tuamotus, which was closer and also reputedly the site of the first pearl farm in the Tuomotus. She was anxious to get there in daylight. The entrance was only about 20 metres wide with strong currents

They arrived the following morning, some four days out from Ua-Pou, and Linda was hoisted up the mast to con *Gipsy Moth*

IV through the entrance. Any sailor's first experience of entering a lagoon pass in the South Seas is unforgettable.

First there is the distant sound of the pounding of the deep blue Pacific, self-destructing on the coral reef – a constant roar like an express train. On either side of the pass, hundreds of tons of water explode in a shrapnel of white spray and foam. The reef sometimes rises almost vertically off the seabed. With barely enough time to marvel at such a graphic demonstration of nature's force and fury, the current speeds you onwards, with shades of iridescent blue, turquoise and emerald flashing under your keel. Then suddenly you glide into the peaceful, protected, mirror-smooth waters of the lagoon. Here, if you are lucky, you are suddenly enfolded in waters of such crystalline transparency that the yacht will seem suspended in a liquid mirage. The breeze may carry the sweet-scented smell of vanilla, coconut or frangipani.

Outside, the Pacific may rage and roar, but inside the lagoon you are safe – except, of course, for the shallow patches and outcrops of coral, known as 'bommies'.

Antonia Nicholson

Heading for Ua-Pou, in the Marquesas, Gipsy Moth heels to the breeze.

Having negotiated the pass, Linda spotted two reefs, which could only have been seen from mast height, as they approached the anchorage. As soon as the anchor went down, the crew jumped in for a swim. After lunch, Antonia, Linda and Emmanuel got the tender ready to go to the village to top up the water supplies. The water-maker had not been working properly for the last two days and the outboard engine also had a fuel leak, which threatened to turn the quick trip to the village into a marathon row. They got some emergency water from a neighboring boat, *Anthenium*, and in a stroke of luck they hailed a passing local boat which took them to the village to fill the water canisters.

Also on 'to do' list was the primus stove – brilliant when it worked, but they had been reduced to one hob for the last few meals and now none worked. But they were buoyed up after making their first successful long passage and the crew were learning all about maintenance, an essential part of sailing.

Even on the 3,000-mile leg from Galapagos to the Marquesas, *Gipsy Moth IV*'s original primus stove had only worked only on one burner. Now it was Chris's turn to try and coax the stove to life. He spent hours working on it, but the spare parts were a different size and when he primed it a small leak ignited and the flames licked around the deckhead. Kim dashed out of the cabin, shouting: 'Fire! Fire! The paraffin tank is going to explode!'

Antonia, who was visiting a neighboring boat, *Shambalah*, with Linda, promptly jumped into the sea and swam to *Gipsy Moth IV*. Chris managed to douse the flames with wet towels but the deckhead and galley area were covered in black soot. 'We seemed to be faced with one difficulty after another,' Linda wrote in her diary.

Next day was a day of maintenance and relaxation which culminated in one of the crew's most magical evenings. As evening swallowed the horizon, they ate barbecued chicken on the aft deck in candlelight. The water was as still as a millpond and the sunset was reflected in hues of pink, red, orange, purple and violet. Darkness soon followed and the stars returned.

For Emmanuel, Manihi, was 'the most beautiful place I had ever been. It had lovely clear waters and pearl farms everywhere.'

Charlie wrote in the log: 'The trees were swaying in the warm breeze of the Pacific... the sheer beauty of the coral reefs and wildlife was stunning.'

The primus stove only worked on one burner across the Pacific. Now it stopped working altogether, before threatening a cabin fire. RIGHT: Linda on the helm.

Linda Crew-Gee

Linda Crew-Gee

Kim was enchanted by Loana, a local native woman who had taken Linda to her house and given them frozen chicken, coconuts and three tanks of water. 'We met such nice people and saw a wonderful place.'

The crew were up early next morning to prepare *Gipsy Moth IV* for the next passage to Rangiroa, the largest atoll in the Tuamotus, and the second largest in the world. Rangiroa, 90 miles away, means 'Far Sky'.

The narrow pass out of Manahi looked menacing, even at slack water, with its shallows and rip tide. 'We looked in trepidation at whirlpools of water for at least 50 yards but our safe passage through was a true team effort,' said Linda. Loana was also there to help guide them safely out of the lagoon. 'Never before did the deep blue waters of the ocean look so welcoming,' said Linda.

With little wind, they motor-sailed to get to Rangiroa in time for slack current in the lagoon pass at mid-day. 'This had to be one of the most frustrating days for all of us as we were on target for entering Rangiroa lagoon were it not for winds not turning up as predicted and the engine packing up,' said Antonia. 'At some of the atolls, currents of five to nine knots are reported, so arriving on time is similar to arriving at the Needles Channel at the right time. You can't arrive when it suits you.'

Chris and Antonia worked tirelessly on the engine the whole day. Numerous sat-phone calls were made to UKSA with various suggestions on how to proceed. It was eventually established that they had a fuel problem. When Chris found a crab in a water filter and some residue blocking the fuel pipes, he thought the problem was solved. But he checked another bit of fuel piping and found more dirt. Eventually every bit of the fuel system had to be checked and cleaned and engine was restarted at least 10 times during the day as the problem persisted.

With no wind and an unreliable engine to enter the pass, Antonia called another Blue Water Rally yacht and was advised to proceed for Tahiti, since entering the pass was tricky, especially without an engine, and there were no suitable mechanics in Rangiroa. Bernard from *Pauline III* volunteered to get help from French Navy. 'I looked forward to welcoming handsome Frenchman sailors aboard *Gipsy Moth*, but I wasn't sure how embarrassing it would be for us Brits to be rescued by the French!' said Linda.

FAR LEFT: *Chris spent hours working on the engine, made unreliable by contaminated fuel.*

BELOW: *Loana pilots* Gipsy Moth *safely through Manahi's narrow pass.*

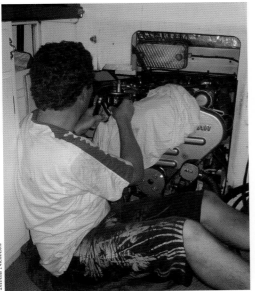

Peter Seymour

To enjoy the tranquil lity of Rangiroa's lagoon, first you must negotiate Tiputa Pass, with its treacherous currents and coral heads.

Antonia decided to alter course for Tahiti and see how far they had travelled by 0500. After a long, tiring and frustrating day, she eventually climbed into her bunk, which promptly fell off its bracket. But she was too exhausted to care. She hadn't slept properly for days in the heat and things were not going well for *Gipsy Moth IV*.

By the appointed time of 0500 they were still only 20 miles from Rangiroa's entrance. They had drifted along with no wind for hours. With no change in the barometer, Antonia didn't fancy floating towards Tahiti with a malfunctioning engine, lack of fuel, scarce water and a tired crew. They altered course for Rangiroa. It was a decision that would change everything.

Half an hour later as the sun rose, they could see the clouds building and

the wind coming towards them. 'We were travelling at three knots and had 21 miles to go so it seemed our arrival at the pass would be perfectly timed for slack water', said Antonia who was on the helm.

Gipsy Moth entered Rangiroa lagoon through Tiputa Pass under sail with a steady 15 knots of wind and the engine as a backup, if needed. They avoided the rip falls and arrived at the anchorage just as the first squall came. '*Gipsy Moth IV* must have known she was going to take us to a new place and that we would be able to give her the attention that she likes,' thought Antonia.

The squall was also a good opportunity to have a shower on deck. 'We were so happy to arrive safely,' said Linda. The snorkeling here was even better than Manihi.

Other Blue Water Rally yachts at anchor generously brought food and water, plus tools to fix the engine. Because of the problems with the primus stove, rally yacht *Tzigane* skippered by John and Jenny Greenwood, invited the crew to come and eat aboard.

Three people tried to help Chris remove the engine filter. Finally, Niels Jahre, skipper of *Blackbird*, succeeded.

'Rangi', as it is known to divers, has some of the best dive sites in the world and fantastic snorkeling, but next morning *Gipsy Moth*'s crew continued to work on the contaminated fuel and tanks.

'We were in one of the most beautiful places in the world – a South Seas paradise, and we were working like slaves,' said Linda. 'The inside of the yacht looked like a garage turned upside-down. Later six of us with ten 20-litre fuel cans squeezed into the three-man inflatable dinghy and rowed ashore to get diesel. But the credit card was declined. We couldn't get money out of the bank either! At least we got some water, but we now needed to save electricity as the engine hadn't been charging the batteries.'

At breakfast next morning they read a fact sheet on fuel contamination sent by the UKSA and prepared, again, to tackle the fuel problem. 'Imagine your living room, kitchen, bedroom and study all crammed into a space the size of a small bathroom. It's boiling hot, rocking up and down and smells of diesel. Someone has lifted the floorboards, leaving a gaping hole with two narrow strips to walk each side. Six people, each with something different to do (working, reading, eating, cleaning, sleeping), in search of a solution,' wrote Linda in her log.

The fuel that was eventually pumped from the tank looked like white coffee with chunks of dark solids in it. The tank had thick, slimy deposits. Working through an inspection hatch, they eventually cleaned the tanks. 'We were plastered in gunk which melted with our sweat. What a paradise!' exclaimed Linda.

With a new filter, clean tanks and a fresh supply of diesel – Klaus Schuback, skipper of *WhiteWings*, gave them four 20-litre cans of diesel – they switched on the engine and it ran smoothly.

Next day they planned to leave for Tahiti. 'We were on a tight schedule to get the crew there in time to fly home,' said Linda. There was no time to stop and repair the watermaker or outboard. Crew morale was at its lowest and Linda was writing an article entitled 'Hell in paradise'.

Klaus Schuback, skipper of fellow blue water rally yacht White Wings, *gave Gipsy Moth's crew 80 litres of clean diesel fuel.*

Linda Crew-Gee

Linda Crew-Gee

Linda Crew-Gee

Gipsy Moth's last night in Rangiroa's lagoon began with a spectacular tropical sunset.

A deadly necklace of coral and motus (islands) surrounds Rangiroa's beautiful blue lagoon.

At dawn next morning they rowed to another yacht, *Numero Uno*, which had also offered to lend them some diesel. 'We got fuel from anyone who had some to spare. Slack water in the pass was at 1530 so we went swimming, scraped barnacles from *Gipsy Moth's* hull and relaxed.'

Two other Blue Water Rally yachts had already left Rangiroa that morning. Furthest ahead was *WhiteWings*, with Klaus and Marlies. *Onyva*, skippered by Glenn MacMillan with his wife Rebecca, had left at lunchtime.

But when *Gipsy Moth IV* came to raise the anchor the chain was twisted around a coral head. Motoring in circles soon untwisted it, but the anchor wouldn't budge and Chris had to dive to free it. They waited for him to surface for what seemed like ages and were beginning to worry when he broke surface to say he had freed it from a ledge. As they

Linda Crew-Gee

Linda Crew-Gee

prepared to raise the anchor chain, one end of a wooden cleat snapped and the chain veered to the side splintering part of the toerail. 'What next?' Linda wondered. 'It was as if *Gipsy Moth IV* was saying yet again – "I don't want to go,"' she thought.

They finally left the anchorage at 1530 and motored up the lagoon to Tiputa pass. Antonia had drawn a plan of the pass and used it in the cockpit for navigation. They were joined by a pod of dolphins escorting them away from Rangiroa. Remaining in Rangiroa's lagoon were rally yachts *Blackbird* (Niels Jahren) and *Baccalieu III* (Mike and Donna Hill).

After hoisting the running foresail to help balance the boat and reduce the rolling they took pictures of the sunset as they motor-sailed at six knots. Antonia gave the course to steer before going below to fill in the log, joining Chris, who was getting supper started. Linda

sat in the cockpit with her laptop computer, writing her notes as they ran down the coast of Rangiroa, off to their port side. 'Charlie was on the helm and I was so engrossed in writing my diary that I don't remember seeing the land, or when it got dark, or which side Charlie was sitting,' Linda recalled. 'When he asked to be relieved of the helm, Kim volunteered. Some time later I heard a screeching noise … it wasn't loud and the boat didn't lurch violently.'

Down below Antonia felt a dreadful crunch as if the yacht had hit something, even though it didn't seem a big impact. 'As soon as I came on deck, I could see *Gipsy Moth IV* was heeling right over and we were in shallows,' she said. 'How on earth did we end up here?' she exclaimed, grabbing the tiller and putting the engine in reverse. But the headsail had backed, pinning the yacht onto the reef. The crew let go the sheets, but it was hopeless. *Gipsy Moth IV* lay over at a crazy angle on her starboard side and was rocking in the surf – and she wasn't coming back up.

The cockpit started to fill with water from the waves. Linda dropped her laptop into the water on the cockpit seat and saw that *Gipsy Moth IV* had been spun around 180° as a wave had swept her onto Rangiroa's reef. She was facing back the way they had come. It was dark, there was no moon or stars, and none of the crew could see land beyond. The boat didn't move or make any

Linda Crew-Gee

*Emmanuel was
on the toilet when
Gipsy Moth
struck the reef.
'I thought I'd
better get out of
there!' he said.*

more noise, but waves sometimes broke over the high, port side into the cockpit. Had the noise of the engine drowned out the warning sound of surf breaking on the reef as they were motor-sailing?

In the subsequent inquiry set up by the UKSA it was reported that *Gipsy Moth IV* was 40° off course when she struck the reef at 1815 hours.

It was certainly a miracle the yacht had been picked up by a wave and dropped, as if by the hand of God, on a cushion of water, some 10 or more metres inside the reef and away from its deadly edge. Here the pounding surf would have certainly smashed her to pieces in minutes. It was also a miracle that the reef was level, with no outcrops sticking up. In daylight Antonia would see that the flat shelf stretched as far as the eye could see in both directions. You could almost drive a car along it.

Meanwhile, Linda noticed a bright flashing white light in the distance. It was Mota Maherehonae lighthouse, a 92ft-tall square white masonry tower marking the end of the reef. The light, flashing every five seconds, had a 20-mile range, but had been hidden behind the headsail.

Emmanuel was on the toilet when they hit the reef. 'I was thrown forward and didn't think it was much. But when the boat didn't straighten up, I thought I'd better get out of there!' he later told a reporter.

Antonia looked aghast at Chris and said: 'God, what's going to happen?'

Antonia told Chris to put out a Mayday distress call and instructed the crew to put on their lifejackets and get their passports and money. Linda went in search of lifejackets in the chaos down below. With the cabin floor at an angle of 45°, she had to climb across the galley lockers. Everything was in chaos on the floor, but she found some spare lifejackets in the heads. In the confusion, she put on her own lifejacket inside out. Next she was sent to the aft-deck locker to get the yellow emergency grab bags and the yellow flare container.

Antonia launched the first of two parachute rocket distress flares, amidst much smoke and hissing. 'I wondered what our chances were of someone seeing them,' thought Linda.

In fact, some seven or eight miles away, the two Blue Water Rally yachts heading for Tahiti, *Onyva,* a Hallberg-Rassy 39, and *White Wings*, an Oyster 485, saw two red parachute flares at about 1900. They could see the white lighthouse flashing on the north-west corner of Rangiroa and estimated the

Blue water rally skipper Klaus Schuback, with his wife Marlies, turned back to stand by Gipsy Moth *when she hit the reef.*

FAR RIGHT:
Bernard Rocquemont and his wife. Dominique relayed the Mayday call to the authorities in Tahiti.

Mota Maherehonae lighthouse, a 92ft-tall square white tower marks the end of the reef.

Paul Gelder/Yachting Monthly

Paul Gelder/Yachting Monthly

flares were from half a mile to the east. Both yachts turned around to head back toward *Gipsy Moth IV*. They knew she was in trouble following a radio call from *Blackbird*, which had received a sat-phone call saying *Gipsy Moth* was on the reef. Klaus, skipper of *White Wings*, was angry that neither *Gipsy Moth IV*'s VHF or SSB radios were working properly – 'two essential tools of communication had not been working properly since Panama,' he said.

Chris, too, was wondering if the radios were working, since no one had responded to his Mayday signal. The SSB had only a weak signal. *Onyva* and *White Wings* later reported they didn't receive any VHF or MF/HF emergency calls from *Gipsy Moth*, despite making several attempts to contact her. All communication now had to be done by sat-phone. *Gipsy Moth*'s EPIRB had also not been activated.

Chris used the Iridium satellite phone to contact David Green at home on the Isle of Wight. It was just after 0500 on Sunday morning in the UK when his wife Pat answered the phone, which was by her side of the bed.

'Mrs Green... is David there? This is Chris on *Gipsy Moth*. We've had an incident.' Scrambling for a pen and a piece of paper, David wrote down the yacht's latitude and longitude and immediately alerted Falmouth Maritime Rescue Co-ordination Centre. Within 10 minutes he'd phoned his deputy, Jon Ely, and was at the UKSA's Cowes HQ setting up an incident room and assembling an emergency team with Anna Symcox, his PA.

By then, Antonia had made contact by sat-phone with her friend Bernard Rocquemont, on the French catamaran *Paulina III*, which was also on its way to Tahiti. This was the yacht she had crewed to the Marquesas. She told Bernard: 'I need your help! I have a problem.'

Bernard relayed their distress call to the French authorities in Tahiti, as well as other rally yachts at anchor in Rangiroa's lagoon, including *Baccalieu III* and *Blackbird*.

'At some point I answered the sat-phone and found the British Coast Guard were calling us. We had lots of phone calls that night,' said Linda.

Deck lights on the mast spreaders illuminated an eerie scene. The torn foresail was hanging over the bow flapping in the waves. Although there seemed to be no urgency to abandon *Gipsy Moth IV*, Linda wondered how long the yacht would survive if the waves got bigger or came closer.

The crew lost track of time, but while Chris inflated the dinghy on deck Linda noticed a 'rescue' boat coming from the south and shining a spotlight. They could also see lights from a yacht coming from the north. It was a reassuring sight.

Gipsy Moth had been stranded several miles from the nearest village of Avatoru, where a duty officer of the National Gendarmerie, a local municipal policeman and the Deputy Mayor were the nearest to anything resembling the UK's RNLI. When the Mayday call was relayed to them from the French authorities in Tahiti, it fell on them and local fishermen to risk their lives in two small fishing boats to try and rescue *Gipsy Moth IV*'s crew from the seaward side of the reef. But first, they had to negotiate the treacherous Avatoru Passe in darkness. Currents rip in and out at of these lagoon passes at up to 9 knots with standing waves and coral heads. Even in daylight they are treacherous.

When they arrived at the scene about 90 minutes after *Gipsy Moth* struck the reef they could see she was stuck fast and not in any danger of sinking. Trying to land in the breaking surf on the ocean-side was too dangerous, so the two vessels returned to Avatoru and one of them went on to try and reach the wreck site from inside the lagoon, towing a fast dory so they could get close enough to pick up the crew.

Linda recalls that, ironically, she was quite relieved to see the rescue boats disappearing. 'It meant we wouldn't have to go into the scary Pacific surf in our tiny dinghy!'

But for the rescuers, now travelling inside the reef, it was still a perilous operation in the

The desolate scene the following day on Rangiroa's unforgiving reef.

darkness, with numerous shallow patches and coral heads to negotiate. After another hour they arrived at a point opposite the stranded *Gipsy Moth* and about a mile away.

They called *Onyva* on VHF radio and asked Glenn to relay a message to *Gipsy Moth*'s crew, requesting them to walk across the reef to meet them. Glenn had to call Niels aboard *Blackbird*, still at anchor in the lagoon, so Niels could relay the request by Iridium sat-phone. The added complexity of mixed communications on this dark, moonless night didn't help matters.

Linda was nominated the 'pathfinder' and set off across the reef with a torch and a lifeline of several ropes tied together – one end tied to the yacht, the other around her waist. She used a boathook to sound the depths and steady herself. Chris was concerned the coral was dangerous and pointed to a group of spiky sea urchins near the yacht. 'With no moon I couldn't see the beach,' said Linda. 'We thought the coral might end suddenly and I would fall into deep water, but after 50 meters it was still only up to my knees and on occasions only up to my ankles. It wasn't slippery or sharp. When I returned to the boat they said I'd walked for 100 metres – that was the length of the three ropes joined together.'

Once it was established it was safe to wade across the reef to the beach, the dinghy was

Peter Seymour

– marking the ketch's desperate position on the reef. In an attempt to limit damage to the hull, Antonia pushed a fender through a hole in the hull on the starboard side.

By now it was about 2100 hours and *Onyva* and *WhiteWings* were standing off, some half a mile from the reef close to perilous waters. They could see the lights of the rescue boat on the other side of the reef and heard from the gendarmerie that the crew had been picked up safely. There was no more they could do, so they were 'stood down' from the rescue and turned around to head for Tahiti.

Glenn, a fluent French speaker, had done a superb job throughout in helping with communications, making a Mayday relay call and passing on *Gipsy Moth IV*'s position to the gendarmerie's rescue team.

'It was really hard to leave Antonia on her own and our thoughts were with her,' said Linda. 'Surely this would be the most horrifying night of her life? I told her how much we appreciated her help and how wonderful she was in rescuing us. We stood on the reef and waved goodbye, but not before one big wave swept me off my feet. I heard the kids calling and asking if I was OK. I shouted back – "I am OK, I am OK!" This was the only moment of panic I experienced.'

They set off wading through the water with Chris and Linda shining torches. Antonia

loaded with rations, grab bags, water and some of their possessions. Linda stuffed Chichester's original hand-bearing compass into her rucksack and she Chris and the teenagers headed for dry land, pulling the dinghy with them. Antonia used the yacht's spotlight to light up the scene for them. After about 15 minutes they saw two strong lights coming from the lagoon beach. Linda wondered if a car was parked there.

For Antonia it was 'like waving goodbye to my little family.' She remained aboard *Gipsy Moth IV*, alone, to keep watch over the yacht and any possible looters. To conserve power, only the masthead light was left switched on

Paul Gelder/Yachting Monthly

A superb job in radio communications: fluent French speaker Glen McMillan and his wife Rebecca, from Onyva.

Paul Gelder/Yachting Monthly

Paul Gelder/Yachting Monthly

Base camp on the beach, where skipper Antonia spent two nights, before John Jeffrey took over guard duty on the wreck of Gipsy Moth.

shone a light at them all the way. 'As I looked back at the surreal sight of *Gipsy Moth*, I felt incredibly sad that she had ended up there as part of our negligence,' Linda later wrote.

Eventually, after about 500 metres, the landing party reached a beach and were met by two men with an aluminum dinghy. They crossed to the inner lagoon, wading through water sometimes up to their waists and negotiated a maze of rocks while pushing the dinghy, until they were able to climb into it and transfer to the waiting fishing boat. It was the lights from this boat that had looked like a car parked in a distance. This was also the fishing boat that had come to the rescue on the Pacific side of the reef.

'They offered us drinks, blankets and food, but we were not hungry, thirsty or cold,' said Linda. Soon Charlie and Kim fell asleep. The trip across the lagoon to Avatoru village took almost an hour. They were taken to a dormitory by the gendarme who laid mattresses and beds for them. There were also five plates of food with coffee and tea. 'I was probably the only one who devoured the full plate of pasta and fish,' said Linda.

Niels and Arial from *Blackbird* were waiting to greet them. That night it was difficult to sleep and Chris spent a lot of time on the phone to the UKSA and the Blue Water Rally. Peter Seymour, back in Papeete, the capital of

Tahiti, reassured him that arrangements had been made for the crew when they got to Tahiti and he himself would be flying out to Rangiroa next day.

Back on *Gipsy Moth IV*, Antonia dozed fitfully on the starboard berth, until she was woken by a creaking noise. 'I turned my searchlight on and noticed a bulkhead was splitting apart. I thought she was starting to break up around me. Although I knew *Gipsy Moth IV* was strongly built, I moved up to the companionway.' Here, Antonia huddled in the cockpit, drenched by waves still breaking over the yacht's cockpit and listening to the heartbreaking sounds of wood crunching on coral and the creaking of split bulkheads and frames.

When dawn broke at 0500 she said: 'I've never been so glad to see daylight… until I saw the state of *Gipsy Moth*. I wept. I couldn't bear to look at her. I climbed over the side and walked ashore…'

Chris, returned in the morning to take over the vigil so that Antonia could go back to Avatoru to organise the departure of Linda and the three young crew. During the long night, Blue Water Rally director Peter Seymour, who had been called in by the UKSA as the 'man-on-the-spot', liaised with the Tahiti-based rescue authorities and the gendarmerie in Rangiroa. The fact that he spoke fluent French, proved a big help, especially with the ongoing task of finding suitable contacts for the salvage operation in Tahiti on a Bank Holiday weekend. Peter had many contacts, having shepherded five previous rallies across the South Pacific. Soon he was in touch with the Head of the Port Authority and the French Naval Commander, asking about the availability of tugs for the planned salvage operation.

By now many of the rally yachts had arrived in Papeete and were shocked and saddened to hear the news of *Gipsy Moth IV*'s stranding.

The morning after, Peter flew to Rangiroa to assist the crew and assess the damage to *Gipsy Moth IV*. He was met at the airport by Antonia, who was in the process of arranging flights back to Tahiti for Linda, Charlie, Kim and Emmanuel.

Together with Antonia and accompanied by Rangiroa's Deputy Mayor and the local policewoman, he went to the wreck site to see the yacht 'lying against a backdrop of black storm clouds and roaring surf.' Chris was still in a state of shock and broke down crying.

With the policewoman and mayor he helped make a crude shelter for the crew near some bushes, using the yacht's boom cover to make an awning. Inside, Antonia laid some mattresses from the boat's bunks. Here she would spend a second night, this time with Chris, guarding the boat. They were plagued by sand flies and throughout the night there were crabs scuttling through the bushes. Antonia found one on her pillow.

Valuable equipment from *Gipsy Moth IV* was carried ashore through the surf to the 'campsite', which was by then taking shape under the guidance of the Deputy Mayor. They also bought ashore a considerable amount of the crew's soaking wet clothing, which Peter took back to Tahiti.

'Air Tahiti were not very impressed with this cargo, nor with my own soaking wet condition in their seat!' Peter recalled.

Gipsy Moth's crew arrive safely in Tahiti, with the traditional Polynesian garland of flowers.

Annette Seymour

Annette Seymour

After the perils of paradise came the pleasures, with Polynesian native girls dancing at a Blue Water Rally reception in Tahiti.

He encouraged Antonia and Chris to lay two anchors from *Gipsy Moth IV*, in the hope of preventing her being damaged any further by waves washing over the reef.

By now communications with the UKSA were by mobile phone and Antonia had to walk out onto the centre of the reef, up to her knees in water, to get a good signal.

Back in Tahiti, Linda and the three crew were met at the airport by Peter's wife, Annette, and a press gang of local TV, newspaper reporters and cameramen. Annette escorted the crew away to a three-star local hotel where she had booked rooms. She also loaned them fresh dry clothing. The only 'complaint' was from Emmanuel, who thought the jeans he'd been loaned by Annette, spoiled his 'street cred'. They had flowers and bows on them!

John Jeffrey, one of the UKSA's training skippers for the project, who had arrived in Tahiti hoping to sail on *Gipsy Moth IV* as first mate to Tonga, flew out to Rangiroa to take over 'guard duty' on the stricken *Gipsy Moth IV*. He, too, was extremely grateful eventually to be relieved by the local gendarmerie who were probably immune to the local mosquitoes and sand flies.

Meanwhile, Antonia and Chris flew back to Britain a few days later to face an inquiry into what had happened. They were told not to talk to the media.

'Throughout the whole of our ordeal nobody was hurt, nobody showed any signs of panic or fear. Nobody shouted and we were all calm,' said Linda. 'When so many people asked in the days to come "What happened?" we truly didn't know what went wrong. It was so sudden and surprising.'

Saving Gipsy Moth IV

Everyone involved with the *Gipsy Moth IV* project remembers where they were when they first heard the news that she had struck a reef in the Pacific. I was just 250 miles away, on a boat lying at anchor in an idyllic, mirror-calm, picture postcard blue lagoon on the island of Raiatea, the second largest island in French Polynesia. I'd flown to Tahiti with my wife, Anne, to meet *Gipsy Moth IV* and celebrate *Yachting Monthly's* 100th birthday in May, looking forward to sailing aboard the ketch to the nearby island of Moorea. While we waited for her to arrive,

I'd chartered a 42ft catamaran from The Moorings with a local French skipper.

Then I got the phone call that none of us wanted to receive. Peter Seymour had been up most of the night handling the crisis and broke the news to me. Straightaway, I could picture the scene at Rangiroa, since our catamaran was anchored just inside Raiatea's barrier reef, a few hundred yards from the roar of surf thundering on the reef. It was a sound that haunted me all day. The one consolation was that *Gipsy Moth IV's* crew were all safely ashore.

Lorry tyres, planks of wood and sand bags — these were some of the simple supplies on the mercy mission to save Gipsy Moth. *Bruno Videau, from Techni-Marine in Tahiti, sits on the right.*

Paul Gelder/Yachting Monthly

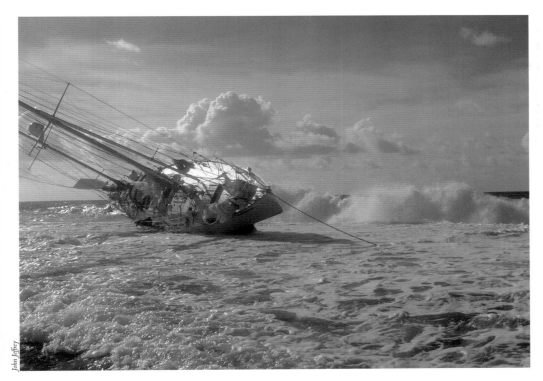

John Jeffrey

*At the mercy of
the Pacific breakers,
Gipsy Moth lies
near the edge of
Rangiroa's wild,
barren stretch
of reef – 10,000
miles from her
safe dry dock in
Greenwich.*

A flurry of phone calls were made to see what salvage options might be available. The Moorings charter company was also a supporter of the *Gipsy Moth* project and Dimitri Zoellin, our skipper, rang the base to see what could be done. But this was a French Bank Holiday weekend and everyone was off enjoying a three-day holiday, as Peter was also discovering back in Tahiti. Eventually, we weighed anchor and sailed back to the marina base to catch an hour-long flight to Tahiti.

Back at the UKSA in Cowes it had been a case of 'all hands on deck' since David Green had taken the first phone call. 'Normal life was put on hold,' remembers Anna Symcox, Green's PA and PR manager for the project. A round-the-clock emergency response team was set up and was soon besieged by the world's press, all wanting details of what happened. The official website was getting thousands of hits each day. 'There were lots of pizza deliveries, for the next few days and nights,' said Anna. Now it

was a race against time to save the ketch while the weather in the South Pacific remained stable. The cyclone season officially ended on 30 April, the day after *Gipsy Moth IV* went aground, though storms can form at any time. Any strong winds or an increase in the ocean swell would put *Gipsy Moth IV* in further peril. Lead skipper Richard Baggett had been booked on the next available plane to Tahiti and the search for a suitable salvage company had begun.

When the UKSA rang Dutch marine salvage company Smit, one of the world's most experienced salvors, and told them they had a yacht aground on a South Pacific reef they were asked: 'How many tonnes in the vessel?'

Jon Ely replied: 'Twelve.'

'Just leave it with me and I'll call you back,' they said.

With the next phone call, they were told: 'We've just been on your *Gipsy Moth IV* website and we like your little boat. We'd like to help you!'

PPA

Internationally renowned, Smit are used to salvaging rather bigger craft that *Gipsy Moth IV* – like oil tankers, cruise ships and the £50m salvage of the container ship MSC *Napoli*, driven ashore in Devon in 2007. Their man from Rotterdam, Bert Kleijwegt, known as 'the Red Adair of salvage', was on a plane to Tahiti within a few hours.

Three days after the grounding there was a tsunami warning, following a seaquake in Tonga. This caused everyone to hold their breath. We watched television in Tahiti at breakfast and in the evening, awaiting developing news. Mercifully, it turned out to be a false alarm. Meanwhile, *Gipsy Moth* lay patiently on the reef for the next six days and nights, at the mercy of the elements and just out of reach of all but the biggest waves, while the international rescue plan was formulated.

On the fourth day, at a waterfront hotel in Papeete, Tahiti's capital, I joined the rescue team as they convened for their first meeting. After flying to windward for 20 hours on a jumbo jet, Richard Baggett had arrived, as well as Bert Kleijwegt. The local salvage expert, brought in by Peter Seymour, was Bruno Videau, a marine surveyor based in Papeete. John Jeffrey was back from Rangiroa, having left the local gendarmerie watching over *Gipsy Moth IV*.

The rescue plan was simple. It had to be. The remote Tuomotu islands have only basic facilities. But at least Rangiroa had a JCB-type excavator, the only one on the island, which was being loaded onto a barge and sent across the lagoon – some 40 miles long – to the wreck site. The JCB would be used to lift the yacht so a plywood patch could be put over the damaged hull to make her watertight.

It had been arranged that a port authority tug would stand by in Tahiti, ready to head for Rangiroa, almost 200 miles away, to tow her off into deep water if the operation was successful.

Paul Gelder/Yachting Monthly

The cost, including the tow, was estimated to be £100,000 and the local salvage team wanted signatures on contracts before the work could begin. Faxes flew back and forth between Tahiti and the UKSA's insurers and lawyers. The manpower on the reef alone would be US$5,000 a day; the tug would cost US$105,000.

During the discussions, Bert raised the spectre of possible compensation payments to the local Government for damage caused to Rangiroa's coral reef by the JCB. Reef protection and ecology is a highly sensitive subject, of course, but having seen dead coral reefs around Raiatea and Bora Bora, I thought we had enough problems. Bert said more than a million dollars compensation was paid for reef damage in the Red Sea during a salvage operation. Bruno Videau, the local French surveyor, didn't think it would a problem. Richard and Bert would fly to Rangiroa that evening and Bruno and I would fly out next morning.

As the meeting was breaking up, I got a phone call from Miles Kendall, my deputy at *Yachting Monthly*. In London it was 10pm on Monday night and he was attending The Periodical Publishers' Association (PPA) national magazine awards dinner at London's Grosvenor House Hotel, in Park Lane. He'd rung to tell me that we'd just won the 'Campaign of the Year' award for our 'Save *Gipsy Moth IV*' project. We had been nominated several weeks earlier, but the irony didn't escape me that that star of our award now lay shipwrecked 10,000 miles from her 'safe haven' in Greenwich dry dock. The shipwreck obviously happened too late for the judges to change their mind, but perhaps it was appropriate that Miles had been presented with the award by Ian Hislop, editor of the satirical magazine, *Private Eye*. It didn't seem an appropriate moment to mention our award to the salvage team – let alone celebrate.

Next morning, as the plane flew over Rangiroa I looked down to see if I could spot *Gipsy Moth IV*. Instead, I saw the wreck of another yacht that had obviously been stranded some time ago on another part of the coral reef that encircled Rangiroa's beautiful blue lagoon like a deadly white necklace.

A few steps from the tiny airport, Bruno and I were met by a large dory with a 50hp outboard and some of the men from Techni Marine's eight-strong salvage team, already on the spot with local helpers. We sped across the lagoon to the wreck site, 40 minutes away. On the way we stopped twice to load up with sand bags, 14 lorry tyres and long planks of wood – the planks would be used to make the sledge on which *Gipsy Moth IV* would be dragged back into deep water.

A dramatic, desolate scene as the sun sets after the first day's salvage work.

Gipsy Moth IV's name on her transom and bows had been covered up with duct tape. It seemed a further indignity for this stricken old lady. The sail covers, with the sponsors' logos, had also been removed. Later David Green explained he had given the order to 'cover-up' to save the crew being harassed by the media. He granted Paul Gelder's request to remove the tape on the second day of the salvage operation.

My first glimpse of the yacht was heartbreaking. A mile or so away, through a gap in the mangroves and palm trees, I spotted her in the distance, lying forlornly on her side on a wild, barren stretch of reef. Her red ensign fluttered proudly from the mizzen mast. She hadn't lain at this angle since Chichester suffered his capsize in the Tasman Sea in a 40-knot gale during Tropical Cyclone Diana. It was the night of Monday 30 January, just one day and 185 miles after leaving Sydney. He'd estimated the mast had gone 40-60° below horizontal. 'Thank God the water was warm!' he wrote. 'I was damned lucky,' he said of that wild night. 'Yet, I could not be more depressed, everything seems wrong about this voyage.'

His crisis of confidence didn't last long, of course. And I hoped and prayed we, too, would overcome this unexpected crisis. It was unthinkable that after the last 15 months, her final resting place would be a coral grave on this remote atoll.

Arriving on a rocky beach, we waded through the shallows. A few hundred yards away, was the crude A-frame shelter which had been 'home' for skipper Antonia, Chris

and John Jeffrey, as they'd kept vigil. *Gipsy Moth IV*'s lifebuoy, fuel and water jerry cans and some of her sails, plus Chichester's old paraffin stove, formed a sort of 'base camp' for the Everest task ahead. A damp, salt-stained copy of Ellen MacArthur's book, *Race Against Time*, about her solo voyage round the world, lay in the sand, its pages fluttering in the wind. Beyond, on the horizon a quarter-of-a-mile away, *Gipsy Moth IV* lay on the edge of the reef. We had seven hours daylight left to begin the salvage operation.

From the bushes and scrub behind the camp, a JCB emerged, trundling across the beach like some prehistoric creature, belching smoke as its caterpillar tracks crunched on the coral. It reminded me of the fire-breathing 'dragon' in the James Bond film *Dr No*. And, yes, it was dead coral. The JCB was loaded with the first equipment needed for the salvage – oil drums, tyres and sacks, which were being filled with sand from the beach.

From base camp I waded through knee-deep water to get my first close-up sight of *GMIV* since I'd stepped off her deck in Gibraltar. I don't mind admitting that, like

Ace/PPL

Chichester's Gipsy Moth V never escaped her 'grave' on Gabo island, where solo sailor Desmond Hampton ended his round the world race after falling asleep when the wind changed direction.

Work begins in yet another race against the clock to save Gipsy Moth, before the weather deteriorates causing a bigger Pacific ocean swell with waves which could cause further damage to the yacht. INSET LEFT: The damaged area was some three metres long and a metre high. With seven hours daylight left on the first day of the salvage operation, the stern and bow were raised by the JCB, using crane strops, and sandbags and tyres supported the hull so the damaged area could be patched up.

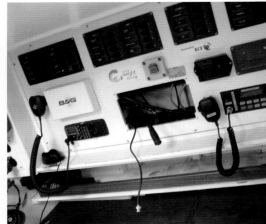

Paul Gelder/Yachting Monthly

John Jeffrey surveys the topsy-turvey world inside Gipsy Moth's saloon. There was a hole in the bulkhead above the chart table, where Antonia had removed the C chartplotter to take back to the UKSA as part of the inquiry into how the accident had happened.

Depending on the size of waves crashing on the reef, the water was up to your ankles or your knees.

... tyres and sandbags supported the raised hull
... salvage workers made it watertight.

Paul Gelder/Yachting Monthly

Paul Gelder/Yachting Monthly

Working in a perilous and confined space in a 'tunnel' under the keel, salvage workers applied three plywood 'patches' over holes in the hull. First two smaller patches, then one big sheet of plywood was used, coated with Sikaflex sealant and nailed and screwed to the hull. It was difficult and dangerous work, with chest high waves washing under the hull. If one big wave had moved the yacht the workers could have been crushed.

Gipsy Moth's orange trysail was readied to cover any further damage when the ketch was dragged off the reef.

Paul Gelder/Yachting Monthly

Paul Gelder, who photographed the salvage operation, pictured at the end of day one.

John Jeffrey

Final preparations as darkness falls. Alain gets spare ropes ready, John Jeffrey looks pensive. Would the patches hold? Would she leak or sink?

Paul Gelder/Yachting Monthly

Paul Gelder/Yachting Monthly

Antonia, I wept a few tears as I got closer and saw her plight. *Gipsy Moth IV*, for all her faults, was a thing of grace and beauty. She had carried Chichester safely around the world to international fame. In the last 10 months she had given scores of youngsters (and adults) adventures they would share with their grandchildren. Boats have a mystique and exert a powerful spell on those willing to succumb. 'They have a soul and a personality,' as blue water cruiser Frank Mulville once wrote. The older the boat, the stronger the power. 'She gains in stature with each new experience … people look and wonder and say "She's been to the South Seas," or "She's just back from the North Cape."'

I had visited *Gipsy Moth IV* stripped bare for her first refit in 1995. I'd ridden in the truck that took her on the unlikely beginning of her second round the world voyage – from Greenwich to Gosport, via the M25 and A3, on a November night 17 months ago. I visited her at Camper & Nicholsons' numerous times to witness her resurrection from the 'almost-dead' during her six-month restoration. I sailed on her from Plymouth to Spain and I had waved her off at the start of her Atlantic adventure from the rock of Gibraltar. We'd shared the dream and now we faced the nightmare. She had been a pathfinder for modern solo circumnavigators. A groundbreaking yacht – and now the ground was breaking her. I felt a unique bond with *Gipsy Moth* and, like Mulville when his yacht was wrecked, 'I felt the dead weight of responsibility settle heavily on my shoulders.'

With hindsight, *Gipsy Moth* had a weak crew on what was undoubtedly one of the most dangerous parts of the voyage – through the Dangerous Archipelago. Knowing this area, I felt a personal responsibility for not involving myself more in the UKSA's crew selection procedure. Having an inexperienced offshore sailor, Linda Gee-Gee, as chaperone to three 16-year-old greenhorns only added to Antonia's burden of responsibility when she already had to coope with the yacht's various faltering systems.

I clambered inside the topsy-turvy cabin. Locker doors hung open and books and clothes were strewn everywhere. Water rushed through a hole punched in the hull where a massive transverse wooden frame had snapped with the impact. The coral reef was visible through the water. There was a hole in the bulkhead above the chart table where the chart plotter had been removed and taken back to the UKSA by Antonia as part of the investigation into the accident. There were signs of the crew's 'last supper that-never-was'. A plastic rubbish bag swayed from the cockpit lifelines in the cool breeze.

Gipsy Moth IV was a ghost ship. I'd been looking forward to photographing her against the exotic backdrop of Cook's Bay, Moorea, with its verdant green spires. Not here. Not in this desolate state, struck down like a wounded animal. Her name on the bows and transom had been covered with duct tape. 'David's orders!' Richard explained. The mainsail boom cover and spray dodgers, with the sponsors' logos, had also been removed and the UKSA's logo covered up. It seemed a further indignity for this stricken old lady.

Using crane lifting strops, first the stern was raised by the JCB's giant claw, so that sandbags and tyres could be positioned under the hull. Then she was lowered again. Then the JCB moved to the bow to repeat the operation. An oil drum with a sand bag on top to protect the hull, crumpled under the weight of *Gipsy Moth IV*. Gradually, the damaged area below the waterline on the starboard side was raised high enough for the workmen to crawl underneath to assess the damage: one broken frame, plus a hole 30cm across and several smaller holes. The total area of damage was 2.5m long and a metre high.

Three acro props (telescopic scaffolding poles) were positioned at the stern on a block of wood to raise *Gipsy Moth IV* higher off the reef. As the work went on, Bert smoked his Dutch cheroots, people walked out on to the reef to find a better mobile phone signal and one of the salvage workers, Punoa, who

The ocean-going tug arrived from Tahiti, some 200 miles away, and used a rocket launcher to send a 'messenger' line for the main towing hawser (heavy rope). This was attached to a bridle made from the JCB's lifting strops. Richard Baggett, John Jeffrey and salvage worker Nerou, scrambled aboard Gipsy Moth as she was towed off the reef in three heart-stopping manoeuvres. Pulled through the crashing surf, a big wave broke around her to cushion the drop from the reef edge as she slid into the deep blue Pacific – her mast suddenly sprang upright to loud cheers from the salvage party ashore.

seemed to be the local 'Mr Fixit', posed in one of the crew's bikini tops, found washed off the yacht's lifelines!

By 1500 the first of two big plywood patches coated in Sikaflex sealant were nailed and screwed to the hull. It was difficult and potentially dangerous work. Waves breaking on the edge of the reef constantly washed around the keel, and some of the bigger ones left the workmen struggling in chest-high water. If one big wave had moved the yacht, they could have been crushed. Another big plywood patch was placed over the others – a sort of giant 'band-aid'. By now it was 1800 and the moon, peeping out from behind a bank of trade wind clouds, illuminated a bizarre scene. It was getting too dark to work safely and the JCB clanked and clattered its way back across the reef to dry land, followed by a weary but satisfied band of workers.

Richard, John, Bert and myself were dropped off at the local Novotel, about half-an-hour away by fast boat. Sir Francis Chichester's reputation had even spread to this remote atoll, where the French hotel manager quizzed us about the day's events. Our evening meal was dominated by the gnawing suspense of wondering what tomorrow would bring. With a one-metre swell (0.5 on the reef) predicted, John joked: 'It's either good for surfing or getting a boat off a reef!'

That night I rang David Green and he explained he'd asked Antonia and Chris to cover up *Gipsy Moth IV*'s name and remove the sponsors' logos to save them being harassed by the media, because she was such a famous yacht. He gave me permission to remove the tape from her name. As we slept, a harbour tug was already on its way from Tahiti – an 18-hour, 200-mile journey.

Early next morning, long planks of inch-thick wood were nailed to the hull, as a kind of sacrificial skid on which *Gipsy Moth IV* could be pulled across the reef back into deep water. I thought of the shipwrights at Camper & Nicholsons, who had laboured so lovingly over the seven layers of mahogany cold-moulding as the hammers struck home three inch nails. Quick setting cement was poured into the damaged hull area from inside the hull to make

Techni-Marine's salvage team: Marine surveyor Bruno Videau (back row left), and Alain (third from left back row) with Bert Kleijwegt, the 'Red Adair' of salvage, fourth from left back row.

Paul Gelder/Yachting Monthly

everything watertight. An orange trysail was lashed to the sidedeck, with a line under the hull, ready to use in an emergency if the hull was further damaged with the threat of leaks. Crusader Sails had already emailed the UKSA offering to sort out a new sail wardrobe.

The moment of truth, 'mission critical point' as Burt called it, was close. The tug was due to arrive from Tahiti. Would *Gipsy Moth IV* break her back as she was pulled over the edge of the reef into deep water? Would the patches hold? Would she leak, or sink? 'The most critical time is on the edge of the reef as she enters deep water,' Burt warned.

The breaking surf made it impossible to board her after she was dragged off the reef. And if she did leak, who would pump her out? It was decided that Richard Baggett and John Jeffrey would be aboard as she was pulled off. We'd run out of time and options to consider anything else. A second boat would be stationed off the reef with a high-powered pump, in case it was needed. Two divers had also been employed at 4,500 CPF an hour, in case any stray tow lines fouled the tug's own propeller. This was where Bert's expertise and foresight into the worst-case scenario came into play. If necessary, the yacht's liferafts would be deployed for floatation. If the yacht came off and remained watertight, she'd be towed straight to Tahiti. If not, she'd be towed to the anchorage on the atoll.

Burt was 'cautiously optimistic.' 'These rescues are by their nature full of risk and we have done everything we can to secure the safety of the vessel. I know there are many people around the world wishing us well and we all have the same feeling here. We have done all we can in this remote area with the limited resources at our disposal.'

We carried the yacht's safety gear, lifebuoy etc, back to *Gipsy Moth* from base camp. The inflatable Avon dinghy was tied to the yacht as a 'liferaft' and lifejackets were found for Richard and John. At 1215 local time a smudge on the horizon slowly became the massive Voith Schneider ocean-going tug.

Paul Gelder/Yachting Monthly

A towing bridle was made from the lifting strops and the tug, stationed as close to the reef as possible, fired a messenger line to pull ashore the much heavier tow line, which was attached to *Gipsy Moth IV*.

Bert and I shook hands with Richard Baggett and John Jeffrey as they scrambled aboard for what John described, with typical British understatement, as 'A boys' own

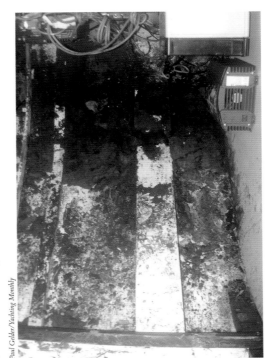

Paul Gelder/Yachting Monthly

Exhaustion or relief after the successful salvage? Punoa found a 'plunge pool' on the coral reef to relax in.

Quick drying cement was used to seal any potential leaks in the plywood patches.

adventure!' One of the salvage workers, Nerou, a muscular, bearded Polynesian, accompanied them and lay flat in the cockpit. As the tug manoeuvred to take up the slack tow line, Bruno on the reef talked to the tug skipper via hand-held VHF radio. For the first time in six days *Gipsy Moth IV* started to edge back towards her natural element in three heart-stopping manoeuvres.

Against the noise of crashing surf on the reef, came a ghastly screeching sound of wood grinding on coral as she was unceremoniously dragged around so that her bows faced the open sea and freedom. Thank God it was the sacrificial planks that were taking all the punishment, not *Gipsy Moth IV*'s hull. She looked an ungainly sight, as she lurched sideways, like some stricken sea creature in a final, desperate struggle to escape a trap.

A second pull bought her closer to the crashing surf as Richard and John braced themselves on the high side of the cockpit. 'Despite a lifetime of military flying, I don't recall many occasions when I have felt more tense,' said John afterwards. 'Although we were wearing lifejackets, we did not clip on. If she was going to sink, we wanted to be able get clear, fast!'

The captain of the tug waited for a big wave to break around *Gipsy Moth IV* and cushion her fall. This was it, then. Bruno talked calmly into his VHF radio to the tug ... the engines went into reverse and the tow line suddenly went taut again. As the surf from a third, bigger wave broke around *Gipsy Moth IV*, she was given a final heave off the reef. Suddenly it was all over. She slid gracefully back into the deep blue Pacific and her mast sprang upright. Cheers from us all drowned out the noise of surf.

On board, Richard, John and Nerou rushed for the companionway to check that the hull patch was holding. 'It was, though a trickle of water continued to come in past the quick drying cement for the next 20 hours,' said John. A RIB from the tug took Nerou off and left them a high-capacity pump, which they rigged and tested but never needed.

Paul Gelder/Yachting Monthly

Within minutes a radio call from Richard on *Gipsy Moth IV* confirmed that there were no bad leaks aboard. A RIB was launched from the tug and divers checked everything. At that moment, 1240 local time on 5 May, *Gipsy Moth IV* was granted a reprieve and a third lucky life. A new chapter was about to begin. Just 321 days after she was re-launched at Camper & Nicholsons on 20 June 2005, after a £300,000 restoration, she was on her way to Tahiti and her third restoration.

From the middle of the reef, I phoned David Green at the UKSA, where it was late on Friday night. He had moved a mattress into the incident room to spend the night there. The relief and euphoria from 10,000 miles away was tangible. '*GMIV* OFF THE ROCKS!' was the headline on the website.

As we walked back to base camp, two figures in the distance were scrambling ashore from a boat in the lagoon. Sky television reporter Derek Tedder and his cameraman Mostyn Price had spent nearly 30 hours travelling from London to Tahiti, via Los Angeles, and now Rangiroa, to 'get an exclusive story'.

'Where's *Gipsy Moth*?' Derek asked, excitedly. 'There!' I said, pointing to a dot on the horizon. 'You just missed all the drama!'

ABOVE:
The moment of truth. Richard and John, huddle down in the cockpit as the ketch is dragged off the reef.

LEFT:
Gipsy Moth begins her 200-mile tow to Tahiti – creaming across the Pacific at 10 knots.

Anne Gelder

The tug arrives in Tahiti to a welcoming committee with the French Harbourmaster

RIGHT: Sky Television reporter Derek Tedder and camerman Mostyn Price finally get their 'scoop'.

Gipsy Moth *is lifted out of the water.*

Derek and Mostyn grabbed the tripod and camera equipment and dashed and splashed across the reef – two intrepid reporters in search of the story they'd missed by minutes – a case of literally 'missing the boat'. They were due to sail as crew on the next leg from Tahiti to Tonga. But they wouldn't be the first to face disappointment.

As *Gipsy Moth* was towed to Tahiti, creaming across the Pacific at 10 knots, darkness fell and Richard and John began solo watches, the two-hourly clatter of the bilge pump acting as a wake up call.

I flew back to Tahiti that evening in time to meet *Gipsy Moth* when she arrived at Papeete's harbour next morning. Papeete is a crossroads for sailors. A place to get things fixed and change crew after the long haul from Panama. It's also known to tradewind sailors as 'Heartbreak Harbour'. Arriving yachts disgorge crew that have been cooped up together for weeks. As sailor Herb Payson observed: 'Often people explode out of yachts like shrapnel, manic with gratitude that they've neither gone crazy nor killed each other... Papeete was the scene of decisions, crew swaps, divorces, marriages, recriminations, congratulations. Those who didn't adapt to cruising went back to where they came from, some sadder, some wiser. Tahiti was a threshold. Many who crossed it would decide they'd be happy to cruise for the rest of their lives.'

For *Gipsy Moth* it was to be a different crossroads. But she had a welcoming committee, which included the French Harbourmaster, dressed in white shirt, shorts, socks and shoes, accompanied by his elegant wife, plus two reporters from the two local newspaper and TV and, of course, Derek and Mostyn from Sky News. We all cheered as *Gipsy Moth IV* came around the breakwater. But it was quite a shock to see the extent of the damage when she was lifted out of the water on the Travel-hoist. The rudder and keel had both been badly chewed up on the reef, with chunks gouged out. The splintered sacrificial planks showed

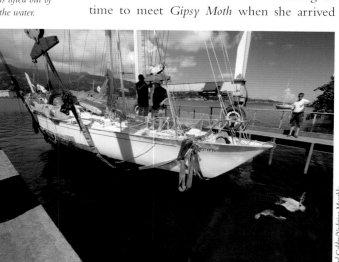

Paul Gelder/Yachting Monthly

Paul Gelder/Yachting Monthly

The sacrificial planks of wood nailed to the hull, and used as a sledge to drag her off the reef, took the brunt of the damage.

they had done their work, taking the brunt of the damage. Bruno and the salvage men from Techni-Marine had known exactly where the planks needed to be nailed – on the balancing point of the hull – and had done a superb job in saving *Gipsy Moth IV*.

John Jeffrey said: 'This has been one of the hardest weeks of my life. I'm bruised, battered and extremely tired, but I couldn't be happier.'

Later, Sir Robin Knox-Johnston, one of our patrons, who was preparing his open 60, *Grey Power* (later *Saga*), for a second solo non-stop circumnavigation in the Velux 5 Oceans, emailed me: 'Desperately sorry about *GM*, but glad she has been saved...'

Giles Chichester sent a heartwarming text message: 'Very sorry to read of *Gipsy Moth IV*'s mishap. The Pacific region does seem to have it in for *GMs**. My father told me you need little accidents to keep you on your toes and reduce statistical chances of a big one.'

Some days later, Peter Seymour returned to Rangiroa to thank Felix, the Deputy Mayor, his policemen and Punoa, and everyone who

had played an important part in assisting with the *Gipsy Moth IV*'s crew and the recovery operation. Felix assured him that, '*C'était rien*'.

Everyone on the *Gipsy Moth IV* project profoundly disagreed!

---

* Sir Francis' Gipsy Moth bi-plane crashed at Lord Howe Island in 1931; *Gipsy Moth IV* had her knockdown in 1967 and *Gipsy Moth V* was wrecked on Gabo Island in 1982.

LEFT: Peter Seymour with Punoa, the local 'Mr Fixit'.

BELOW: The Deputy Mayor, Felix, and the gendarmerie.

Peter Seymour

Peter Seymour

Kiwi miracle
The race to repair Gipsy Moth

'Crunch time for *Gipsy Moth*' was the headline in *The Daily Telegraph* newspaper. The original plan had been to sail her from Tahiti to Tonga and then on to Auckland, followed by 'The Big One' – crossing the Tasman Sea to Sydney, Australia, Chichester's one stopover. But now legs 12 and 13 were abandoned and *Gipsy Moth* would arrive in New Zealand as deck cargo on a freighter. There would be little more than a month to get her repaired and seaworthy for the 1,400-mile leg to Sydney.

Gipsy Moth was loaded onto the freighter, *Thor Simba*, 11 days after being towed into Tahiti from Rangiroa. John MacDonald, a marine surveyor, had flown from Auckland to assess the damage and Bob Bradfield, one of *Gipsy Moth*'s ardent supporters, arrived in Tahiti to assist Richard Baggett.

A big morale booster was when top New Zealand sailor Grant Dalton, himself a seven-times circumnavigator and then running the America's Cup Emirates Team New Zealand, offered to help. Chichester had been his boyhood hero. He ordered one of the America's Cup sheds in Viaduct Harbour to be made available for *Gipsy Moth*'s repairs, and offered facilities and assistance from his team.

James Blake, son of the late Sir Peter Blake, New Zealand's biggest sailing hero, was due to sail on *Gipsy Moth* from Auckland, adding an even greater impetus to getting the boat seaworthy. I had a special interest, too, since I was joining James and skipper Richard Baggett on passage across the Tasman Sea.

At the UKSA, 500 emails and letters of support were received, while in New Zealand Chris Fewtrell, a friend of David Green, who was co-ordinating the refit with Richard

Plywood patches stuck on in Rangiroa were removed and the damaged area needing repair was eventually a gaping hole 3.5 metres by 1.5 metres.

Richard Gladwell

Richard Gladwell

Lead skipper Richard Baggett with Chris Fewtrell, who co-ordinated the refit after Grant Dalton offered help from his America's Cup Emirates Team New Zealand.

Baggett and Bob Bradfield, had no shortage of offers of help. Chris, who had set up the deal with Dalton, soon found a project manager for repairs, Bob Wilson, from Brin Wilson Boat Builders Ltd.

By the time *Gipsy Moth* arrived from Tahiti, everything was in place and shipwrights began work in round the clock shifts. On the first morning, the plywood 'band-aid' covering the hole in the hull was ripped off and the galley and other furniture removed to expose the damage. The rudder was taken away to repair at Wilson's facility in Gulf Harbour. SP Systems once again made

materials available via Gurit (New Zealand) Ltd, as did International Paint. Some two tons of African mahogany were shipped from Sydney to Auckland for the hull repair.

Viaduct Harbour, in the heart of Auckland's waterfront business district, has world-class facilities with just about every marine skill and service available. Richard was impressed by the Kiwi's 'can-do' attitude. Materials and time were given at discounted rates, sometimes free of charge, by companies in the Westhaven Yacht Refit Destination Group. Electronics Afloat Ltd stripped out *Gipsy Moth*'s wiring, electronics

Richard Gladwell

The galley and other interior furniture was stripped out to repair the damage.

Richard Gladwell

and communications equipment from the damaged area. The cracked main bulkhead was cut away and replaced. The re-skinning of *Gipsy Moth IV*'s damaged starboard side was the major task, with six layers of veneer to patch a hole 3.5 metres by 1.5 metres. The lead keel was separated from the hull ready for new keel bolts. The work moved forward at a blistering pace.

Against all the odds, another *Gipsy Moth* miracle re-fit was performed, thanks to the Kiwis. The work was finished in less than three weeks, ahead of schedule and under budget, but the bill was some £120,000.

On 23 June, to celebrate her re-commissioning, *Gipsy Moth IV* sailed a lap of honour in Auckland Harbour, accompanied by a fire-fighting tug, naval training yachts and a fly-past by a vintage Gipsy Moth bi-plane. Bob Bradfield organised an auction at The Royal New Zealand Yacht Squadron, where *Gipsy Moth IV* memorabilia, including an original winch, raised more than NZ$13,000.

Meanwhile, Antonia Nicholson and Chris Bruce were facing a UKSA board of inquiry into the Rangiroa grounding incident. A three-man panel comprised David Green, his deputy, Jon Ely and John Walsh, a Yachtmaster Ocean Examiner and the project manager of the restoration.

The result was that Antonia and Chris were dismissed with a right of appeal. A statement issued by the UKSA said: 'The passage plan constructed by the skipper and the mate, which gave a two-mile offing from the reef, is considered to have been ill-conceived, particularly given the navigational challenges of the area and the approaching hours of darkness. The last plotted position of the vessel was at 1615 and all the necessary navigation equipment, pilot books and charts were aboard the vessel. The skipper and the mate had available to them all necessary means to navigate the vessel safely.

'From that point there was a gradual deterioration in the course made good towards the reef which was not detected. At 1800 the vessel was already perilously close to the reef. Although a lat and long position was taken from the GPS at that time and written in the log, it was not plotted on the chart. A change in helm after 1800 may have resulted in an exacerbation of the course error. The Skipper and the Mate did not supervise this change in helm. The vessel continued towards the reef which it struck at around 1815.

'Had the skipper or mate navigated the vessel at any stage during that two-hour period, by the simple means available to them, the course error and the potential danger to the vessel would have been detectable and an alteration of course would have been possible thus resulting in this incident being avoided.'

Throughout the ordeal on the reef, and afterwards, Antonia never sought to blame anyone else for the accident. Many sailors on the Blue Water Rally and readers of *Yachting Monthly* thought the inquiry should have been more wide-ranging and should not have been conducted behind closed doors.

Opinions over Antonia's dismissal were sharply divided in the sailing community. Many thought she deserved more support with the pressures she had been under with engine problems and malfunctioning equipment. 'Post traumatic stress-counselling, rather than the sack,' was suggested by two correspondents. Chichester, of course, would have been aghast at such modern-day notions. He coped single-handedly with his 'cantankerous' craft, but then he didn't have three teenage crew to look after with a daily sat-com web log to edit!

It was undoubtedly a huge embarrassment for a sailing school, priding itself on teaching seamanship, to be suddenly in the spotlight after the near-shipwreck of such a national treasure. The total bill for the incident, if you added up everyone's involvement, would be getting on for half-a-million pounds and it had been a massive setback. The UKSA faced a difficult choice. They were damned if they made an example of the crew and damned if they didn't.

Later Antonia explained: 'On that day, I had been up since 0600 getting fuel. I hadn't slept properly for days because of the workload, plus the heat, and I was concerned the kids would miss their flights home. The new crew were already on their way to the airport so there was no down time for me or the boat. The Blue Water Rally support was excellent but I was disappointed in the UKSA. They were really supportive at first. The *Gipsy Moth* project was a big part of my life for over a year. I put a lot into it. Ultimately, the whole thing was a big bump in the road – but just that. The road does go on.'

After the inquiry Antonia had her Commercial Yachtmaster's qualification suspended for six months by the RYA. 'Everything I had learnt from the incident was brushed aside. I was unable to teach when I felt I had experiences to pass on to others. I had lots of work offered to me from other sailing schools but I couldn't take it. I don't think suspending me was the solution – it was punishment.'

A year after the grounding, Antonia, having retaken her Yachtmaster exam, flew out to Fort Lauderdale to deliver a 76ft ketch to Greece with husband Ray, who had resigned from the UKSA in sympathy.

'Getting rid of that image of *Gipsy Moth* stranded on the reef took a long time,' said Antonia. 'Now I see her sailing in the Solent, I remember the wonderful people and amazing places we saw on our voyage and the special moments shared with so many young people. To me that's what sailing is all about. I would never have changed any of it – except for that one particular moment.'

In less than three weeks, and against all the odds, Gipsy Moth *was relaunched.*

Richard Gladwell

Following the reef incident, there was an outcry from some quarters about 'risking such a priceless British maritime icon in dangerous waters'. Ironic, since it was coming from some of same people who hadn't cared a jot when *Gipsy Moth* was rotting away in dry dock. Questions were raised about the suitability of the boat for novice sailors.

There were lessons to be learned from the grounding incident beyond the dismissal of the skipper and mate. We could so easily have been facing a public inquest into lives lost, rather than an internal UKSA inquiry into a navigational blunder.

In the aftermath, I wrote a five-page memo to David Green expressing widespread concerns passed on to me by marine industry pundits, my own staff who had sailed on *Gipsy Moth* and readers. All had raised issues which I felt couldn't be ignored if we were to be above criticism. I listed more than 20 points, including the unsatisfactory original compass and primus stove, plus watch-keeping, sleep deprivation, crew selection and slab reefing.

At the end of my memo I wrote: 'The success of the *Gipsy Moth* project should be measured by a safe, seamanlike voyage. If success is to be measured by the amount of publicity generated, it should be remembered that the

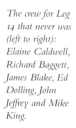

The New Zealand stopover was a good opportunity to take stock and make safety modifications, like adding a bulkhead compass.

The crew for Leg 14 that never was (left to right): Elaine Caldwell, Richard Baggett, James Blake, Ed Dolling, John Jeffrey and Mike King.

Titanic made one of the most successful voyages of all time!'

The New Zealand and Sydney stopovers offered a good opportunity to take stock and make safety modifications. A new bulkhead steering compass was fitted with a new diesel stove replacing the unreliable paraffin stove. Radar would also be fitted in Darwin (though it would have made no difference in the grounding incident). The pressure on skippers to provide daily video clips and photographs by sat-com was discussed, as well as better integration with the Blue Water Rally from Cairns onwards. We were all on a steep learning curve with this project. But I strongly believed the daily video for the website added an unnecessary and unrealistic workload for skipper and mate.

By now David was in Sydney making arrangements for *Gipsy Moth*'s royal engagements. He stopped off in Auckland on his way home to visit the repair team and witnessed severe winter weather, with winds of over 100mph in the Tasman Sea.

When he got back to the UK we held a meeting at *Yachting Monthly* with David, Jon Ely, myself and Dick Durham. It was three days before I was due to fly to Auckland to join *Gipsy Moth* for the Tasman crossing. Out of the blue, David dropped the bombshell that he'd decided to abandon leg 14. Instead, *Gipsy Moth* would go to Sydney as deck cargo on a ship. It seemed that the combination of my memo, winter weather in the Tasman, plus a royal appointment, conspired to make this the safest option. It was a bitter personal disappointment. But I understood that risking *Gipsy Moth* in the Tasman Sea, where Chichester suffered a serious capsize, might be seen as a risk too far, even though we had a strong crew. No less disappointed were skipper Richard Baggett, who had worked so hard on the refit and John Jeffery, who had flown out early, and was frustrated to miss his third leg of the voyage! Ed Dolling, from BT and Mike King, from the Isle of Wight partnership, were also in New Zealand hoping to go sailing, together with James Blake.

At Buckingham Palace on 1 June, Princess Anne hosted a fund-raising reception for the *Gipsy Moth* project where Laura Walsh, Maria Turner and Barbara Kennedy, the three young ladies from the Ellen MacArthur Trust who had recovered from cancer and sailed to the Galapagos, spoke eloquently about their adventures.

Later that evening a gala dinner and auction was held at the Royal Thames Yacht Club in Knightsbridge, raising £85,000 towards the project. Items sold included an oil painting of *Gipsy Moth* by Tim Thompson (£14,000); an original Barlow primary winch (£2,500) and a Corum watch (£5,800).

The New Zealand repair team, led by Chris Fewtrell, Bob Bradfield and Bob Wilson, were delighted when Princess Anne stopped off in New Zealand, on her way to Sydney, to say a big thank you for all their hard work.

Gipsy Moth sailed a lap of honour in Auckland Harbour after her repairs were completed.

Richard Gladwell

Wizard in Oz

Gipsy Moth in Sydney

While Britain slept, hundreds of sailors on the other side of the globe were welcoming *Gipsy Moth IV* back to Sydney Harbour for her second arrival on a glorious sunny Sunday afternoon in July. Forty years previously, Chichester sailed through Sydney Heads at 4.30pm on 12 December, 1976 to a tumultuous welcome after 14,100 miles non-stop. 'The whole town went crazy. It was a sight that bought tears to the eyes of many who watched,' said one observer. 'Some voyage! Some man!' was the London *Evening Standard* headline. 'The lone conqueror of the sea is here!'

Sydneysiders were eager to welcome the most famous mariner to reach their shores since Captain Cook anchored the *Discovery* at Botany Bay almost 200 years earlier. But Chichester, 65, couldn't start the yacht's engine and was worried about being rammed by the TV and press boats, before being taken in tow by a launch from the Royal Sydney Yacht Squadron.

Giles Chichester was the first to jump aboard, giving his father a hug. 'Giles is much taller than I am and pretty husky and the photographs made me look like an old man weeping on his shoulder,' Chichester said.

Later, *Gipsy Moth* berthed at the yacht squadron, where Chichester stepped ashore on wobbly legs for the first time in 107 days. 'I feel a bit wonky and very humble,' he told reporters. Later, when he saw the press photos, his verdict was: 'I looked like the oldest inhabitant of Little Teapot by the Sea being helped towards his 110th birthday cake.'

These 'ghastly photographs', together with some of his outspoken criticism of *Gipsy Moth*, were published in the press and he got a telegram from Tony Dulverton, principal owner of the boat, saying that on no account should he continue with the voyage.

Forty years on, our Sydney welcome in 2006 demonstrated how much Sir Francis had touched the hearts of Australians with his heroic passage. The front-page headline in *The Sydney Morning Herald* was: '*Gipsy Moth*'s back, minus a crusty old salt!' The Australian newspapers dubbed our second circumnavigation 'an against-all-odds voyage', especially in the light of the grounding in Rangiroa.

Sydney's second welcome for Gipsy Moth, *40 years on, showed how much Chichester had touched the hearts of Australians.*

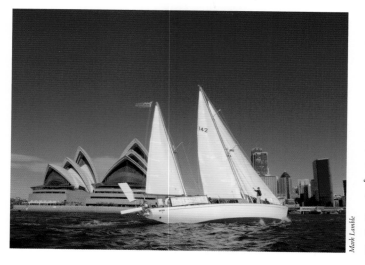

Mark Lamble

As *Gipsy Moth* sailed into the harbour, I was aboard. But I'd be lying if I didn't say I felt a complete fraud! Instead of revelling in the achievement of making landfall after crossing 1,400 miles of treacherous Tasman Sea in winter, I'd flown first to Auckland and then to Sydney, stepping aboard *Gipsy Moth* in Noakes Boatyard, west of Sydney Harbour Bridge earlier that morning

Here, *Gipsy Moth*'s masts had been re-stepped after she'd been craned off a cargo vessel from Auckland and a couple of days were spent sprucing her up for her parade of honour.

The crew were skipper Richard Baggett, mate Simon Hay, Elaine Caldwell, 23, with whom I'd sailed from Plymouth to Bayona on the first leg, and James Blake, from my home town of Emsworth, where *Gipsy Moth* had taken shape on Illingworth & Primrose's design board at 36 North Street.

Elaine had written a poignant message at the time of *Gipsy Moth*'s grounding on the reef in Rangiroa which inspired the entire project team: 'It's important everyone remains upbeat about *Gipsy Moth*,' she said. 'This is her first trial since she left Plymouth in September. It could have been worse! Chichester never gave up and I'm sure he wouldn't want us to either. She can be fixed. She lay in a dry-dock for long enough before being resurrected. If it can happen once, it can happen again. Keep the spirit of the voyage alive! This project has taught me something new. You get knocked down and you must just keep getting back up. That's why I'm so gripped by the *Gipsy Moth* experience. Perseverance and people out there doing things for the greater good.'

All of us aboard *Gipsy Moth IV* that day were privileged to be in the grandstand seat for her big Sydney welcome. After breakfast we motor-sailed under Sydney Harbour Bridge, past the Opera House and out beyond Sydney Heads to see whales breaching in the distance. At lunchtime we turned around to make our staged 'grand entrance' into Sydney at the appointed hour of 1400.

This fabulous sterling silver model of Gipsy Moth, *made by Benzies of Cowes, flew first-class to Sydney!*

Gipsy Moth *(to the right of the lifeboat) sails though Sydney Harbour on a July Sunday afternoon.*

Yacht designer
Warwick Hood
(left), who helped
Chichester
make changes
to the ketch in
1996, with Jack
Christofferson.

RIGHT:
Chichester arrives
in Sydney in
1967.

TV news channel
helicopters buzzed
Gipsy Moth on
her staged arrival
in the harbour.

David Green was out in a fast RIB shepherding his 'flock' with a hand-held VHF radio and walkie-talkie at the ready. He was a sort of sea-going stage manager for our re-enactment of Chichester's arrival having dubbed himself: 'Master Event Co-ordinator.'

Soon we were flanked by a flotilla of vessels, including Sydney-Hobart race boats, classic gaffers from the city's Maritime Museum, water taxis, ferries, an RNLI lifeboat and a vintage steam tug. Overhead, TV helicopters and two Gipsy Moth bi-planes buzzed the yacht as part of her spectacular welcome. Alex Whitworth, the intrepid Sydney sailor in his 60s, was there singlehanding *Beremilla*, the yacht he'd sailed with his friend from the Sydney-Hobart Race to the Fastnet in England and back to take part in the next Sydney-Hobart.

We berthed alongside at the Royal Yacht Squadron in Kirribilli two hours later, just as Chichester had done. Among those on the pontoon to take our lines was Warwick Hood, the Australian naval architect who, with the late Alan Payne, helped Chichester make valuable improvements to *Gipsy Moth IV*'s keel in 1966 by adding two metal plates screwed and riveted to the existing keel to give more directional stability.

Forty years on, Warwick had already stepped in to help the yacht's second circumnavigation by responding to an appeal by the UKSA for a new propeller. He organized a collection at the squadron and raised £1,500 to buy an Australian Hydralign folding prop, made by Jack Christofferson of JCB Engineering. It proved a big improvement on the original 'egg whisk'. *Gipsy Moth*'s original propeller was polished up and presented to Warwick and Bruce Gould, mounted on a plaque as a memento of our arrival. Payne's daughter, Rosetta, also came to visit the yacht.

Throughout the coming the week, many visitors shared photographs and memories of Chichester's Sydney stopover. Bill Psaltis, who was club Commodore in 1966 and one of the first people to talk to Chichester, was another sailor for whom the sight of *Gipsy Moth* 40 years on evoked fond memories.

It was during his Sydney stopover that Chichester was told of the knighthood bestowed on him by Queen Elizabeth. The actual ceremony would take place six months later in Greenwich.

Events during our stopover included a dinner at the Royal Sydney Yacht Squadron, where I reminded the Aussies of one of the comments shouted by a fan at Chichester's Sydney press conference in 1966: 'You little beautie Chich – we knew you'd bolt it in mate!'

Rex Harrison, Commodore of the RSYS, was presented with a special limited edition bottle of *Gipsy Moth IV* Mount Gay Rum. A centrepiece at this dinner, and at other functions, was a fabulous sterling silver model of *Gipsy Moth IV*, made by senior craftsman Will Souter, of Benzies, in Cowes, known as 'the Yachtsmen's Jeweller'. It had been flown first-class to Sydney by Emirates Airlines.

'I'm looking forward to a decent dinner when I get to Sydney,' Chichester wrote in his log book. 'I've lost about 40lbs on this trip and can hardly keep my pants up.' Actually, it turned out he had lost 18lbs.

Two nights later we enjoyed a fund-raising black-tie gala dinner with Princess Anne at Darling Harbour. The occasion was part of the annual Australian Yachting Awards. Elaine Caldwell spoke eloquently and Nick

Bonham conducted an auction which raised $42,000AU for the project.

The Queen sent Chichester a telegram before his departure in January 1967, saying: 'My husband and I send you our warmest good wishes for the completion of your journey round the world in *Gipsy Moth IV. Bon voyage.* Elizabeth R.'

Now it was her daughter, Princess Anne, who wished the new crew fair winds.

A keen yachtswoman, she relished the opportunity next morning to go sailing on *Gipsy Moth* for the first time, after opening a display of Chichester memorabilia at the Australia National Maritime Museum.

Kitted out in sailing jacket and sporty sun shades, she took the helm for a tour around majestic Sydney Harbour. There were a few jokes aboard about avoiding 'any more incidents', especially with our highly experienced crew, which included James Stevens, RYA training manager, Phil Jones, CEO of Yachting Australia, skipper Richard Baggett, David Green, a barefoot James Blake, two royal protection officers in suits, and myself.

LEFT:
Pippa Blake takes Gipsy Moth's *helm.*

ABOVE:
The Royal Sydney Yacht Squadron in Kirribilli.

Bruce Gould from the Royal Sydney Yacht Squadron.

As well as a 'press exclusion zone', *Gipsy Moth IV* was shadowed by an Australian anti-terrorism squad armed to the teeth in a black RIB. Under full sail, with mizzen staysail, and later, cruising chute, the yacht heeled to gusts of 18 knots – which blew off Phil's hat – quickly recovered by the men in black – and sluiced water down the sidedeck, soaking one of the protection officers!

We sailed from Darling Harbour to berth some 90-minutes later at the Cruising Yacht Club of Australia (CYC), in Rushcutters Bay. Here, as president of the Royal Yachting Association, Princess Anne was guest of honour at a ceremony to launch RYA Australia.

A cheeky Australian reporter wrote: 'Members of the club are better known for

their rum consumption than their dress, but they brushed up a treat as they lined the marina awaiting the Princess Royal's arrival. Blazers replaced salt-encrusted sailing shorts.'

Another link with *Gipsy Moth* and Australia is that her co-designer John Illingworth founded the famous CYC Boxing Day Sydney–Hobart Race in 1945 when he was a Royal Navy officer based in Sydney.

Next day, *Gipsy Moth* moved to the Maritime Museum at Darling Harbour where she was open to the public until her departure.

Chichester spent seven weeks re-fitting his yacht and regaining his strength in Sydney, before leaving on January 29. 'Of course, I'm taking my smoking jacket – I couldn't possibly do without that. It has been on every major voyage of mine,' he was quoted in *The Times*.

On the eve of his departure he told a reporter: 'I have tarried too long, there will be no more delays. A spot of dirty weather should help me get back into trim quickly.'

The 'spot of dirty weather' he referred to was the cyclone Diana which had been forecast. Its backlash was to give him a terrible pasting and cause *Gipsy Moth IV*'s capsize in the Tasman Sea.

Forty years on, history repeated itself when *Gipsy Moth*'s new young crew sailed from Sydney on a Sunday afternoon, after a stopover of less than two weeks, into the worst storm of 2006.

Gipsy Moth *berthed in Darling Harbour for the Australian Yachting Awards gala dinner with Princess Anne.*

Sydney to Mooloolaba

By Chris Bray

Riders on the Storm

Leg 15

Distance:

400 miles

Skipper:

Simon Hay, (37)
UKSA

Mate:

Gordon Berry
(61), UKSA

Crew Leader:

Chris Bray (23)

Crew:

Elaine Caldwell
(25),
David Thackray
(18) and Nicole
Starling (17)

Bullets of windborne water pelted loudly against my oilskin hood. Just ahead of me, illuminated by the spreader lights in the dark, skipper Simon Hay glanced back. 'OK, are you ready mate?' he shouted above the gale. 'This is NOT going to be fun.' We both knew what we had to do. Against every instinct, I clipped my lifeline to the jackstay and crawled out along the sidedeck. 'Incoming!' First mate Gordon Berry shouted the warning from the cockpit as a wave picked up our stern, surging us forward. Clinging to a shroud, I could feel it writhing in my hand like a tortured snake as we careered down the crumbling face of another giant wave. My heart was racing. Despite the fact that we only had one sail up – the No2 working jib – *Gipsy Moth IV* was hurtling down waves at almost 12 knots, much of her deck buried under white water.

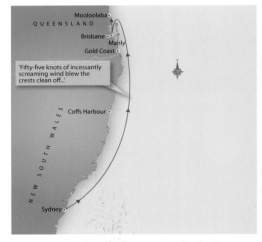

'Fifty-five knots of incessantly screaming wind blew the crests clean off...'

In strong winds, waves don't just get bigger, they get angrier, too. Despite being pitch black, I could see the glowing white water of these ogres falling over each other in their hurry to dash themselves against us. 55 knots of screaming wind blew the crests clean off, streaming them along the surface like spindrift. Towering as high as our first spreaders, five metre waves bore down directly into the open cockpit as we rocketed our way towards Brisbane in the worst storm to ravage the New South Wales coastline in 2006.

History was repeating itself. Chichester suffered some of his worst weather in *Gipsy Moth IV* not far from these waters 40 years ago, when he was capsized on a wild night in the Tasman Sea the day after leaving Sydney for Cape Horn. It was on 30 January and he was seasick a few hours after passing Sydney Heads

Mark Lamble

Gipsy Moth
sailing past a
moody-looking
North Head.

and took to his bunk that night, lying ahull in 'a series of savage bursts of wind... it was too rough, even for a storm jib.' He hoped the thumping was the self-steering gear and not the new false keel.

'White breakers,' he wrote in his log on the Monday night, 'showed in the blackness like monstrous beasts towering high in the sky. I wouldn't blame anyone for being terrified at the sight.' But he did bravely venture on deck next afternoon to finally set a storm jib.

When the capsize came at 2230 he was down below in his bunk, bombarded with crockery, cutlery and bottles in the pitch dark. He wondered if the boat would roll over completely. Switching on his bunk light he was amazed it worked and had a feeling of something normal in the world of utter chaos suddenly illuminated. The cabin was two foot deep with a jumble of tins, bottles, tools, shackles and two sextants. The five foot bilge was not quite full. Fearing his radio might stop working, he called Sydney Radio just after midnight on the distress frequency – 'to get a message out that I was okay ... and if they didn't hear from me again it was because the telephone had been swamped.'

He later estimated – from the trajectory of a bottle of Irish whiskey and its embedded fragments of glass – that *Gipsy Moth IV* had been knocked down to 131° and the mast would have been 41° below the horizontal.

Forty years on, Simon and I continued to edge closer to the bow. Every time the yacht plunged downwards, I felt myself becoming weightless as my knees lost contact with the deck, until we struck the next wave. Squinting through salt-blasted eyes at the headsail, our fears were confirmed. At least five hanks had pulled off the forestay. The sail was clinging on merely by the tack, head, and a few scattered points in between! We had to get it down – now.

Drenched at the helm, 17-year-old Nicole Starling expertly guided *Gipsy Moth IV* into a turn, so that when I released the halyard the headsail would fall on the deck, instead of being blown over the side. 'Now!' Simon's mouth formed the words and I released the halyard.

The battered headsail fell to the deck, bristling with bent and mangled hanks. We sprang on top, quickly subduing it with sail ties. Then the shrieking wind tried to snatch the bright orange storm jib, which we were to put up in its place, from under me.

Under bare poles, Nicole grimly held our course, while Simon attached the halyard and I tied on the sheets. 'OK, pull her up!' Driving spray stung my face as I pulled and the sail thrashed violently, whipping and cracking. 'One of the sheets has come off!' shouted Simon.

'We have to drop it ... Drop it! Drop it!' I've never seen a bowline thrash itself apart before. Simon retied it with an extra long tail before giving the signal. 'Pull!' Again the angry orange sail rose from the deck and flailed like a thing possessed. The sheet lashed around at everything, including me, as I clung on by the mast trying to winch the halyard up tight. 'Pull in the sheet!' Simon roared back to the cockpit, where there was a problem bringing it under control. I dived for shelter behind the mast.

Thirty minutes after leaving the cockpit, Simon and I returned grinning like idiots. 'Was that fun, or what?' Simon asked Nicole.

Chichester had not been so lucky during his 'big shemozzle'. One of his big 600ft genoas was swept overboard, plus a drogue and 700ft of inch-and-a-half plaited warp.

Skipper Simon Hay: 'Yeah mate! She's blowing 50 knots.'

Chris Bray

'I longed to be back in Sydney tied up to the jetty,' he admitted in his account of the voyage. 'I hated and dreaded the voyage ahead. Let's face it, I was frightened and had a sick feeling of fear gnawing inside me. If this could happen in an ordinary storm, how could a small boat possibly survive in a 100-knot greybearder?'

For me, too, the start of leg 15 of *Gipsy Moth IV*'s second circumnavigation was not quite what I was expecting. 'Just a little sail up to Queensland...' I was told, 'You know... write a few words... take some photos for *Yachting Monthly*.'

But no one could dispute the fact that all six of us taking part were having the time of our lives.

As a child, I had sailed around the world with my family for five years on my dad's homebuilt 44ft aluminium *Starship*, but I had never seen conditions like this. We'd always sailed conservatively – waiting for the weather – but on *Gipsy Moth IV* we were running to a timetable that discouraged delays. 'At the end of the day', Simon said, 'this project is about getting young crew to overcome challenges and gain confidence in themselves. So long as it's safe, given the choice between this gale, or flapping our way slowly up the coast in light winds – I'd pick strong winds every time – ideally after a brief settling-in period of better weather.'

And that's exactly what we'd had.

Roller reefing the mainsail on a golden evening.

Chris Bray

Chris Bray

Chris Bray

FAR LEFT:
*Chris Bray
was expecting
'a gentle sail to
Queensland.'*

LEFT:
*Red sky at night
did not follow with
a sailor's delight.*

So long, Sydney!

Just two days earlier, on Sunday afternoon, 16 July, *Gipsy Moth IV* slipped from her berth in front of Sydney's National Maritime Museum in Darling Harbour, sailed under the Harbour Bridge and headed out to sea.

Our accompanying fleet of well-wishers thinned out, just as Chichester, too, suddenly found himself alone and eventually even the news helicopters abandoned us. A lone humpback whale slowly puffing north from Antarctica caused a brief sensation, before darkness closed in around us. There were three young crew aboard from Sydney on this leg, myself, Nicole and David.

On *Gipsy Moth*'s new Wallas diesel cooker (the original Primus stove having been retired), we heated up a spaghetti bolognese, pre-made by Nicole's mum Dianne and divided into two teams, with Simon, Nicole and I taking the first watch of the voyage: four hours on, four hours off at night; six hours on, six hours off by day.

'Have you ever been sailing at night before?' Simon asked Nicole. 'Never!' she grinned. 'I've not even sailed outside the harbour before.' The excitement burning in her eyes started to sparkle through the veil of shyness and uncertainty.

The wind was a mere seven to eight knots northwesterly, and with such a short fetch the rolling swell remained a docile two to three metres as we sliced into them. However, this was still enough to turn Nicole and me

green. We willed those first four hours past, until at last Elaine and David – both looking ill, came up to change watch, followed by the perpetually jolly Gordon.

I lay on a saloon bench, trying to ignore the rising feeling of dread within me – being seasick was no longer a question of 'if' but 'when'. As Hugo Vihlen once commented: 'I don't know who named them swells. There's nothing swell about them. They should have been named awfuls.' Back on watch, as I leant over the leeward lifeline and the churning water tore past in front of my face, I shared my dinner with the fishes. Once the nausea passed, I slunk back to the cockpit to relieve Nicole of the helm. 'Steer her 030°,' Simon cheerily nodded at the bulkhead-mounted compass – just one of the new additions to *Gipsy Moth IV* after her refit in New Zealand. It was great to have this most famous of yachts back on track after her encounter with a reef in French Polynesia and the indignity of being carried across oceans as deck cargo.

By next morning the wind had slackened, and we fired up the engine to pick up the pace, charging the batteries and flushing the watermaker – something that needed to be done every few days.

'We want to put as much distance as possible between us and what's astern,' Simon said from below. 'There's a 35-knot southerly chasing us, with seas up to 4m,' he added, before turning back to the weather chart on the laptop.

Chris Bray

Chris Bray

Elaine (left) and Simon on watch as Gipsy Moth encounters the worst storm to ravage the New South Wales coastline in 2006.

If you're offshore, there's a strong current of 3–4 knots running down the east coast of Australia, hampering progress northwards. It's similar to the treacherous Agulhas current off South Africa, the second swiftest current in all the world's oceans (the Gulf Stream is the worst). It can be avoided by staying closer inshore, but that means running the gauntlet of a minefield of crab-traps, fishermen's floats and lines – so we opted to stay well offshore. In the southerly we'd have wind–against–current, translating into a nasty sea. 'It should hit us about midnight,' said Simon, shutting the laptop down. And so the waiting game began.

Peering around the deceptively flat ocean, Nicole spotted the dorsal fin of a shark slicing through the water, followed at an alarming distance by its tail fin. A shower of little baitfish

'I don't know who named them "swells". They should have been called "awfuls".

Chris Bray

boiled from the surface in front of him as he cruised along. Yes, definitely a good idea to stay offshore away from those crab-pots – I couldn't imagine any of us volunteering to leap over the side to cut us free.

As dusk gave way to darkness, the stars perforated the sky above, burning brilliantly for us away from the light pollution of civilisation. Already that night I'd spotted three shooting stars. 'Where is this so-called gale?' was the question on all our lips – there was no sign of the ominous nightmare chasing us from behind.

Four hours on, four hours off, and I was back on watch again, the moon's glowing orb rising above the horizon, as Nicole and I watched its silver reflection dancing over the gently rolling ocean towards us. The odd wave slapped hard against the windward side, sending a shower of water pattering against the back of our oilskin hoods, momentarily jerking us back from the sleep-deprived void through which we drifted.

Next day from morning until noon we watched keenly for signs of the storm. Simon's eyes narrowed as he peered at a thin tongue of cloud spearing past us to starboard. Then, all at once, the rest of the cloud rolled into view – a smothering ashen blanket galloping towards us. 'It's alright mate...' Simon sniggered cheerfully. 'It's midday now, we're off watch!' We couldn't help but laugh at the look on Gordon's face as he led his crew into the cockpit for the watch and we three dropped below decks.

Unfortunately, sleep was not an option. We braced ourselves as the dial on the wind speed anemometer was behaving more like the hand of a clock: 20 knots, 25, 30 knots. What were initially just whitecaps soon became full-on breaking waves, emptying into the cockpit. Suddenly, wave after wave ripped along the sidedeck into the cockpit, or broke over the stern. Our impressive seven knots of boat speed rose to eight then nine as we shot onwards, rolling from side to side. Below decks none

A fly-past by two Australian Gipsy Moth bi-planes as the ketch sails into Mooloolaba after an eight-day passage from Sydney.

of us got a wink of sleep. You might as well try napping inside a washing machine, as the contents of the chart table or a galley drawer was emptied into the mix.

Conditions steadily deteriorated. Simon relieved David, who resembled a drowned rat, at the helm. As he retreated below, an almighty wave followed him along the cockpit and spilled down below. 'Put the washboards in!' Simon called. The sheer force of the waves sometimes sprayed through the washboards as if a fire-hose was being held against the outside.

After a hearty pasta and Irish stew dinner prepared by Nicole in the tumultuous galley, Simon called David Green, at the UKSA, on the satellite phone.

'We're all ok, having a whale of a time out here,' Simon said. Sure. I could see the similarities. A whale: an air-breathing mammal, immersed in water for long periods of time. In truth, spirits were at an all time high and the unmistakable spark of adventure flashed in everyone's eyes. This was what it was all about.

As daylight ebbed away, those in the cockpit were left with nothing but the howl of the wind and the crumbling white waves around us. I couldn't see the really big ones coming, but there was no need to look back, a quick glance at Nicole's face was plenty of warning. If she was looking worried, upwards and astern it meant trouble. A thundering roar in the darkness would reach a crescendo and an immense body of water would collapse into the cockpit. Spluttering, we'd regain control, wipe the water out of our eyes, count the number of people still harnessed on, and smile in relief. 30 knots of wind, 35, 40.

'If we're registering 40 knots...' I yelled into Simon's ear, '... and we're sailing downwind at 10 knots...'

'Yeah mate!' Simon's grin flashed in the darkness. 'She's blowing 50 knots!'

Nicole, especially, was in her element – she loved it and could now hold a course firmer than any of us in this gale. It was incredible to see how much her self-confidence and skill had risen in just the last three days. The shy girl I'd met when I first boarded in Sydney was gone. Sitting beside me now was an extremely capable and dependable ocean sailor. A particularly violent wave flushed the cockpit and Simon shone his torch forward to the headsail, quickly turned it off, and sat there in silence. 'That doesn't look quite right does it?' I ventured. 'The hanks aren't pulling off are they?'

After the foredeck drama that night, not much changed in the next 24 hours. The gale kept raging, we kept getting drenched and bruised but held ourselves together. I wish I could say the same for *Gipsy Moth IV*. Moving around down below involved carefully timed transfers from handrail to handrail, until eventually – as we found out – you ended up on your back with the handrail no longer attached to the deckhead. Meanwhile, Gordon fell through his pipecot berth in the forepeak and was later hurled through the cabin door, taking the hinge with him.

Gipsy Moth gets an escort into port after the storm.

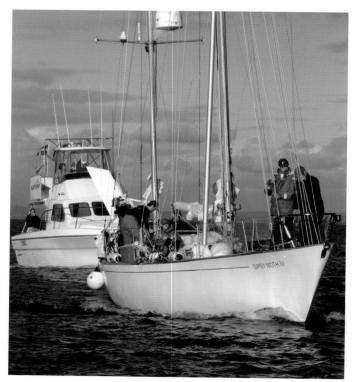

Gipsy Moth IV's stern looked like a war zone, too. The danbuoy was snatched by the sea during the night and both horseshoe lifebuoys hung at tormented angles. The dodgers emblazoned with sponsors' names were ripped off the lifelines and flailed around. Mercifully, though, the hull and rig held together.

As the storm settled it was time to head into Manly, a small town on the outskirts of Brisbane. A few brave boats escorted us to our marina berth. All six of us were exhausted and longed for a hot shower and a dry bed. It was mind-boggling to think Chichester sailed this yacht solo around the world for 226 days. We relished our stopover in Manly, culminating in a delicious dinner at the Royal Queensland YC before continuing on to Mooloolaba the next morning, where the UKSA has its Australian base.

Despite relatively calm seas, from force of habit the crew still adopted what became known as the 'Gipsy Moth Posture' – moving around in a pre-brace position, ready to fend-off walls or bulkheads that might suddenly spring at us from all directions. With fair weather and no need for structured watches, the crew shared tasks and laughs and we enjoyed ourselves, too. While living within a boat length of each other, we'd been isolated on opposite watches. Now, for the first time, I got to know Elaine and the other half of the crew. When the weather was ugly, Elaine, who sailed on *Gipsy Moth IV*'s first leg from Plymouth to Gibraltar, had told me: 'You'd think once would have been enough in Biscay!' Now, as our journey came to an end, she admitted, 'Actually, I wish we could sail further.' I couldn't have agreed more.

With less than two miles to Mooloolaba breakwater, two Gipsy Moth bi-planes made a fly-past salute and the air filled with the sounds of foghorns. Simon skillfully slid us alongside our VIP berth and we leapt ashore, flicked the warps around the cleats and brought *Gipsy Moth IV* to a standstill. We'd made it. 'Welcome to Mooloolaba!' said the marina manager, who shook our hands heartily.

After eight days of unforgettable experiences we would all soon fly home, leaving skipper Simon to meet his new crew for the next leg of this remarkable journey. For all of us, it had been an unforgettable voyage. Comfortable? No. But I believe the only reason comfort zones are defined is so we know what boundary to step outside when we want to feel truly alive.

Chris, Elaine and Nicole go surfing in something smaller!

The calm after the storm. Gipsy Moth at journey's end.

Mooloolaba to Cairns   By Andrew Eccleston

Living the dream

Leg 16

Distance:
900 miles

Skipper:
Simon Hay (37)

Mate:
Andrew
Eccleston (54)

Crew Leader:
Jeremy Graham
(45)

Crew One:
Sean Mayers
(18), Jonny
Dawson (16) and
Daniel Elvin (16)

Crew Two:

Crew leader:
Julian Gillies
(42)

Crew:

Sophie Hedman
(16), Emma
Aldridge (18)
and Natalie
Crawford (17)

Here I was at last – living a dream that I never actually had – on board *Gipsy Moth IV*. When I was a teenage schoolboy in Birmingham, if anyone had suggested that one day I'd sail on board the yacht that inspired a nation, I'd have dismissed the idea as absurd.

We were alongside in Mooloolaba for a week getting the boat ready to sail up the coast of Australia to the Great Barrier Reef and beyond. There were still a few minor things left to put right after the refit in Auckland, plus the bad-weather leg from Sydney. It was a chance to get to know the boat and crew in a part of paradise called the 'Sunshine Coast'. The young crew had been scuba diving with sharks, sea-kayaking and visited Steve Irwin's Australia Zoo, where they fed the crocs and Daniel communed with kangaroos. They had

also carried out a few previously unknown activities – like cleaning and cooking.

This boat takes a lot of looking after – I had to go back to the supermarket for two more bottles of Brasso to get the job done. 'If only I had invested in Brasso shares,' said crew leader Jeremy. But the yacht does look good and this is appreciated by everyone who stops by to share their memories of Chichester. On Sunday's official Open Day we showed more than 250 people over the boat. Simon said Mooloolaba had given *Gipsy Moth IV* one of the warmest welcomes she'd had anywhere.

We went for a shakedown sail to learn about the winches, sheets, halyards and other parts of the rigging and would soon be on our way with provisions for eight days at sea. When we finally put to sea I soon gained numerous bruises and bumps from my first ride on what others call 'the vomit comet'. I was caked in salt from the frequent dunkings on deck when reefing during the night. At least in these latitudes the water is warm. After a spell on the foredeck helping Jonny change a headsail, Jeremy was seasick and in quite a state (not to mention the colour of the sail). He spent several hours prostrate on the floor of the heads. Simon had a brief chat with him to make sure that he was not seriously ill.

As the sun rose in a blue sky over a blue ocean, the weather eased and Simon hoisted the mizzen. Sean, from The Academy, Peckham, South London, was having his first day as 'mother' – looking after all the cooking and cleaning. For someone not used to cooking, let alone for six people on a two-burner stove, it's an extreme challenge. We entered tropical latitudes again at breakfast time.

After some sleep, the first job I tackled was fixing my bunk, the top one on the port side in the main saloon. It's very comfortable, except it has now given way twice. This meant drilling a couple of holes in part of our national maritime heritage, so it was done with great care.

I had a mental list of 'Chichester moments' to tick off on this voyage – and one of them was to see the Hasler self-steering working. For Simon and me, with our shared appreciation of what all this means, it was a magic moment

when it took over helming the boat downwind. Working up a sextant sun sight on the first day at sea was another tick in the box – and finding a flying fish on deck the night before.

Sitting in the saloon with my copy of *Gipsy Moth Circles the World*, that I was given as a schoolboy, it felt quite remarkable to be looking at the photo showing Sir Francis sitting on the bench opposite me leaning against the chart table bulkhead as he sewed the mizzen stays'l. I glanced astern at the view out of the companionway with the mizzen mast and three winches framed against the Pacific sky.

On watch with Jeremy and Jonny in the moonlight we were now well inside the Great Barrier Reef, although it was over 20 miles away. It was 40 years ago this week that Chichester departed Plymouth to write a page in our maritime history.

In four days we covered the 668 miles north to Airlie Beach. We had winds of 40-plus knots and big following seas. Apart from the wild ride, the most wonderful thing to see was how the young crew changed almost before our eyes. Although they thought they were tough and cool, they had never faced anything like this. My respect for Chichester, and the boat, has multiplied. She is a racing yacht, built to survive. She rolled and heaved like a crazy thing, but never ever felt over-pressed. There was also some interesting navigation to do

FAR LEFT:
A tender moment for Julian with Emma, Sophie and Natalie.

BELOW:
Motor-sailing up the 'Sunshine Coast'.

Catching fish was exciting. Gutting them was not always so popular.

FAR RIGHT: Andrew, Gipsy Moth's official Meteorologist.

along the way. We have been relying on GPS rather a lot. I had intended to do some astro navigation, but having to look after the boat and the young crew took priority. There were some tricky moments as we were passing through island groups with unlit rocks at night when I had a chance to do some old-fashioned 'running fixes' to get a check on the GPS.

Arriving at Airlie Beach in the heart of the Whitsunday islands – where it was race week – was an uplifting experience after the rigours of the voyage. In Abel Point Marina, we fixed the various bits of damage, above and below decks, and polished the old girl up again and hosted a drinks party for the local yachties with plenty of Mount Gay rum. *Gipsy Moth IV* received over AU$300 of donations and we sold over AU$1,000 of merchandise. Sean, Dan and Jonny did a great job, promoting the project like true professionals.

Later we relaxed aboard *Gipsy Moth IV* in Butterfly Bay, Hook Island, the second largest island in the Whitsundays. It has spectacular steep-sided tree-clad hillsides plunging into a coral-edged blue sea, under a blue sky. Nearby is Luncheon Bay and Sawmill Bay. Many of these intriguing names derive from James Cook's great voyage of discovery, when he found the excellent anchorages in these islands.

We started the day with the usual routine of cleaning and polishing, while I continued with the endless list of bosun's tasks. We managed to get the dodgers repaired in Airlie Beach after blowing them out again on the trip from Mooloolaba. This time they were rigged with bungees so that next time *Gipsy Moth* takes a sea down the afterdeck there's a bit more give in the system.

Jeremy had recovered from his prolonged seasickness and served bacon sarnies with choice of brown sauce/ketchup and a cup of hot coffee. After lunch, the snorkeling gear came out and the beautiful and highly-coloured underwater world of the Whitsundays was revealed. While the youngsters cavorted with coral and tropical fish, we entertained some people from a charter boat who knew about *Gipsy Moth IV* and wanted to see the yacht. More brochures sold and another AU$20 in the kitty!

It's winter in Australia, so we had some cloud, and even rain, but much of the time the sea and sky were a beautiful blue. At our anchorage you could see the sandy bottom. As soon as your head was beneath the water the transition to a gaudy, multi-coloured world was quite a shock. It was like looking at one of those popular screen savers.

Julian finds a new cuddly friend.

Our next stop was Hamilton Island, where we would change to an all-girl crew. We said goodbye to Sean, Jonny and Daniel and I recorded and edited final video interviews with the boys for the website. They spoke quite profoundly about their experience on *Gipsy Moth*. Two of them, Sean (from Peckham) and Daniel (from Barnados), were from a tough background, but found that sustained physical work, discipline, cooking, cleaning and the challenge of the elements was a new place to visit. Jonny, by contrast had enjoyed a privileged upbringing and attended Dr Challoner's Grammar School and lived in Little Chalfont, Buckinghamshire, but was also significantly affected by his experience and said that he would be much more tolerant of other people, and their views, in the future. What all of them discovered was the joy of working as a team, getting on together, and getting the job done – in the face of whatever challenge the day throws up.

So this project is not just about restoring an old boat and sailing it round the world again. It's also about exposing a new generation to the Chichester legend and inspiring them to go down the same road I discovered 40 years ago.

Our new crew leader was Julian (Jules) Gillies (42) and the new crew of teenage girls – Sophie Hedman (16), Emma Aldridge (18) and Natalie Crawford (17) – bumped into the boys at the airport. They already knew Jonny from their training weekend at the UKSA and enjoyed catching up on the news. But the first thing Natalie noticed was how absolutely shattered they looked. 'This had me worried. Was it really going to be that hard work?' she wondered. They also warned her about Simon's obsession with Brasso – little did Natalie realise how relevant this warning was going to become!

Sophie was from the Harris City Technology College, Peckham, sponsored by Lord Harris of Peckham, and Emma and Natalie were from Portsmouth Grammar School. Having three girls aboard was a huge change for me and the skipper. They were soon put to the same regime as the previous crew. Having already brought up two daughters, I was going through the same loop. One memorable moment was having to unplug the hair straighteners to get at the valves to change over fresh water tanks!

Andrew Eccleston

Gipsy Moth
*'dressed overall'
in port.*

On the first night Natalie got a mobile phone call with her AS level exam results – four straight A grades! Next day, Emma, who usually spends her Saturdays in a supermarket stacking shelves, had to winch Sophie up the mast. And later Sophie got a phone call from her mum, halfway round the world, to get her GCSE results.

Meanwhile, everywhere *Gipsy Moth IV* went she attracted attention. In the anchorage the people on the next boat, who had been following the project on the web, wanted to come and have a look round. We sold our commemorative brochures at AU$5, T-shirts, GMIV jackets and ties to help raise funds to keep the project going.

Hamilton Island, known locally as 'Hamo', is the epicentre of wealth and sailing in the Whitsundays and *Gipsy Moth IV* was a guest at the annual race week where top boats in Australia come to compete in the winter. The island is owned by the Oatley family and their boat *Wild Oats* was competing here. This boat won the last Sydney-Hobart Race, which is one of the world's top ocean races. George Harrison also owned a property on the island.

With all these yachties in one place, we met some very knowledgeable people during Open Day on *Gipsy Moth*. It was a real privilege to be part of this project, going round the world and making so many people happy. Those who saw *Gipsy Moth* when she was entombed in London are delighted to see her alive again, and there are lots of questions about how she sails etc.

One of the visitors was an extremely generous man called Norbert, who has a property on Hamo as well as another overlooking Sydney Harbour. He invited us to go for a sail on his boat – a Swan 57. For those of you who don't know boats, this is a bit like saying 'would you like to come for a ride in my Bentley Continental?' So the first time our new crew actually went sailing it was on a boat where there was a fridge, freezer, plasma TV, carpets, deep cushions and all the sails were controlled by pressing buttons – a bit different to our spartan *Gipsy Moth*! Norbert took us to

Whitehaven Beach and Hills Inlet. This is a five kilometre pure white beach with a walk up to a lookout point where the view rendered us speechless. We even saw two whales having fun on the way back.

At an exclusive prize-giving dinner for the top sailors at Hamilton Island the *Gipsy Moth IV* crew managed to raise AU$5,300, selling one of Sir Francis Chichester's original winches, mounted on a mahogany plaque, plus some other items, including a pendant.

When we were in Hamo one of the many visitors to *Gipsy Moth IV* invited us to visit Townsville on the way to Cairns, as a guest of the yacht club. The 24-hour sail up from Airlie Beach was an interesting trip. We did most of it under cruising chute during the day and running sail at night, averaging about five knots overall. This was a first experience of night sailing for Emma and Natalie, as well as a chance for us all to enjoy the '*Gipsy Moth* roll' running downwind.

We enjoyed another warm welcome from another group of very friendly Queenslanders. Townsville was quite different to other places we had visited – it was a 'real' town, not just a place for tourists and backpackers to enjoy themselves. But it had some beautiful buildings and a picturesque Strand along the seashore with palm trees – all rebuilt after a devastating cyclone some years ago. Our host, Colin White, took me and the girls to the top of Castle Hill, a sheer-faced rock behind the main town and we had a fantastic view over the surrounding area – including being able to see the Moth dressed overall alongside at the yacht club.

On 25 August, it was Simon's turn to say goodbye to *Gipsy Moth IV*, after skippering her for two legs, plus Sydney, with 12 young crew. It had been quite an adventure since taking over from Richard Baggett in Sydney Harbour seven weeks ago. Our new skipper, Steve Rouse (51), was a regular aboard having skippered the yacht on legs 3 and 8. He took over for the final 170 miles hop up the coast to Cairns – and the start of *Gipsy Moth IV*'s final Australian leg to Darwin in the Northern Territory.

Paul Gelder writes:

On Tuesday 8 August, while *Gipsy Moth* had been heading up the East Coast of Australia for the Whitsunday Islands, dramas had been going on behind the scenes at the UKSA HQ back home in Cowes. On Tuesday 8 August I got a phone call from David Green's deputy, Jon Ely, warning me that a press release was about to be issued announcing the departure of David Green, their CEO for 16 years, and Gipsy Moth's Global Project Manager.

It was a bolt from the blue. 'David is standing down to launch his own fund-raising and sponsorship company,' he told me. The chairman of the UKSA's trustees, David Lister, wrote in a letter: 'It was clear when the *Gipsy Moth IV* project started that David had found a new challenge in fund-raising...'

Throughout the 18 months' I shared with David on the *Gipsy Moth* project, he had always remained something of an enigma. A driven man, but driven by what? He enjoyed the limelight, the TV cameras and the radio microphones and promoted the *Gipsy Moth* project with boundless energy. He was capable of inspiring great loyalty among his staff and equally others found he could be dismissive, insensitive, conceited, and boastful. He was criticised by some for the decision to sack, rather than support, his skipper, Antonia, after *Gipsy Moth*'s grounding incident in Rangiroa. My only disagreements with him had been

when he tried to 'manage the news' or manipulate events to show things in the best possible light. He also ignored much useful advice from the Blue Water Rally organisers.

But David always had the best interests of the project at heart. In the days following the UKSA's arrival on the scene as *Gipsy Moth*'s new owners, many of his staff told me that it was as if 'stardust had been sprinkled on the academy' and David had been given 'a new lease of life'. Now *Gipsy Moth* was to be his springboard for fresh challenges. The UKSA had signed up as the first client of David's new company, 3greenlights, so he could continue to find sponsorship and funds for the remaining 16 legs of the voyage. He remained as Global Project Manager.

One thing was certain. Without David's passion, enthusiasm and 'can-do' attitude, *Gipsy Moth* would never have sailed in time for her 40th anniversary voyage and we all owed him a great debt. While day-to-day operations now switched to Jon Ely, David phoned me to say: 'I've given up the day job to look after your boat!'

Graham Snook/Yachting Monthly

David Green, who was succeeded as CEO of the UKSA by Jon Ely.

Cairns to Darwin

By Andrew Bray

Cook's tour

Leg 17

Distance:
1,312 miles

Skipper:
Steve Rouse
(50)

Mate:
Bob Bradfield
(54), Stephen
Thomas Trust

Crew Leader:
Andrew Bray
(57)

Crew:
Richard Benady
(17), Katie
Brewins (18)
and Rebecca
Holdstock (18)

Leg sponsor:
Isle of Wight.

As the only Australian aboard for Leg 17 from Cairns to Darwin, I brought along a packet of large leaf tea to remind the rest of the crew of our shared heritage as we followed in the wake of Captain Cook. We rationed it to a morning cuppa for 1,300 miles and it lasted all the way to Darwin.

On board, we marvelled at how Chichester, aged 65, kept his sanity aboard this cramped ketch with her poltergeist self-opening drawers and relentless rolling, which can be triggered simply by a vigorous course correction. *Gipsy Moth IV* may be bristling with the latest hi-tech satellite navigation gear, plus a sat-com dome to transmit emails and video of life aboard back home, but she's still the same stubborn, skittish thoroughbred that tested Chichester's patience to the ends of the earth, literally.

For my British shipmates, the most remarkable aspect of this leg was the lack of civilisation and mobile phone coverage on this coastline. North of Cooktown (15°28'S) there's nothing but a few isolated fishing or mining hamlets and Aboriginal communities in the 380-odd miles between there and Thursday Island, in the Torres Strait.

We slipped our lines and left Marlin Marina, Cairns with Australia in mourning for Steve Irwin, a wildlife promoter who became global news after being killed by a stingray the day before – and at the very anchorage we were heading for... a tiny cay in the Low Isles. Irwin's friends told how the celebrated Crocodile Hunter pulled a deadly stingray barb from his own chest before dying.

There are more creatures in Australia that can kill you than anywhere on the planet – from snakes to spiders, exotic blue-ringed octopus, stone fish, cone shells, box jelly fish, crocodiles, not forgetting the Great White Shark. They're all known as 'Australia's assassins'. Not surprisingly, when we later anchored at the popular day-tripper island, where Irwin died, the crew restricted their snorkeling as large shark-like fish circled the boat.

This was a conservation area but we were able to fish for our supper outside the restricted zone and caught something every time we deployed our 'killer' lure. In fact, we'd caught our first Spanish mackerel only a couple of hours after leaving Cairns. It was a reasonable size and Steve introduced the youngsters to gutting and filleting fish. We managed to get six good sized fillet steaks off each side and shallow fried them in garlic and olive oil on a portable burner on the aft deck with sundowners. Gaffing and filleting the fish was a gory process which Becky and Katie initially found disgusting, but Becky eventually became a fully participating 'savage', catching and preparing the third fish almost unaided.

Becky, from the Isle of Wight, and Richard, from Gibraltar (on the Stephen Thomas Bursary) had some previous sailing experience, but Katie, from Yorkshire, had never been on a yacht before, except for a few hours during her selection process at the UKSA.

First Mate Bob Bradfield had become involved with the *Gipsy Moth* project through his late friend, Stephen Thomas, who made the first big donation. Stephen died in a tragic accident in the Antarctic and, with help from Peter Seymour of Blue Water Rallies, Bob had raised funds for a bursary in Stephen's memory. Our crew member Richard had been awarded the first bursary.

Steve's plan was to day sail up the inside of the Great Barrier Reef so the crew could enjoy its marvels. He reckoned it would take about six days to get to Cape York, the northern tip of Australia, from where we'd sail direct to Darwin, where the tides equal those

of the Channel Islands in the UK, with ranges of some seven meters.

The *Gipsy Moth IV* experience was a radical departure from the young crew's normal comfort zones and they had profound personal adjustments to make. First there were the physical discomforts of living on a small, rolling yacht in the tropics. Then food aboard proved a challenge – no hamburgers and chips here. I doubted whether Katie had ever eaten fish not covered in batter before!

I'm sure some mums of the *Gipsy Moth IV* crew around the world got a pleasant surprise when their teenagers returned home with more worldly appetites – perhaps even eager to demonstrate new cooking skills.

TOP:
Katie Brewins polishing brightwork on deck.
ABOVE:
Crew leader Andrew ('Oz') Bray, a freelance sailing journalist from Sydney, sailed round the world in his home-built boat, Starship, in 1990-93. His son Chris crewed on leg 15.

Steve Rouse and Richard catch supper.

Skipper Steve Rouse was a master at juggling three saucepans on the small hotplate and turned out very tasty meals. *Gipsy Moth IV* hadn't sailed these waters before, but many other historically important vessels crewed by British sailors had, and the signs were not hard to find. The charts we used from Cairns to Torres Strait are strewn with places named by, or commemorating, early British navigators. Fitzroy and Green islands, near Cairns, were named by Cook, and the inlet where he careened *Endeavour* in 1770, after she was badly holed on nearby Endeavour reef, is now the northernmost town on the East Australian coast. The Cooktown Museum features one of the cannons jettisoned to lighten his stricken ship. Cook also named the Low Isles, Cape Bedford and our third stop, Lizard Island, from the peak of which he spied an escape route through the Great Barrier Reef — now known as Cook's Pass. We arrived at Cape Bedford just before

Bob Bradfield on engine checking duties.

last light and were invited onboard Christoph Rassy's Hallberg Rassy 62, *Bamsen*, which was also sailing with the Blue Water Rally.

Lizard is about as far north as many Australian cruisers go, as there are no coastal towns beyond. Boats tend to wait here in October and November for the trade winds to slacken, so they can get south again without a long haul to windward. Most yachts would have moved on to Darwin earlier in the season, but among the 30-odd cruising yachts and dive boats in the anchorage were several from the Blue Water Rally, *Golden Eye, Saoirse K, Fennella* and, of course, *Bamsen*.

We took the portable gas BBQ ashore for an evening feast on the beach — not far from the ruins of Mrs Watson's house. This ill-fated woman, and her maid and daughter died on a desolate islet 34 miles downwind, nine days after setting themselves adrift in a cooking tank to escape Aborigines. That was back in 1881. But this is still no place to find yourself drifting.

That evening the VHF radio Channel 16 was dominated by the search for two missing divers — we never learned the outcome.

We left Lizard at 0500 and had a perfect downwind sail, covering 87 miles in 12 hours, to anchor in the lee of Stanley Island, in the Flinders Group. Here we witnessed the elusive 'green flash' — a rare phenomenon prized by sailors and sometimes glimpsed when the last of the setting sun's orb dips below the horizon.

Later, passing close to Restoration Island, we looked through the binoculars at the beach where Captain Bligh landed after the first stage of his epic long boat voyage following the famous *Bounty* mutiny.

Soon after anchoring in Margaret Bay, Bob spotted a large crocodile a few metres astern. Saltwater crocs can exceed 6m (20ft) in length and may be found anywhere within the reef. They mostly lurk in turbid, mangrove inlets and coastal bays like this one. Protected species, they are quite common and also cunning. They'll include people in their diet if given the chance. The crew declined to take the inflatable dinghy ashore unaccompanied until we reached Darwin. Perhaps this is why Australia is the home of the lightweight and almost indestructible aluminium dinghy. Steve wished he could take one home!

Given the shallow anchorages we visited and the lightweight ground tackle, Steve used the crew to lower and weigh anchor on all nine occasions. A cheap hallway carpet was rolled out on deck to protect the paintwork as the chain was flaked onto it, ready to be paid out by a team of gloved hands.

Chichester's Danforth-style anchors are uncommon on cruising yachts, perhaps because they are awkward to stow on a bow-roller. I was surprised when late one night the GPS revealed we were dragging rapidly out of our anchorage at Adolphus Island, Queensland. After deploying more chain, Steve slept on deck! We were in good company. Even Captain Cook dragged anchor along this coast.

Our passage through Torres Strait, past Cape York and the top of the Gulf of Carpentaria made use of the tides, which even at neaps can flow at 3 knots. The whole Torres Strait area is reef-strewn and dangerous. In 1791 the *Pandora*, bringing home HMS *Bounty* mutineers for trial, was wrecked 60 miles eastward.

As *Gipsy Moth* sailed west into another sunset, Steve was in awe of those great seafarers, Cook and Bligh, who went before us. 'The whole coast is steeped in maritime history

Becky became a fully participating 'savage' – catching, gutting and preparing fish without any help.

and I guess that's one reason why *Gipsy Moth* fits in so well... In our own special way, we're making history too,' he said.

After turning the corner at Cape York, *Gipsy Moth* was truly on her westward ho' way home back to Europe. Our passage planning paid off and by evening we were past Booby Island, sailing under working jib and double-reefed main and making eight knots over the ground.

The crew were now divided into three rolling watches (three hours on, six hours off), which advanced everyone's watches by three hours per day, so even on a passage of a few days we'd all get to experience the full range of night watches, seeing satellites after sunset, meteors after midnight, plus the magic dawn watch. The teenagers were suitably impressed by the grandeur of the southern night sky.

Cook and Bligh's routes diverged after Torres Strait, although both eventually got to Timor. Our route skirted the Wessel Islands and converged on the Australian mainland again, 700 miles west at Cape Don.

Northern Australia is a hot, harsh land, and although some of it gets plenty of rain in the wet season, few white people choose to live in these parts. Apart from mining and Aboriginal settlements, there are no coastal towns anywhere between Cooktown on the east coast, and Darwin, which Steve called 'the jewel in the crown of Australia's Northern Territory'.

The Spanish mackerel is filleted by Richard as master chef Steve Rouse cooks al fresco on a portable stove.

An exhilarating sail for young crew aboard the veteran 53ft ketch.

As an Australian, I understand the damage the sun can do to the human body and I cover up carefully. This earned me the nickname 'Dr Livingstone'. The lack of a proper bimini on the yacht certainly made life difficult.

By now, as Steve observed in the log: 'The young crew were moving about the boat like old sweats from years gone by... the daily routine of changing watches, cooking, cleaning up the boat and polishing the brass-work was done automatically.'

Having spent a month in Auckland helping with the major repairs to *Gipsy Moth IV* after her shipwreck in Rangiroa, Bob found it particularly rewarding to see the 'sharp end' of the project – the youngsters facing up to the challenge of weeks aboard a cramped, poorly ventilated boat in a hot, humid tropical climate.

There was another beautiful sunset with smoke from bush fires blown by the trade winds from Arnhem Land, adding a deep red cast. It was eerie motorsailing at dawn through Dundas Strait into Van Diemen Gulf, with no swell, depths below 30m and strong currents.

There were few signs of the low-lying land in any direction until we raised Cape Hotham late in the morning. This was crocodile country and drowning if you fall overboard is the last of your worries.

We used our two chartplotters for some careful pilotage through an area that skirts tidal overfalls and invisible reefs. With a landfall in Darwin beckoning by nightfall, we scrubbed the boat and spruced ourselves up for the return to civilisation. Darwin, demolished by a cyclone on Christmas Day 1974, has been rebuilt into a modern, prosperous city with several marinas. We anchored half a mile offshore in the cruising roadstead of Fanny Bay and were very grateful for the showers, beers, and cheap meals available from Darwin SC, which made us honorary members.

Chichester also made a landfall in Darwin – but in his bi-plane, after a storm-tossed journey to Java and some thrilling island hopping to the edge of the Timor Sea. He 'touched down at Darwin to the surprise of a few leathery gentlemen who appeared to be using the airfield as a spitoon!'

ABOVE:
Oz cover-up from the sun.
RIGHT: Gipsy
Moth *was in good company when she dragged her anchor.*

Next morning, *Gipsy Moth*'s crew met the owners of Buzz Café, at Cullen Bay Marina, who loaned the yacht a berth, so the public could visit her and we could attend to various tasks. Radar was to be installed and the engine, heads, and other saltwater plumbing had to undergo a 14-hour chemical treatment to prevent Asian Green Mussels, which are present in Cairns, being introduced to these waters.

Becky summed up the voyage thus: 'Sailing across oceans brings a completely different meaning to life. Your life is no longer your own. You're part of a close-knit team and if you fall, everyone will fall with you. It's given me a different outlook on life. I've have been inspired by everyone and will take a small part of their tuition with me into everyday life. When I wrote my application letter, I just wanted to sail on *Gipsy Moth IV*. But I've snorkeled on the Great Barrier Reef, seen dolphins on the bow nearly every day, eaten crocodile, caught tuna and spanish mackerel... It's a hard life on a boat and there are few comforts. Physically life will be easy when I go back home, but I don't want to leave this different way of life. I've achieved so much and I feel I'm leaving a little bit of my heart behind. Life is a lot bigger than it was before.'

Katie Brewins described 'the many highs and lows. The highs have been indescribable, exciting and unforgettable and the lows have been challenging and hard. Every day was different. I felt different, thought differently, ate differently and even smelt differently! I'm sure this story will be passed down for generations in my family as sailing on GMIV has made my family and me extremely proud.'

For my part, too, I'd enjoyed the romance of sailing aboard *Gipsy Moth IV*. I'd wrestled with the same weather helm as Chichester. But unlike his lonely passage, I took home with me fond memories of a shared experience with my shipmates. It's people, not yachts, that make voyages memorable. I won't be surprised to learn that Richard takes up a professional sailing career, or that Becky's determination turns her into an offshore sailing instructor one day. Like all the youngsters who sailed aboard this iconic yacht, horizons have been widened. As Chichester's biographer Anita Leslie wrote: 'The story of Francis Chichester will last because every man who reads it will find that he is touching facets of himself.'

TOP: *Katie Brewins, from Scarborough, enjoyed 'the romance of sailing Gipsy Moth.'*

ABOVE: *Becky from the Isle of Wight, said: 'Life is a lot bigger than it was before.'*

Sunset over Fanny Bay, Darwin, the city where Chichester landed his Gipsy Moth bi-plane to refuel in 1930, on his record-breaking flight.

Darwin to Kupang

Leg 18

Distance:
420 miles

Skipper:
John Jeffrey (62)

Mate:
Noel Little (55)

Crew Leader:
Victoria
Blackmore (24)

Crew:
Melanie
(Swampy)
Kendall (18),
Jay Shirlaw (17),
Alice Burton (18)

Leg sponsor:
Isle of Wight.

John Jeffrey was *Gipsy Moth's* 'fourth-time lucky' skipper. Five months earlier, he'd flown to Tahiti, expecting to sail to Tonga as *Gipsy Moth's* mate, only to find himself part of the salvage team on the reef in Rangiroa. He had also been due to skipper the leg from Tonga to Auckland and then sail as mate on the leg to Sydney – both legs cancelled when the yacht was shipped as deck cargo, instead. John had flown thousands of miles only to face disappointment.

Now, he had *Gipsy Moth* entirely to himself as he waited for her new crew to arrive in Cullen Bay Marina, Darwin. 'It's slightly eerie, having the old girl to myself,' he thought. But there was plenty to do, showing visitors around and preparing for the soon-to-be-installed radar. Mate Noel Little, from Emsworth, arrived with the four crew: Victoria and Melanie, from Plymouth, and Jay and Alice, from the Isle of Wight. There was also 'Humphrey' the mysterious seventh crew member.

'When six crew live in one another's pockets, stuff happens – lights get left on, lids are left off food containers and ropes are not made up securely . . . You can point fingers at one another and get defensive or ratty, or you can lower the temperature by blaming a seventh, imaginary, crew member,' said John. 'Just ask him nicely not to do it again. Every crew, and every household, could find a place for Humphrey.'

On her first day, Alice tried two new things: sleeping on deck and eating kangaroo – even though she was a vegetarian! 'But I don't think I'll be doing it again,' she said.

With the Blue Water Rally fleet in town, Darwin's normally relaxed pace was being stretched to the limit. Twenty-plus yachts all wanted jobs done by Friday. Noel drilled a hole in *Gipsy Moth's* 'sacred timbers' for the radar

installation. 'No thunderbolts struck, so we carried on and the display was soon installed, ready to connect to the radome as soon as it was mounted on the mast.'

John had lost count of the number of journeys various people had made up and down the mast to fit the radar, but finally the job was complete. *Gipsy Moth's* navigation station looked like something out of Star Trek. 'With such an attractive display, the trick will be to stop the crew relying on it to tell the whole truth about what's outside, without bothering to look for themselves!' John observed.

Finally, after almost two weeks in the marina, *Gipsy Moth* sailed from Australia for Kupang, in West Timor, Indonesia, some 400 miles away. Under full sail, she looked a picture, but there was no one to admire her. 'We wondered if the ever-vigilant Australian authorities might pay us a visit – they check a lot of boats in these waters, looking for illegal immigrants,' said John. 'But the only visitor we had was a large black and white seabird which settled on the guardrail and bit my finger as I tried to feed it!'

The night watch had bright moonlight for their first night sail aboard *Gipsy Moth IV* and the crew later had their first visit from dolphins. Alice tried helming *Gipsy Moth IV*. 'Quite a challenge as the yacht steers like a brick,' was her verdict.

On day two John came on deck with the chart plotter manual, tripped and it flew out of his hands, disappearing overboard and sinking

without trace! Since John is an expert in astro-nav and there was a sextant aboard, it was no problem. The danger of over-reliance on clever, hi-tech electronics was also highlighted with the failure of *Gipsy Moth's* engine alternator, which charges the yacht's batteries. The Ampair Aquair 100 towing generator, helped, but the crew were still short of electrical power, most importantly for the Wallas diesel stove which had electric ignition. Normal communications to the UK ceased, with no more daily logs or photos sent to the website.

On arrival in Kupang, John sent out a plea for help until a replacement alternator arrived. Christoph Rassy, founder of the Swedish boat-building firm Hallberg-Rassy, who was sailing his 62ft *Bamsen IV* on the Blue Water Rally, immediately offered assistance. Within a few minutes, he had raised anchor and *Bamsen IV* was alongside. Her walk-in engine compartment was larger than *Gipsy Moth IV's* saloon and her main generator the size of a small chest of drawers and made barely a whisper of noise. With *Gipsy Moth's* shore-power cable plugged in, her flat batteries were re-charged, just like a jump-start for a car. This 'power sharing' exercise is what blue water sailors call 'rallying round'. John's message for everyone back home was: 'We're fine. We just love having problems to solve and it's great to have people to help us solve them, too. That's life at sea.'

On a flying visit, this bird bit the skipper's finger.

Power sharing: Gipsy Moth *recharges her battery bank from Christoph Rassy's* Bamsen.

Kupang to Bali

Leg 19

Distance:
450 miles

Skipper:
Sam
Connelly (31)

Mate:
John Jeffrey (62)

Crew Leader:
Nigel
Stilman (49)

Crew:
Gregory
Amman (18)
and Kirstie
Blackwood (20),
both from the
Chichester Trust

Leg sponsor:
RWE Npower
and Isle of
Wight

Sam Connelly was back aboard as skipper, following his Panama-Galapagos adventures on leg 9, with the girls from the Ellen MacArthur Trust. The first thing he noticed, was the remarkable repair job to *Gipsy Moth*'s hull carried out in New Zealand. 'You wouldn't know anything had happened,' he said. 'I hoped they'd left the computer back on the reef, but no!'

The crew took the '*bemo*' (bus) into Kupang town. *Bemos* are used in Indonesia to transport anything and everything you can imagine. There was loud music from speakers under the seats and the ticket collector was hanging on outside.

Kupang was a significant port for Europeans in the 18th century. Captain Cook, wary of its reputation for debauchery, sailed on by in 1770, but Captain Bligh headed

for there in 1789 after the mutiny on HMS *Bounty* and had nothing but praise for Kupang's hospitality after his six-week 4,000-mile voyage in a 23ft open boat with 18 men.

At the *pasar* (market) *Gipsy Moth*'s crew enjoyed a breakfast of rice, noodles and fish before casting off for the ten day trip to Bali. With battery problems, skipper and mate tinkered with the boat's electrical system, wriggling into a tiny cupboard in pitch darkness to investigate with a new 'tool' – Blu-Tack on the end of a bread knife.

Greg began his first three-hour night watch just after midnight and had the perfect wake-up call – going on deck to find the yacht surrounded by beautiful islands. They spent most of the day motor-sailing, stopping at lunchtime at the village of Trong, on Adunara island, to top up the yacht's diesel tanks. There was enough wind later to try the spinnaker. They anchored at Larantuka village, Eastern Flores, for the night. 'It's not even vaguely a tourist spot,' said John. 'And five Europeans provoked great curiosity.

"Hey Mister!" is as common here as "No Worries" was in Darwin. I'm sure the lean-to "restaurant", where we enjoyed rice, fish and chicken must have doubled its takings as people dropped by to try out their English on the foreign visitors!'

Next day Sam promised the crew a secluded bay for a swim and a snorkel when they anchored off Tanjung Gedong. There wasn't a soul in sight, just the towering mountains and coconut trees lining the coral beaches. But within 15 minutes they were joined by several dug-out canoes and were soon swamped by local kids and their fathers playing water polo with the crew. 'By the afternoon we had half the village out,' said Sam.

Gipsy Moth's crew were the first Europeans many villagers had seen. 'And they delighted in showing us how to get coconut milk, how to light fires (they use a cigarette end!), roast seeds and grill fish on the beach,' said John. 'I tried a lot of new things today: climbed a coconut palm, paddled a dug-out canoe, inspected a boat being built, caulked with coconut fibre. Imagine how much fun I've had saying "I have three grandchildren" – "*Saya punya tiga cucu*" – especially since *cucu* is pronounced "choo choo"!'

John was on a personal mission when he ran the water-maker on passage next day to Sea World, a German-run diving resort in North Flores. When *Gipsy Moth* anchored and the crew had gone ashore, he took advantage of the privacy of *Gipsy Moth IV*'s deep cockpit to use a bucket of fresh water to wash the salt out of himself and his clothes. 'The clothes aren't exactly clean, but at least they bend a bit now. Bliss!'

Long night watches offered the chance to strike up interesting conversations. John found out all about working in a vet's practice from Kirstie and discussed astrophysics while star-gazing with Greg.

On day 6, *Gipsy Moth* stopped at Rinca Island, where there were rumoured to be komodo dragons. The crew found tracks, but no dragons, so they sailed on to the nearby island of Komodo, where they met Rahlai, a local native. He told them the park where dragon sightings were 'guaranteed' was just closing for the day. As a consolation, he invited them to supper at his waterside home in the fishing village built on stilts. While Rahlai's mother cooked over an open fire in the corner, several neighbours dropped by to 'check out the foreigners'. As dusk deepened, Rahlai lit an oil lamp and the crew were treated to a stunning display. 'The fishing fleet, now formed up in a line across the far side of the bay, turned their lights on. The effect was like a diamond necklace strung along the horizon. In the background, we could hear the sounds from the mosque as the faithful were being called to prayer,' said John. 'Dinner was soon ready and we moved into the main room of the house. This is the one with electricity, powering a single long-life bulb and a small fluorescent tube giving us enough light to see what we were eating as we sat cross-legged on the carpeted floor. A bowl of rice (*nasi*) and another of noodles (*mi*) formed the basis of it, and to go with these staples there were dishes of fish and omelette. Isn't this kind of experience of someone else's culture one of the main reasons why we travel?'

By day 10 *Gipsy Moth* had made good progress before hitting a foul six-knot tide on the western channel of Lombok. They crept along a narrow channel, beside tall cliffs and shallow reefs. 'With the GPS playing up, the newly installed Simrad radar was a blessing!' Sam observed.

Finally, on day 11, 25 October, *Gipsy Moth IV* arrived at Benoa Marina, Bali. John relished the convenience of stepping onto a pontoon for the first time since Darwin, instead of using the dinghy. Here they were reunited with old friends from the Blue Water Rally, all sharing tales of their adventures.

One thing, however, was just like home. 'Whenever you find a good spot in a marina, a man with a hat will come along and make you move!' said John.

Beautifully painted Javanese shadow puppet

The elusive Komodo dragon

Nigel installing the watermaker pump

Bali to Singapore

Leg 20

Distance:
900 miles

Skipper:
Sam
Connelly (31)

Mate:
Gordon
Berry (61)

Crew Leader:
Gareth
Cowell (52)

Crew:
Bryn Hugh-
Jones (17)
Iwan Ellis-Jones
(17) and Rhodri
Owen (17)

Leg sponsor:
Corum

*G*ipsy Moth left Bali with two extra crew members – a couple of live chickens bought in a local market (see photo below). 'I wonder what an Isle of Wight taxi driver would say if I hailed him outside Tesco's with two live chickens!' thought Gordon, licking his lips at the prospect of chicken curry.

Skipper Sam Connelly and mate Gordon, from the UKSA, were joined by 'crew Cymru' – a quartet from Gwynedd, North Wales. Crew leader Gareth was a teacher at the school of Bryn, Iwan and Rhodri. The trio had won their place on the voyage through a North Wales Watersports Challenge at the Plas Menai National Watersports Centre.

Three hours' surfing at Bali's Kuta beach soon banished their jet lag after the 18-hour

flight from the UK to Bali. But the crew's faces turned white as the *Gipsy Moth* roll took effect when they left Benoa Marina and motor-sailed through the swell, bound for Singapore.

'The smell of chickens in a basket on the aft deck didn't help!' said Iwan, who was not looking forward to killing them. A cheeky note in Welsh in the ship's log stated: '*Cowell yn 'cyfog!*' (translated as 'Mr. Cowell pukin'!') On the fifth day out, *Gipsy Moth* anchored off the east coast of Madura island, where the crew went ashore to the village of Jurangan.

Nothing could have prepared them for the delight of their welcome. 'The local school staff and children exuded optimism and enthusiasm. I'd love to teach here!' said Gareth.

Iwan saw only happy faces, though the villagers had hardly any possessions or wealth.

'It was a real eye-opener,' said Rhodri. 'Many of them were so excited because they hadn't seen white-skinned people before. We were probably the first westerners to visit the area for some time, having arrived by sea.'

Next day Gareth tried his hand at paddling a dug-out canoe, loaned by a local native. 'It was classic bronze age (by our definition!), something akin to what our ancestors in the Menai Straits would have paddled 3,000 years ago. I loved the stability and gracious movement that accompanied it. I'm going to copy it and open a franchise! Look out Dickie's of Bangor!'

The eighth day out 'curry night' was declared. The chickens' date with destiny was more of a problem for the crew, it seemed. While the Indonesian way of life is intertwined with suffering and death, 'chicken in a basket' had a different concept for *Gipsy Moth*'s crew. Names were placed in a hat to choose the 'executioner'. Somehow, the skipper and mate's names were selected. Sam slaved over a hot stove, even fulfilling a request for curry and chips! 'It's like going to Wales and asking for Haggis,' observed mate Gordon.

By day nine *Gipsy Moth* had cleared the Java Sea and was in the South China Sea, heading through the Selat Karimata, the 40-mile wide channel between Kalimantan and Indonesia, renowned for piracy. 'It's nice to be putting this area behind us as we head into open water,' Sam wrote in the log.

Skipper Sam takes a noon sight in the Java Sea.

After four days non-stop motoring, *Gipsy Moth*'s crew enjoyed the ancient 'crossing the line' ceremony as she headed north over the equator. Coincidentally, Sam had been skipper on the equator crossing between Panama and the Galapagos islands, 12,000 miles to the west. This time the crew celebrated with synchronised swimming as they flew '*Y Ddraig Goch*' (the Welsh Dragon flag) above the waves.

Gareth observed: 'When I told people I was going to Indonesia I was met with warnings and concerns about our safety. How misplaced this has turned out to be. We've been welcomed with warmth and interest. What we share in common with these people unites us and crosses all divisions, just as the equator runs through lakes, seas, mountains, deserts and jungles on its course around the world.'

Balinese wood carving of a dragon.

RIGHT: Flying the Welsh flag as Gipsy Moth *crosses the equator.*

BELOW: Blade runners Bryn and Iwan on propeller cleaning duties.

BELOW:
Welsh assembly on deck shower duties in the rain.

RIGHT:
Beach party surf trio.

At anchor off the island of Bintan, in the Straits of Singapore, Sam learned about the inaccuracies in the charts they were using. *Gipsy Moth*'s position was one mile inland! Fortunately, he knew the area well because he'd worked at the water sports resort in Mana Mana, where they had stopped for a visit.

Gipsy Moth cleared out of Indonesian waters at Nongsa Point Marina, on Batam Island, a few miles south of Singapore, where other Blue Water Rally yachts gathered. The marina is a waterfront playground for the wealthy, with sprawling sandy white beaches, shops bars and restaurants.

Just two weeks after leaving Bali, and after crossing the busiest shipping lanes in the world, the Straits of Singapore, *Gipsy Moth* arrived at her berth at the Republic of Singapore Yacht Club. The Welsh lads were treated like celebrities and met the British High Commissioner at a presentation held by *Gipsy Moth*'s official time-keeper, Corum.

They also saw another side of Singapore life when a friend of Sam's took them to a night club and they encountered 'lady boys' ('men that had changed into women' as Bryn described it). 'Bryn was considering it as a career!' joked Iwan.

After a Blue Water Rally party hosted in *Gipsy Moth*'s honour, the Welsh lads' three-

week adventure was over. Their verdicts were unanimously favourable.

'I've seen and done things I could only have dreamed about,' said Rhodri.

'The *Gipsy Moth* voyage has opened a whole new world to me and drastically changed my views on career options,' said Iwan.

'What an experience! Taking part has changed our lives and given all of us a sense of independence. We have seen things that we wouldn't have imagined seeing at home,' said Bryn.

Their teacher, Gareth, said: 'They've experienced more in three weeks that most people do by the time they are 30!'

Gipsy Moth's arrival in Singapore proved a critical moment in the *Gipsy Moth* project, which desperately needed more cash and sponsorship and had been haemorrhaging money. The cost of long-haul flights for the crew, plus the unexpected bills to get the show back on the road following the accident in the South Pacific, had all taken their toll.

Jon Ely, now the new CEO at the UKSA, telephoned me to say the UKSA was down to a contingency 'get-you-home-fund' of £30,000, set aside for any unseen problems which might strike. Jon admitted: 'The sensible thing to do financially, would be to put the yacht on a ship and bring her back home as deck cargo... but that's not in the spirit of the project.'

It was not a realistic option to let down the hundreds of sponsors, let alone the teenagers, who had clearly been gaining so much from the voyage. Just as Chichester's original voyage had set new records, now *Gipsy Moth* was helping to change young lives and open a unique window on their world.

Yachting Monthly and the UKSA advertised crew places 'for sale' aboard *Gipsy Moth* at Phuket in Thailand during the Christmas holiday period. Two seven-day voyages and one 10-day voyage were planned.

As a result, four individuals contributed £11,500 to the funds over Christmas 2006. Two other people had already contributed more than £8,000 to sail aboard *Gipsy Moth*.

Just as Chichester held his nerve and showed defeat was alien to his nature, so *Gipsy Moth* would sail on in a voyage that was proving, in some ways, to be almost as desperate and magnificent as his own 40 years ago!

TOP:
The young crew were presented with expensive Corum watches – just for a week!

BELOW: Gordon in a rain squall.

FAR LEFT: Gareth tries paddling a dug-out, canoe borrowed from a friendly local native.

LEFT: A midday dip to cool off!

Singapore to Phuket

Leg 21

Distance:
600 miles

Skipper:
Sam Connelly
(31)

Mate:
Gordon Berry
(61)

Crew Leader:
Greg Amman
(18)
Chichester Trust

Crew:
Elaine Chua,
John Wong (23)
and Enrico
Clerici (75)

For the 600-mile passage from Singapore to Phuket, Thailand, *Gipsy Moth IV* was joined by one of Asia's top professional sailors, Elaine Chua, who a few months earlier had competed successfully in the solo 2,600 mile race to the Azores and back, from Les Sables d'Olonne, home of the Vendée Globe. It's an event similar to the solo Mini Transat.

Elaine had also competed at Cowes Week, sailed with Chay Blyth's BT Global Challenge on *Save the Children* and taken part in the famous Raja Muda International Regatta and the King's Cup in Thailand, where *Gipsy Moth* was bound.

'It's fantastic to be onboard one of the first boats to circumnavigate the world and to be part of such a national maritime treasure,' said Elaine, who a few months earlier sailed with Ellen MacArthur's team during their Asian Tour from Shanghai to Singapore on her trimaran *B&Q*.

Thirty hours after leaving Singapore on 21 November, the wind gods were not doing *Gipsy Moth* any favours. They were still under engine power.

'Classic Singapore to Malacca delivery,' noted Elaine. 'No wind. Or if there is, it's on the nose!' It was a good job *Gipsy Moth* had 200 litres of diesel fuel in jerry cans strapped to the deck. On day two, as they motored past Langkawi, Elaine noted that *Gipsy Moth* was definitely designed for the cold weather. She 'sweated buckets' as she tried cooking potato pancakes on the diesel stove down below.

After more than 50 hours, she couldn't believe they were still motoring. It was beginning to look like 'a power boat trip aboard one of history's greatest sailing icons!'

Chichester Archive/PPL

Sam Connelly

Deck shower Gipsy Moth-style. The original famous photograph of Francis Chichester (far left) is re-enacted by Enrico with an uncanny resemblance.

Skipper Sam was wondering why anybody would choose to cruise the Malacca Straits. 'The pilot book warned about salt-water crocodiles up to 20 miles offshore. The crew spotted hundreds of jellyfish the size of dustbin lids and encountered masses of floating debris – including tree trunks as big as *Gipsy Moth*, washed out to sea from coastal rivers. There was a lot of shipping and unlit fishermen's drift nets floated at night waiting to snare unsuspecting yachts.

Finally, on day three-and-a-half, the crew enjoyed a couple of hours of sailing as they approached Phuket. While they were enjoying deck showers, Sam remembered a picture of Chichester taking a shower in the cockpit and Enrico re-enacted the scene.

Finally, on 24 November, *Gipsy Moth* sailed past the breathtaking outer islands of Phuket which rise majestically out of the water, like some semi-submerged sea serpent, and tied up safely in the Yacht Haven Marina.

'Believe it or not, it will be nice to get away from the diesel cooker in the tropics and arrive home to the cold weather!' said Gordon.

Asia's top sailor Elaine takes a sextant sight and prays for wind.

Phuket Christmas cruise

Leg 22

Distance:
250 miles

Skipper:
Tim Magee (29)

Mate:
Mikaela
Zehnder (23)

Crew One:
Brad Osman (49)
Ben McGill (30)
and David
Eyles (50)

Crew Two:
Jonathan
Zorichak (62),
Kirsty
Maltby (17) and
Kate Abigail (16)

Leg sponsor:
Lord Harris

Gipsy Moth IV's Christmas stopover in Phuket proved the perfect opportunity for the UKSA to raise funds by selling berths to sailing enthusiasts during the holiday period. The ketch was based in Phuket Yacht Haven, a 'home from home' for the Blue Water Rally with two independent cruises planned.

Gipsy Moth's skipper was Tim Magee, who would remain with the yacht until the next stopover in Sri Lanka. First Mate was Mikaela Zehnder, a psychology graduate from Santa Cruz, California, for whom this was her first assignment after completing her Professional Crew and Skipper Training (PCST) at the UKSA.

The first of two crews included Brad Osman, from Fordingbridge, Hampshire, whose wife Judy bought him the week on Gipsy Moth as his 50th birthday present, Ben McGill, from

Southampton, who had also been treated to this tropical adventure as a Christmas present, and David Eyles, a keen sailor, was enjoying a break from his work with the London Metropolitan Police. Brad, originally from Plymouth, remembered seeing Chichester's return in 1967 as a schoolboy.

Gipsy Moth's first assignment was to join a sail parade of honour at the King's Cup Regatta off Kata Beach to mark the 79th birthday of the King of Thailand. Then the ketch sailed for Ko Phi Phi Don, described as the third most beautiful island in the world. Nearby Ko Phi Phi Leh was made famous as the backdrop for the 2000 Hollywood film *The Beach*, based on Alex Garland's book, with Leonardo DiCaprio as the young American backpacker. Much of Phi Phi Don and other parts of the western coast of Thailand were devastated by the 2004 Boxing Day Tsunami.

Two years on, sightseers would never guess that 23,000 tonnes of debris had been removed from this island alone – 7,000 tonnes cleared by hand so they could search for passports and indentification for those still missing, presumed dead.

When the tsunami struck, 10 Blue Water Rally Yachts had been anchored off Maya Beach, Phi Phi Don and American sailors Helen and Ed Muesch were swept inland. Helen nearly died. 'The faces and screams of the people in Phi Phi Don continue to haunt me,' said Ed months later. 'I'll never forget the face of the man who helped me pull Helen from the water.'

Tim Magee

Now all was a scene of perfect tranquillity as *Gipsy Moth*'s crew enjoyed snorkeling, sunbathing and swimming in the crystal clear waters. Later they sailed to the Similan islands, 60 miles north-west of Phuket in the Andaman Sea – nine granite islands covered in tropical jungle with some of the world's finest beaches.

David had a broad grin on his face as *Gipsy Moth* broad-reached across the clear blue tropical ocean: 'Who says heaven is a place you only visit when you're dead?' he asked.

Here there were amazing underwater rock formations, eroded by the sea over thousands of years and providing divers with spectacular passages, caves and gorges as well as being home to an amazing variety of marine life, including leopard sharks and manta rays. Ben dived and fell in love with a moray eel which he named Emma!

Soon Tim and Mikaela were back in Phuket welcoming their second crew to this tropical paradise. This time the crew leader was Jonathan Zorichak (62), a university

lecturer from Llanwenog, Wales, who had bought a 43ft yacht in 2006 and planned to go cruising. An occasional mountain climber and skier he was also a life-long reader of Chichester's books. The young crew were Kirsty Maltby (17) and Kate Abigail (16), both from Lord Harris's City Technology College, South Norwood, London.

Soon Mikaela had introduced the girls to elephant trekking before they headed offshore for a 10-hour sail back to Ko Miang, in the Similan Islands for Christmas. Tim moved *Gipsy Moth* to a more protected mooring on Christmas Eve at Ko Similan, with its white sandy beach.

The previous Christmas, *Gipsy Moth* had been in Barbados, now in Asia her miniature Christmas tree was decorated with small coloured elephants and Tim, Mikaela and Jonathan were up at dawn on Christmas Day decorating the boat with tinsel.

Christmas dinner was a tuna with cous cous salad, cooked by Jonathan, and later that day the girls went ashore to collect firewood for a bonfire on the beach and Tim arrived, dressed as Santa, with a sackful of presents.

Gipsy Moth's crew were joined by an Austrian couple who marvelled at the eccentric British behavior, with Tim dressed as Santa Claus and Jonathan in a silk smoking jacket with the temperature still 27°C!

The Christmas day finale was launching 'good luck' hot air lanterns into the night sky and each making a wish. When the Thais performed this ceremony the 100th day after the tsunami, a minute's silence was observed at the time the tsunami's first wave struck and each lantern represented a human spirit.

It was a poignant, magical end to a momentous holiday. *Gipsy Moth*'s crew had seen dolphins, flying fish, sun bathed with monkeys, ridden on elephants and in tuk-tuks and visited buddhist temples. There was just time for a last lively night out of music and dancing in Patong. And the best Christmas gift for the UKSA was that £11,000 had been raised.

Christmas day in the tropics. Tim Magee plays Santa to Kirsty and Kate in the Similan islands.

Mate Mikaela Zehnder from Santa Cruz, California.

Phuket to Galle

Problems with *Gipsy Moth's* Wallas diesel stove, which replaced Chichester's original paraffin stove, delayed her departure from Phuket by over a week while the crew waited for a spare part to flown from Finland. 'The idea of cold baked beans and sandwiches for 10 days didn't appeal' said skipper Tim, who had 'Plan B' up his sleeve – and fitted an inverter (an electronic device that converts 12 volt battery (DC) current) so a microwave could be used if the 'wonky' primus failed.

Meanwhile, the new crew enjoyed the bonus of taking a long-tail boat to visit Ko Tapu island, in Phang Nga Bay, better known as James Bond island, since the filming there of *The Man with the Golden Gun* back in the 1970s.

After a week they fitted the new cooker part, enjoyed their first hot meal cooked on board, and cleared customs and immigration in Ao Chalong before sailing for Sri Lanka.

First Mate Steve Chipperfield, from Devon, was an experienced sailor, who had competed in the 1976 Cape to Rio Race, the 1979 Fastnet and sailed his Hustler 30 to the Caribbean in 1978. His current boat was a Nicholson 40 ketch. Steve was also a trustee of the UKSA. His first 24-hours aboard *Gipsy Moth* left him 'feeling like a miscreant in a Spanish prison yard, enduring the fierce heat with no protection, just insults from the warders!' In the tropics, the lack of a bimini for sun protection continued to take its toll. 'All I could focus on was getting below at the earliest opportunity. Maybe that's why my noon sunsight was a little wide of the mark!'

Leg 23

Distance:
1,100 miles

Skipper:
Tim Magee (29)

Mate:
Steve
Chipperfield
(59)

Crew:
Shannon
McWilliam (18),
Richard Talbot
(19), Steven
Routledge (18)

Leg sponsor:
Isle of Wight

On the second day they enjoyed glorious sailing with a top speed of 9.7 knots and a NE Force 5 wind just aft of the beam. Richard and Steven, both keen sailors from the Isle of Wight, relished the conditions. Richard, from Ryde, had represented Britain in the 2004 world 4.7 Laser championships and Steven, from Shanklin, sailed a Dart 15 catamaran in national championships.

On the horizon were the Nicobar islands – a chain of 22 islands lying between the Andaman Sea and the Bay of Bengal. After the 2004 tsunami, some scientists estimated the undersea earthquake had moved the islands as much as 100 feet (30m). The wave had devastated island villages and at least 6,000 people were killed.

That night as *Gipsy Moth* headed through the Sombrero Channel between the islands at up to 10 knots, Richard cooked pasta and retired to his bunk exhausted. The islands were in almost complete darkness and so was the surrounding sea, apart from white wave crests and the odd burst of phosphorescence. Shannon, a scout from Fife in Scotland, who had suffered some seasickness, was hauling on the tiller in big seas. For a while, a pod of dolphins swam a few feet away alongside *Gipsy Moth*.

Gipsy Moth's passage across the eastern Indian Ocean gave wonderful, fast reaching trade wind sailing, averaging 7-8 knots, with one burst of 11.4 knots. After one 12-hour run of 105 miles, dawn bought fresh squid

Amazing rock formations around Phuket offer an exotic backdrop.

Chichester Archive/PPL

ABOVE:

Chichester fried flying fish for breakfast. After night 'attacks' by these ocean 'Exocets', Tim was thinking of adding crash helmets to Gipsy Moth's *safety gear*

and flying fish on deck. Chichester would have fried these up for breakfast, but Tim was thinking of adding crash helmets and goggles to *Gipsy Moth*'s night safety equipment as the crew were subjected to a nightly barrage of 'attacks' by flying fish. The Exocet missile is said to be named after this fish's Latin name, *Exocoetidae*!

These kamikaze creatures are found in all the world's tropical and sub-tropical waters and use their gliding ability to escape predators. They can be anything from four to 18 inches long and glide for 200 metres or more. They

have been found on the decks of big ships more than 40ft above sea level and some species can accelerate from a swimming speed of about 22mph to as much as 45mph in air.

Closer to Sri Lanka, the wind backed giving *Gipsy Moth* a nice angle of approach to Dondra Point, the southern-most tip of the island. The crew sighted *Saiorse K*, a fellow Blue Water Rally boat and they chatted on the SSB radio. Steve noticed other signs of land, a long-tailed, parakeet-like bird which tried to land on the masthead, a tanker and some fishing boats.

A typical Thailand boat, decorated with ribbons.

Dick Durham/Yachting Monthly

A day out from landfall, Tim declared war if the cooker committed one more misdemeanour. 'It's delayed us by a week, tried to starve us by withdrawing services – even after expensive new parts were fitted – and attempted to murder us in the night with its fumes,' said Steve. 'This stove is a psychopathic recidivist ... I'm sleeping with a large wrench under my pillow!'

As *Gipsy Moth* sailed round the south of the island into sheltered waters, the white dome of one of Galle's mosques greeted the crew. They anchored off the breakwater to await clearance into port by the Sri Lankan Navy. Less than three months earlier, Galle's harbour had been the scene of a suicide attack on a naval base by Tamil Tiger rebels who exploded their boats damaging Navy vessels. The Tigers have been fighting for a separate homeland in Sri Lanka's north for 25 years. To stop similar attacks, the Navy closed the port between 2000 and 0800 and exploded depth charges during the night to discourage sabotage by divers.

Lying at the heart of Galle is the ancient walled Galle Fort, with a lighthouse, a church, two mosques, a Buddhist shrine, plus 400 houses and a hotel. It was declared a World Heritage Site by UNESCO in 1988. Here on the surf-pounded ramparts, tourists promenade, snake charmers play their pipes and children fly kites or play cricket on the green, while in its bustling narrow streets *Gipsy Moth*'s crew found a maritime museum.

Steve was impressed by the Sri Lankan's stoicism, hospitality and bravery in the aftermath of the tsunami which had devastated Galle two years earlier. 'Surfing in the afternoon was made a special experience thanks to an invitation to join a local family to a very British tea and cake at a little house on the beach.'

The ancient walled city of Galle, on Sri Lanka's south-west coast, is a World Heritage Site.

The Nicobar islands in the Andaman Sea.

Galle to Djibouti

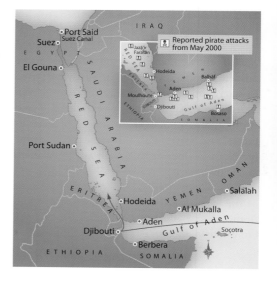

Leg 24

Distance:
2300 miles

Skipper:
John Jeffrey (63)

Mate:
Flight
Lieutenant
Robert Soar (28)

Crew Leader:
Peter
Cooper (33)

Crew:
Glen
Hymers (27)
Danny Walton
and Dominic
Clarke (28).

Leg sponsor:
RAF Sailing
Association

The UKSA deliberately chose not to put young crew on *Gipsy Moth* for legs 24 and 25, which took the yacht through the Gulf of Aden, an area known for a risk of pirate attacks. As one of the Blue Water Rally yachts, *Gipsy Moth* would sail the latter part of leg 24 in convoy, operating in radio silence with secret waypoints. Under John Jeffrey, who skippered leg 18, the ketch's all-male crew was hand-picked by the RAF Sailing Association, of which Rob Soar was training manager. They also provided the funding.

Before leaving Galle on Sunday afternoon to head across the Arabian Sea, *Gipsy Moth*'s crew were invited with other rally sailors to a bizarre Burns Night Supper where, with an obvious shortage of bagpipers in Galle, the Haggis was 'drummed' in by two Sri Lankans. The drum roll was nothing compared to *Gipsy Moth*'s ocean roll which soon had Glen and Dom turning green. Worse still, the cooker soon gave up the ghost and even the back-up microwave failed to get hot enough to scramble eggs. It seemed the crew would be on cold tinned food until Djibouti.

Mid-afternoon, three days out of Sri Lanka, Peter Cooper made the time-honoured call 'Land Ho!' as the first golden sand bar of the paradise islands of the Maldives shimmered on the horizon. The Maldives consist of more than 20 atolls and 1,000 islets, lying just above sea level some 400-miles south-west of Sri Lanka. Only 200 are inhabited.

As the smallest crew member, Danny was hoisted up the mast to pilot *Gipsy Moth* through the coral reefs as they entered the lagoon of Ihavandhippolhu atoll, at the extreme northern tip of island chain.

On his 63rd birthday, his first spent at sea, John opens presents from his wife Jean and family.

The atoll, 12 miles long, had 24 islands around the boundary reef and *Gipsy Moth* anchored in the shelter of Uligamu island, a popular stopover offering fuel and food supplies for yachts en-route to the Red Sea.

'It doesn't get much more like the Bounty advert than this!' thought Rob as they surveyed a holiday brochure scene of white sand, palm trees and nearly 20 Blue Water Rally yachts gently swinging at anchor. Instead of traffic noise, the background rumble was the roar of surf as the Indian Ocean pounded the reef protecting the anchorage.

With a population of just 450 there were only three tiny shops, no restaurants and certainly no bars. The population was almost entirely Muslim and the muezzin's call to prayer echoed across the anchorage several times a day. The crew ate ashore in two different private homes – paying, of course. The people were courteous and hospitable.

One family even tried to pair off mate Rob with one of their daughters!

After a four-day stopover, *Gipsy Moth* left for Djibouti, 2,000 miles away. They were heading for a rendezvous (RV) point in the ocean to sail in company with other rally yachts. On Wednesday 31 January it was John's 63rd birthday, his first spent at sea. With no stove to bake a cake, the ingenious substitute made by the crew was a Citronella candle – normally used to repel mosquitoes – surrounded by six sponge fingers!

John's other unexpected 'gifts' on this passage were being soaked a couple of times by unexpected breaking waves landing in his bunk by the cockpit companionway.

The biggest problem faced by *Gipsy Moth's* crew was that they were eating their way through the tinned rations twice as fast without a stove to cook rice and pasta. Dom also found a weevil in his breakfast cereal and four boxes of bran cereal had to be ditched.

Evil weevil in biscuits

Anchoring by committee! RIGHT: Sunset duties for the crew.

After sailing alone for over a week, *Gipsy Moth* suddenly saw five rally yachts steaming over the horizon together. The voyage now took on a quite different feel as they sailed in convoy. The sun was well up on the eastern horizon as the flotilla of six yachts headed into 'pirate alley' in the Gulf of Aden in a loose rectangular formation, as advised by rally organisers.

The fleet was divided into flotillas of six so average cruising speeds could be matched. Secret waypoints were used and a daily roll call exchanged positions which were passed to UK rally control by e-mail. Low power VHF radio transmissions were used in case pirates were monitoring the airwaves. Rally control maintained a 24-hour 'red alert' during the transit period and yachts were advised to set off their EPIRBs in the event of a pirate attack to alert the maritime rescue centre in Bahrain and

the French Navy in Djibouti. The advice for sailing in this area is: Never carry guns. Do not offer any violence, but carry some 'mugging' money to pay off pirates. It was, perhaps, welcome light relief that the yachts held a daily radio group quiz at 1500!

Twenty miles east of Djibouti, a rally lookout spotted a rapidly approaching dot to the south. The sighting was relayed by VHF radio to the other yachts, which closed up into an even tighter formation, as pre-arranged. The 'intruders', who hadn't shown up on radar, were soon close enough for *Gipsy Moth*'s crew to count four menacing-looking characters in a RIB with a powerful outboard.

The two rally boats on the starboard wing of the formation were *Askari*, a Shearwater 39, sailed by American couple Dick and Nancy Brown, and *Gipsy Moth*, her sails goosewinged to catch the 12 knots of breeze.

'The intruders were a few hundred yards away,' said Jeffrey. 'We sheeted in, and with the wind on our beam, picked up speed. I imagine the sight of her heeled over with a bone in her teeth, coming straight at them, was a bit alarming!'

A second, larger craft appeared and both boats shadowed the convoy. Believing they might be under threat from pirates, Peter and Val Newns aboard *Valhalla*, the smallest yacht in the fleet, sent out a 'Securite' message on VHF Channel 16.

Before the suspected pirates could make their next move, the American warship USS *Oak Hill* appeared dead ahead and hailed the flotilla. 'It was like a scene from Apocalypse Now!' said one of *Gipsy Moth's* crew. As the suspect vessels faded from sight, a US Navy fast patrol craft, bristling with armed men from the warship, draw alongside *Valhalla* to debrief Peter, a retired wing commander.

In the last 12 years the Blue Water Rally has taken 140 yachts through this hotspot without incident, despite numerous pirate attacks on cruising yachts in the same period. This was the sixth fleet to pass safely through the Gulf of Aden, waters which have a long

Keeping up with the daily blog for Gipsy Moth's fans back home.

tradition of piracy from the lawless regions of Somalia and Yemen. In ancient times they made their living attacking Arab dhows. Today they target big ships, even cruise liners, attacking with small open boats with powerful engines. In 2005 British sailors John and Andrina Cossey were rammed and boarded by knife-wielding pirates while sailing their 40ft ferro-cement ketch, *Sara of Hamble*, off the Somalian coast. The nearest port was 900 miles away. Luckily, they were unharmed, but electronic equipment cash and clothing was stolen.

Peter and Val Newns on Valhalla *thought they were under pirate attack.*

Arabian nights and a golden sunset at sea.

Djibouti to El Gouna

Through 'The Gate of Tears'

M oses may have parted the Red Sea around 1300BC, but today it is still a major test of yachts and crew. Not for nothing is the entrance to the sea for northbound yachts called the Straits of Bab El Mandeb, which translates from Arabic into 'The Gate of Tears'.

Nearly 1,400 miles long, 200 miles wide at its greatest width, the Red Sea has a fearsome reputation. Pilot charts foretell contrary winds, dangerous reefs and wayward currents. Mirage effects, refraction and haze from windblown sand, make sun sights unreliable. The Red Sea also has higher than average salinity. Spray and sea air is more corrosive than usual.

As Stephen Davies and Elaine Morgan's *Red Sea Pilot* cautions, horribly short seas test your rigging and find any weaknesses in the mast. Horrendous slamming and pitching will also test rudder, steering gear and engine

Leg 25

Distance:
950 miles

Skipper:
John Jeffrey (63)

Mate:
Lieutenant Colonel Alan Flavell (49)

Crew Leader:
Jason Hadley (35)

Crew:
Johannes Maree De-Kock (21), Jonathan Riley (21) and Rebecca Hince (20)

Leg sponsor:

Army Sailing Association

mountings. A cocktail of sediment shaken in fuel tanks, guarantees to block suspect fuel filters. Dust storms turn the windward deck and rigging reddish brown.

Finally, if all this isn't enough, the Red Sea is a major commercial shipping artery with giant freighters lumbering past in the dark with the dangers of collision.

Dawn found *Gipsy Moth*'s new crew, half of whom had never set foot on a yacht, raising the anchor and creeping out of an isolated anchorage. The crew were all drawn from the Army Sailing Association of which Lieutenant Colonel Alan Flavell, *Gipsy Moth*'s mate, was secretary. Having left Djibouti, their next stop was a tiny fishing 'port'. 'Forget Grimsby, the bustle of Whitby, or the enchanting ambience of Fishguard,' thought John, as he felt his way in, trying to line up a signal tower with a minaret that was on the chart but seemed to have disappeared. What this place did have is street lights, both of which were working. Travel not only broadens the mind, but as Rebecca added, 'It makes you grateful for what you've got.' Poverty in this region is endemic. With Africa to port and Arabia to starboard, *Gipsy Moth* had almost 1,000 miles to cover before Egypt.

Despite having a replacement Wallas diesel cooker (the not-so-old one had given up the ghost), the crew were eating cold food out of packets again. The ketch was bouncing and rolling so much that it was safer not to have hot pans flying across the cabin. At least this was downwind sailing, with the wind around 30 knots, gusting to 40, making steering interesting. Even with just a small staysail, they were barreling along at 6 or 7 knots. The crew were enjoying it 'despite all the hard work, such as having to get up at strange hours, and sleeping when normal people are out clubbing,' said John drolly. They were buzzed by a patrol aircraft which called up on VHF radio with the callsign 'Coalition Aircraft'. 'Nice to feel we're being watched by friendly eyes,' said John.

Shortly after leaving Djibouti, *Gipsy Moth* had a rendezvous with two Royal Navy warships on security patrol, HMS *Cornwall* and Royal Fleet Auxiliary replenishment ship RFA *Fort Austin*. First, *Gipsy Moth*'s crew spotted a Lynx helicopter flying towards them. Then came a VHF radio call from HMS *Cornwall* inviting the young crew members aboard for a tour. 'Yes please!' said Jonathan. The Navy dispatched a RIB to pick them up, and sent two engineers to fix *Gispy Moth*'s broken water-maker and deliver several jerry cans of water, plus eggs, bacon, sausages and other much appreciated supplies.

Gipsy Moth's crew for Leg 25 were drawn from the Army Sailing Association.

Navy RIBS, like this one, from HMS Cornwall searched Arab dhows for weapons.

While skipper John and mate Alan entertained the Navy's repair team, Chief Petty Officer Briggs and Petty Officer Winfindale, *Gipsy Moth*'s four crew were offered hot showers on HMS *Cornwall* (which two of them accepted!) and given ice cold drinks ('Bliss,' said Jonathan). 'We looked back at *Gipsy Moth* from the main deck and it didn't look that appealing. Did I mention that HMS *Cornwall* had air-conditioning, too?' added Jonathan.

Later HMS *Cornwall*'s captain Commander Jeremy Woods, told John Jeffrey over the radio: 'It was a privilege to sail with *Gipsy Moth* for a few hours. The size contrast between a 53ft sailing yacht and a 480ft long warship was apparent. But it's clear we both need teamwork and dedication to set to sea! We wish you luck on your adventures north!'

HMS *Cornwall* was on her way south to the Arabian Gulf as Flagship to Combined Task Force 158, where her duties included protecting Iraqi offshore energy installations. Later she would be at the centre of a publicity storm when 15 of her sailors and marines on a RIB were ambushed at gunpoint by the Navy of the Iranian Revolutionary Guards after searching an Arab dhow. They were held hostage for 12 days before being released amidst controversy over selling their stories to the newspapers.

Soon, *Gipsy Moth* found the wind howling out of the north. Not as strong as it was a few nights ago, but then it had been behind them and the sea was gentle. Now the waves were bigger, the sea rougher. 'I don't want to drive the old lady too hard so we're not carrying very much sail, but even so *Gipsy Moth IV* is leaning over and everything takes twice as long,' said John.

The Red Sea was one of the toughest legs on the round-the-world cruise for strong winds and currents and horribly short seas.

John Jeffery

You catch it,
I'll clean it and
cook it!

BELOW:
Egyptian Temple
God in Karnak.

Gipsy Moth sailed past a *marsa* (natural inlet) where a cluster of other Blue Water Rally Yachts had anchored, waiting for the weather to improve. John told them by radio that the latest forecast showed the 'weather window' they were waiting for not only had shutters across it but was about to be bricked up. 'They were having a jolly social time and didn't seem to care!' John noted.

After about 10 days, *Gipsy Moth* crossed the tropic of Capricorn and was officially out of the tropics. Then land was sighted for the first time for 12 days or so. 'It was the desert mountains of Southern Egypt illuminated by a setting moon and a rising sun about 30 miles in the distance... a spectacular and unforgettable dawn,' said Alan, adding 'our clothes can stand up by themselves with the amount of salt in them. Hair styles are not much better!'

After 14 days at sea *Gipsy Moth* finally arrived in Port Ghalib, the only privately owned marina on the south Red Sea coast of Egypt licensed by the government as an official port of entry.

'It was strange to be on land again,' wrote John. 'Except we were not allowed on land! Six hours later we were still aboard, waiting for our passports to be returned "in ten minutes" every time we asked.' When the crew did get ashore, the restaurant moved up and down and round and round, just like the sea.

Gipsy Moth's sail north to El Gouna saw more headwinds and waves crashing over the

deck. 'By the time we entered the very tight channel into Abu Tig Marina all bodies were encrusted with salt,' said Alan.

The crew may not have realised it, but they had just endured, and won their sailing spurs on one of the toughest legs on the Blue Water Round the World Rally. Drawn from the Army Sailing Association, the soldiers were now true sailors as well as sea dogs.

Jason said: 'Like any elegant lady worth her salt, *Gipsy Moth* kept us on our toes, with plenty of slamming to windward. I was filled with the excitement of arrival in Egypt, but part of me longed to turn her around and keep on chasing that elusive horizon.'

For now, the crew headed for Luxor, and some well earned sightseeing at the Temple of Karnak and other Egyptian antiquities. Soon *Gipsy Moth* would be looking almost new again, after being cleaned, polished and varnished from waterline to masthead, ready for her next crew.

Royal Navy

Gipsy Moth *and* HMS Cornwall *photographed by a Lynx helicopter before their Red Sea rendezvous.*

El Gouna to Crete

Leg 26

Distance:
750 miles

Skipper:
John Jeffrey (63)

CREW NO 1

Mate:
Simon Hall (63)

Crew Leader:
Brian Lewis (70)

Crew:
Hannah Frost
(17), Sarah Lamb
(17), Edmund
Keith (18)

CREW NO 2

Crew Leader:
Mark Lamble

Crew:
Frances
Woolston (14),
Rachel Harrison
(14), Larvell
Gisby (15)

Leg sponsor:

BT Voice of the
Planet; Isle of
Wight and Ellen
MacArthur Trust

As the sun set over Egypt's Sinai desert, hundreds of squawking jackdaws wheeled around the masts of the Blue Water Rally yachts moored at Port Tewfik, waiting to transit the Suez Canal and enter the Mediterranean.

Gipsy Moth's crew found new skills – such as rigging a slip line, riding a camel and ordering an ice cream in Arabic. 'They also took turns at winching things up and down the mast – like the mainsail and me!' said skipper John Jeffery.

First Mate was Hampshire-based yachtsman Simon Hall, 63, manager of a re-settlement centre for MOD servicemen, with crew leader Brian Lewis, 70, a retired MOD engineer, who sailed a Starlight 35 from Port Solent. The teenagers were students Hannah Frost, from Manchester, and Edmund

Keith and Sarah Lamb, both from the Isle of Wight and sponsored by the Isle of Wight Enterprise Partnership.

Leaving El Gouna, *Gipsy Moth* had carefully threaded her way through the reefs, north to spend the night in a bay off the Sinai

shore. The second night was spent in the port of Ras Budran, an oil tanker facility on the eastern bank of the Gulf of Suez, before heading for Port Tewfik.

Gipsy Moth had been having electrical problems for several days. 'Almost a whole week without hot water or hot food!' exclaimed Sarah and Hannah. A sandstorm blotted out the landscape and left the ketch covered in fine dust. The masthead tricolour light had to be removed and washed in fresh water. The critical steaming light was not working and the original wiring core inside the mast had not been completely replaced since Chichester sailed round the world. John spent hours in a bosun's chair trying to fix the problem. The UKSA flew fleet engineer Frank Trotman, 45, out to Cairo, to help. Frank used a fishing weight to drop new wiring down the mast. Frank also replaced the engine's corroded ignition key barrel and fitted a new alternator.

Having faced everything the ocean could throw at them after more than 25,000 miles, the blue water rally sailors were now bottled up in a canal at the mercy of red-tape, bureaucrats and '*baksheesh*', a term used to describe both charitable giving and certain forms of political corruption and bribery in the Middle East.

Yachting Monthly's Dick Durham, who had sailed aboard *Gipsy Moth* from Gibraltar to the Canaries, now re-joined her for part of the 101-mile canal transit. 'Slow boats at the front,'

said Blue Water Rally director Tony Diment, at a skippers' briefing. As the slowest boat in the fleet, *Gipsy Moth* would lead the flotilla and had the 'honour' of carrying the canal pilot. The fastest yacht, a 62ft Hallberg-Rassy, *Bamsen*, skippered by Christoph Rassy, 73, would take up the rear position.

A few days earlier, an advance flotilla of blue water rally yachts transited the canal and sent back a warning they'd been plagued by demands from canal pilots for US dollars, Egyptian pounds and cigarettes. The pilots had become agitated and started shouting when their demands were refused. To prevent a repetition, Tony Diment invited yacht agent

The pretty town of Aghios Nikolas, Crete, where Gipsy Moth made landfall

BELOW:
Rally yachts in Port Tewfik.

LEFT:
Hannah and Sarah visit the pyramids

Dick Durham/Yachting Monthly

The crew prepare to leave Port Tewfik to transit the canal.

Soukar Heebi, known as the Prince of the Red Sea, to the briefing. 'The thing to understand about *baksheesh*,' Tony explained, 'is that it's not seen as a tip, but as your duty to pay under the Koran.' He collected about £8 from each boat and handed it over to Captain Heebi, to pay off the pilots in advance. The only other demands

The Egyptian pilot takes Gipsy Moth's *helm.*

likely to be made would be as the fleet went through Port Said, known as 'Marlboro Alley', where boats have been known to approach yachts demanding cigarettes.

'Do not have a dialogue with them,' warned Tony, 'treat them as you would traders in a *souk* (market). Don't slow down or start arguing. Remember "*lah*" is "no" and "*bass*" is "enough"'. With that, *Gipsy Moth's* crew dispersed into the balmy Egyptian night. Next morning, woken at dawn by the muezzin's call to prayer, *Gipsy Moth IV's* crew slipped her lines and motored out towards the canal entrance. Once under way, John was keen to maintain speed and direction as *Gipsy Moth* is difficult to manoeuvre under power. She was later compared to ex-Prime Minister Margaret Thatcher, as John performed the nautical equivalent of a three-point turn – 'The lady's not for turning!'

A powerful pilot launch ranged alongside hooting his klaxon unceasingly. 'Number one, sir?' yelled a pilot.

'Yes, we are the first boat,' said John.

'Stop!' shouted the pilot.

'Can't!' said John as he carried on regardless, ignoring the buzzing, hooting pilot boat, which itself ignored two other yachts which appeared to have grounded on a sand shoal.

And so *Gipsy Moth* entered the Suez Canal, surrounded by disorganised chaos, none of it produced by the rally yachts.

With a pilot boat ahead and a second one astern of *Bamsen*, the string of 10 rally yachts motored single-file along the 100ft wide and 30ft deep canal. Such regimentation was matched by the soldiers armed with machine guns on the west bank and posted at every kilometre of the route. The early desert chill had them flapping their arms against their sides to keep warm. The huge ramparts of sand on each bank were a reminder of the epic task of digging the canal – carried out over 11 years by Egyptian slaves under French organisation. Thousands of lives were lost from disease and exhaustion.

Sunrise brought the colour of the desert back to ochre yellow from grey as *Gipsy Moth* entered Little Bitter Lake, where 10 giant container ships and two bulk carriers were anchored, awaiting pilots for the transit north.

At Ismailia, the canal pilot came aboard. He didn't speak any English, demanded no *baksheesh* but waved frantically for *Gipsy Moth* to keep up to speed behind the big ships ahead. The 100-mile transit of the canal lasted from dawn to dusk. Under the shadows of the giant mosques of Port Said, *Gipsy Moth* finally entered the Mediterranean Sea, where the fleet dispersed in 30 knots of northwesterly wind for the 470-mile passage to Aghios Nikolaos, Crete. Now that they were back in cooler climes the crew cooked a stew to celebrate and dressed up in their winter woollies. Watch mate Sarah was sitting under the stars driving the ketch across the wine dark sea and humming quietly to herself.

In Crete, *Gipsy Moth* had a crew change as three Nottingham teenagers from the Ellen MacArthur Trust joined for a four-day Easter holiday cruise around the island.

On board were Rachel, Frances and Larvell, with Frank Fletcher, CEO of the Ellen MacArthur Trust, and photographer Mark Lamble. Frank had been in Greenwich

28 months previously 'when *Gipsy Moth IV* was pulled out of the concrete'. She had been a big part his life for over a year when he worked at the UKSA before changing jobs.

Rachel said: 'It's amazing to be sleeping and working in the same boat that Francis Chichester sailed round the world after overcoming terminal lung cancer. I know how hard it is to have cancer, but to achieve something so amazing ... I hope I'll be able to achieve my own dreams.'

Skipper John had the last word: 'This is *Gipsy Moth*'s youngest crew, but they are second to nobody in their enthusiasm.'

ABOVE:
Blue Water Rally yachts steam through the Suez Canal.

LEFT:
Soldiers with machine guns line the canal every kilometre.

John looks anxious as a giant container ship overtakes Gipsy Moth *in the 100ft-wide canal.*

Frank Fletcher
(extreme left) with
skipper John and
the young crew
from the Ellen
MacArthur Trust.

Crew get to grips
with winching and
helming.

Mark Lamble

Mark Lamble

Dick Durham/Yachting Monthly

Simon Hall and Brian Lewis bring the bread rations in Crete.

Mark Lamble

Gipsy Moth *heeling to a Mediterranean breeze.*

Mark Lamble

Frank (left), John and Mark Lamble (right) with young crew.

Crete to Malta

Leg 27

Distance:
540 miles

Skipper:
John Jeffrey (63)

Mate:
Andrew
Eccleston (55)

Crew Leader:
Michael
Jones (21)

Crew:
Charlie
Hatfield (17)
Dan McVeigh
(16) and Jean
Fitzpatrick (68)

*Leg sponsor: Isle of
Wight and B&G*

Ignoring sailors' superstitions, *Gipsy Moth* set sail from Crete on Friday the 13th, parting company with the Blue Water Rally yachts that had been her companions for most of her round-the-world adventure. 'There was hardly a dry eye in the place, though that may have had something to do with the torrential rain,' said skipper John, who had probably sailed more miles on *Gipsy Moth* than anyone, apart from Chichester himself, of course.

For plucky pensioner Jean Fitzpatrick, 68, the first sight of *Gipsy Moth IV* rocking gently in the dusk light at her berth in Aghios Nikolaos, told her she was in for the adventure of a lifetime. 'Even with bare masts, this lady had presence. You could almost feel her eyeing up the new crew,' said the lady who had the distinction of being the oldest, most spirited female crew on the circumnavigation.

Andrew Eccleston, *Gipsy Moth*'s official meteorologist, was one of the lucky people sailing on the 53ft ketch for a second time. 'Same boat, same quirks, new people, new destination,' he said, having last been aboard on leg 16, sailing up the Great Barrier Reef.

Crew leader Michael Jones, was an experienced dinghy sailor, who had flown from his home in New Zealand to join *Gipsy Moth*. Michael was paralysed below both knees, having been born with spina bifida, and used crutches, plus a wheelchair on land. During the first years of his life he was in and out of hospital and had 13 operations by the time he was three years old. He first got interested in sailing as a member of Britannia Sea Scouts in Wellington and then joined Sailability.

'I know that the *Gipsy Moth* voyage will be much tougher and require a lot more of me physically and mentally,' he said in his application letter for a crew place. 'But it will give me the skills to better coach other disabled sailors and act as a role model.' Don Manning, chairman of Sailability Wellington Trust rightly predicted: 'I believe Michael will be a good ambassador for the *Gipsy Moth* project.'

Andrew Eccleston

Michael got around *Gipsy Moth* using plenty of upper body strength and hanging on to anything that wasn't moving already! His parents were there to wave him off, before flying to Malta to greet *Gipsy Moth*'s arrival.

The young crew included teenagers Charlie and Dan. Charlie had lots of sailing experience, but was getting back into the groove after a bad accident. Dan had only done his basic training and so it was all fairly new to him, but he was soon learning the ropes.

'Crete to Malta may sound exotic, because the voyage starts and ends at a popular holiday destination,' said Andrew. However, once the mountains of Crete disappeared over the horizon there was nothing but 400-plus miles of empty Mediterranean sailing due west to Valetta. 'And it really is quite empty.' On the entire trip they saw about a dozen ships, one dead cow that floated past and a small land bird that expired, despite the crew's best efforts.

The beginning of the voyage was an 'Onedin Line' moment for Jean. The sea was choppy and before long Dan looked dreadful and Jean soon joined him at the lee rail. On the second day, Jean was thrilled when a school of dolphins played around the boat for nearly an hour and at nightfall she saw three shooting stars. After her first 24-hours at sea, she was finding the language of sailors quite a challenge. 'So many new words and terms,

each with their own precise meaning: halyard, cleats, topping lifts, mainsheets, genoas... Then there are the knots: bowline, clove hitch, rolling hitch, round turn and two half hitches.'

'When the sea was rough, every plate, cup, knife and fork had a life of it's own and food took to the air in great spiralling arcs landing in the strangest of places,' said Jean. 'After lunch the remains of an onion and tomato salad leapt on to the skipper's oilskins, his bed and into his shoes! He took it very well. I think his threat to keel haul me was a joke?'

Trying to sleep when everything in the cupboards was crashing around had Jean stuffing bedding inside to reduce the noise to a muffled banging. It gave her 'a ridiculous sense of triumph', of which Sir Francis himself would have wholeheartedly approved! Chichester claimed the noise from the lockers was like 'a country fair in full swing!'

As the days rolled by, the breeze came and went. The engine was used when the speed dropped below the average needed to get the crew to Malta in time for flights home, but there were also times when *Gipsy Moth* was doing 8 knots with just one of the running sails set.

The arrival into the spectacular setting of Grand Harbour, Valetta was unforgettable. There can be few harbour entrances more magnificent, with the imposing fortified walls that have seen so many famous vessels come and go. The pilot boat led *Gipsy Moth* to a berth while a TV crew shouted questions at John as the doughty ketch once again became the centre of attention. The crew stood proudly on the foredeck for a photograph wearing their new Tilley Hats, kindly presented by a local agent.

For John, who had brought the yacht all the way from Sri Lanka through three fascinating months, it was a special moment. 'Five legs, three continents, five different crews and all of it a magnificent experience. Including last year's journey from Darwin through Kupang to Bali. That must be over 5,000 miles – and that's not counting the 200-mile white-knuckle ride behind a French tug from Rangiroa to Tahiti!' he said.

The crew in heavy weather gear. At times the ketch was doing 8 knots with just one running sail set.

Crew leader Michael Jones from New Zealand

Gipsy Moth had several flying visitors during her circumnavigation

Malta to Sardinia

Leg 28

Distance:
350 miles

Skipper:
Richard Baggett
(35)

Mate:
Leanna Hill (20)

Crew Leader:
Amy Prime (16)

Crew:
Sam Stone (20),
Noor
Hamza (17)
Josh Clark, (16)

Leg sponsor:
RWE Npower
and Isle of Wight

Having twice played 'midwife' at *Gipsy Moth*'s re-birth – once at Camper & Nicholsons in 2005 and then in New Zealand in 2006 – lead skipper Richard Baggett was delighted to be back at the helm for the short hop to Sardinia.

The ketch left Malta's Grand Harbour with strong winds and for Sam Stone, from the Isle of Wight, one of the highlights of the passage was using the storm sails in Force 7 winds ' ... and watching everyone being sick, washing up at 55° and eating food off my belly, chest and face!'

Noor, from The Academy, Peckham, South London, succumbed to seasickness, but when the weather improved soon enjoyed swimming

in 2,000 metres with Sam and Amy, from the Isle of Wight, and Josh, from Scarborough. The crew experienced a bit of everything, weather-wise, on leg 28. Strong winds on Friday gave way to light winds on Saturday and Sunday, plus a real pea-souper sea fog.

The last full day began as they motored through Sicily's Egadi Islands and out into the Tyrrhenian Sea, bounded by Corsica, Sardinia, Italy and Sicily.

Around 0530 a light north-east breeze filled in so they could set the running sail, main and mizzen and enjoy an hour of peace, watching the most beautiful sunrise unfold.

After carrying out basic engine checks and finishing breakfast, the wind died away as they sailed into a fog bank. With the engine and radar on, *Gipsy Moth* picked her way through the sea for two hours until the sun

Porto Cervo, Sardinia's exclusive yachting centre on the Costa Smeralda

eventually burned off the fog. The rest of the day was spent motoring in calm conditions towards north-east Sardinia while cleaning the boat and carrying out routine maintenance. After lunch, they stopped for a swim and had a perfect finish to the day with a pod of dolphins playing on the bow.

Landfall on Monday was Porto Cervo, often known as Porto Nuovo and the main centre of the so-called Costa Smeralda (Emerald Coast) in northern Sardinia.

Josh, Nor and Sam pose with a local.

LEFT: Writing the daily diary.

Sardinia to Majorca

Leg 29

Distance:
300 miles

Skipper:
Mike Acton
(45)

Mate:
Leanna Hill
(20)

Crew Leader:
Wayne Suttner
(47)

Crew:
Jim Stinson
(17), Cheryl
Osso (16), and
Scott Bruce
(16)

Leg sponsor:
Upper Canada
District School
Board

Mike Acton, who was skippering the next two legs of *Gipsy Moth*'s voyage, had travelled a long way to get to Sardinia. 'I remember *Gipsy Moth*'s Plymouth homecoming when I was six years old in 1967,' he recalled. 'It meant a great deal to my grandfather, who taught me to sail. I read Chichester's book in my late teens so my spiritual journey had been much further than just the trip from the Isle of Wight, where I boarded a ferry to the airport with one of the young crew, 16-year-old Scott Bruce.'

Leg 29 was sponsored by Upper Canada District School Board and crew leader was Ontario teacher Wayne Suttner with two of his 17-year-old pupils, Jim Stinson and Cheryl Osso, from the Thousand Islands Secondary School.

'It's truly an honour to be one of the non-British sailors on this voyage,' said Wayne, a guidance counsellor and geography teacher

who had read about the *Gipsy Moth* project in *Yachting Monthly*. He was a keen sailor and member of Brockville Yacht Club. The fact that Chichester was a cancer survivor made Wayne's journey a personal one, too, since his mother and father both died from cancer and a friend was bravely battling the disease.

Cheryl soon discovered the inconveniences of being a tall person living on a boat – every time she sat up in her bunk she banged her head on the deckhead. Wayne, however, was delighted to discover he'd been allocated Sheila Chichester's portside bunk.

The next few days would bring new experiences for all the crew. They would spend two nights at sea as they sailed to the Spanish Balearic Islands, via Bonifacio in Corsica. 'Forty-eight hours with no land in sight,' was quite strange, Jim decided.

Meanwhile, Bonifacio, was just a day sail away, taking them from Italy's pizzas and pasta to France's boulangeries and croissants.

LEFT: skipper John Jeffrey. Hung out to dry – the crew's wet wet weather gear.

You have to sail into Bonifacio to believe its spectacular setting. The narrow entrance is almost invisible from seaward and lies between spectacular towering cliffs with the buildings of its 12th century citadel precariously perched on ledges. It's not for those who suffer from vertigo!

With a perfect Force 4-5 aft of the beam, *Gipsy Moth* arrived in style and almost as soon as she was moored alongside the town quay, she drew a crowd of sailors and admirers stopping to chat about the famous ketch.

After just one night, *Gipsy Moth* set off for Mahon, the walled city of Menorca, 250 miles away. Wayne soon realised why and how sailors develop close friendships – sharing time together on night watches in the cockpit. 'You're depending on each other for safety and also to fight boredom, fear and loneliness. I couldn't help wondering how Chichester managed. In his writing, he rarely mentioned feeling afraid and alone. Of course, he missed his Sheila dearly, just as I was missing my Patricia.'

Dark clouds gathered and the rains fell as *Gipsy Moth* sighted land after a day-and-a-half and entered the port of Mahon, amidst a thunderstorm one evening. 'We couldn't raise marinas or yacht clubs by VHF radio or telephone. Finally we found a berth at Club Maritimo De Mahon,' said Mike.

Cheryl got to sleep for an entire night. 'It was wonderful. No one woke me up to go on watch and sit in the cold for three hours in the middle of the night,' she said. 'I won't miss night watches, but I will miss the whole *Gipsy Moth* experience,' she said.

Next morning, skipper Mike summoned the crew on deck for a reading from Francis Chichester's book taken from exactly 40 years ago to the day.

'On April 29th I finished the fresh (ahem!) eggs, and I ate my last grapefruit, leaving only one orange and one lemon... My remaining cheeses had to go, too. There was an increasingly horrible smell in the cabin which at first I attributed to rotting fruit or vegetables. But after I had checked all these,

Jim, Cheryl and Scott in Bonifacio.

the aroma steadily became more nauseating every time I passed through the cabin. Then I found that it was due to five cheeses which had been shut in a plastic box. A roll of charts had fallen on to the box and pressed open the lid, thereby letting out the evil genie of the box. Those cheeses were not crawling or humming, they were swimming. It was an ordeal to get them into the sea.'

Henceforth, the crew of *Gipsy Moth IV* decided 29 April would be known as 'One egg, one lemon, one orange and smelly cheese day' – to be celebrated by consuming breakfast pancakes of eggs, cheese, oranges and lemons. A ceremonial piece of cheese was thrown over the side by Jim, the most seasick person of the trip so far.

After spending a day exploring Mahon and being interviewed by the local newspaper, *Gipsy Moth*'s crew left next evening. The real excitement started when the wind howled and the boat did what she does best – heeling over to about 30°. 'Normally, an experience like this only hits me when I look back on the whole thing later. But in those conditions, I was completely "in the moment"', said Wayne. 'And what a moment it was!'

As *Gipsy Moth* arrived in La Rapita on the south coast of Majorca, Wayne was

ABOVE: Sailing upwind to La Rapita in Majorca FAR RIGHT: Deck scrubbing duties for Wayne.

RIGHT: Corsica's beautiful Bonifacio, its citadel perilously perched on towering cliffs.

CBO/PPL

thinking about how well the six crew had got along on their adventure. 'It gets a little cramped sometimes, with a space the size of a bathroom for six people, but Scott, Jim and Cheryl are getting along famously. Shy three days ago, the way they are now, you'd think they'd spent a summer together!'

'Recipe of the day: take three teenagers, put them together on an historic sailboat, add a patient, fun skipper and a glowing first mate, plus a school guidance counsellor – shake it all up (this is *Gipsy Moth* you must remember!) and *voila*! Magic!'

The evening meal became a pasta pantomime produced and eaten with much talk and laughter amidst an atmosphere that, said Mike, 'was priceless.'

'No matter how many bone-headed sailing mistakes I made,' said Wayne, 'Mike and Leanna have been amazing. They ignored them if they weren't life-threatening errors and if they were they politely pointed out what do to – even if they'd just explained the whole thing to me 20-minutes ago! This week has changed me.'

'*Gipsy Moth* had proved a true companion. She's a special yacht, with her own personality. She's carried us safely. *Hasta luego amiga. Yo te quiero,*' was Wayne's parting shot.

Jim's was: 'Sir Francis Chichester may have set a record and made a name for himself, but I guarantee he didn't enjoy himself as much as he would if he had been accompanied by this crew!'

Majorca to Gibraltar

eg 30 kicked off with a serious Thai green curry, cooked by Leanna to match the heat of the Mediterranean. 'I'm not sure the tears streaming down peoples faces were tears of mirth,' thought skipper Mike. The crew soon left bustling Palma for a short 15-mile sail to Santa Ponsa, a beautiful bay with a backdrop of almond-trees and pine forests. They were heading for a berth in the exclusive Club Nautico Marina – hidden down a long, narrow rocky inlet nestling between tall hills.

Flushed with his boat-handling successes in Palma, Mike motored in with confidence but soon came to the conclusion that all the other boats must be equipped with bow thrusters. When it was time to turn back, there wasn't enough space for the 53ft ketch's large turning circle and she lay across the fairway

Leg 30

Distance:
420 miles

Skipper:
Mike Acton (45)

Mate:
Leanna Hill (20)

Crew Leader:
Brian Lewis (71)

Crew:
David Williams (18), Kate Scholes (18), and Mark Reed (20)

Leg sponsor:
Isle of Wight

blocking the channel. Mike, remaining as cool as a chilled cucumber, managed a 30-point turn, with inches to spare, as an array of marina workers shouted unhelpful instructions. With the aid of *Gipsy Moth*'s 'bow thruster', Leanna, they were soon comfortably berthed.

Next morning's passage was somewhat longer – 130 miles due west to Valencia on the Spanish mainland – to visit the 32nd America's Cup sailing regatta. 'It is one of the simplest passage plans I've ever put together – 200 metres from our berth to the harbour entrance and then 270° to Valencia,' said Mike.

Soon, the north-west breeze, kicked up a lumpy sea which made life uncomfortable as *Gipsy Moth* started to buck and rear. Brian and Kate were fine, but Mark's battle with *mal de mer* was impressive. Having lost his breakfast, he felt peckish and ordered up a sandwich from the galley. Mid-way through eating this he was sick again, but paused only briefly to wipe his mouth while proceeding to eat the rest of the sandwich.

That night, *Gipsy Moth IV* motored west under a starlit night at 5 knots, leaving a trail of phosphorescent sparkles in her wake and entertaining three dolphins in the bow wave.

In Valencia, the crew were met by David Green, who secured their entry into the America's Cup Victory Village, where Corum, *Gipsy Moth*'s official time-keeper, was unveiling a new timepiece. The stopover also provided an opportunity for members of Team New Zealand to visit the yacht which had been repaired at their Auckland base after her Pacific grounding when boss Grant Dalton generously donated facilities. Dalton was especially pleased to see the famous yacht back in commission.

Kate, David and Mark watched the start of some spectacular America's Cup racing. 'It was amazing to see how hi-tech the yachts are compared to *Gipsy Moth*,' said David.

Lack of wind meant *Gipsy Moth* motored most of the 380 miles to Gibraltar. Dogged by more battery charging problems, they conserved power by switching off all non-essential items, including the computers

and internet connections, and relied on their Aquair towed generator.

As the sun rose on the Rock of Gibraltar, *Gipsy Moth* officially 'tied the knot' in her second circumnavigation, crossing her outward track from 18 months previously as she headed past Europa Point and into Marina Bay at 0900.

'One of the questions I have asked myself is why Sir Francis Chichester chose to sail alone around the world?' said skipper Mike.

'We all need adventure in our lives. For Sir Francis it meant a huge project – out of the reach for most of us. If my own journey is anything to go by, everyone who has sailed aboard *Gipsy Moth* on her second round the world voyage has had an unforgettable experience. Sailing a complicated boat as part of a team to get from A to B, discovering new places, enjoying companionship and adventures out of the ordinary... put all of these things together and you have a package that's a highlight for young people and could have life-changing consequences.'

Land Ho! announces Mate Leanna Hill.

LEFT: Kate Scholes from the Isle of Wight.

ABOVE: Leanna Hill.

Gibraltar to Plymouth

40th anniversary landfall

Leg 31

Distance: 1,000 miles

Skipper:
John Jeffrey (63)

Mate:
Anson Lane (64)

Crew Leader:
Chris Whitwam (32)

Crew:
Glen Austin (19), Kerry Prideaux (18), Grant McCabe (16)

Leg sponsor:
Isle of Wight

Sailing to a deadline is never a good idea when you have to take the weather into account. 'Wind, wind, wind, where art thou?' pleaded a frustrated Francis Chichester on 28 May, 1967. The 66-year-old lone sailor was 119 days out from Sydney, Australia, sailing up the English Channel towards Plymouth on a Sunday morning.

'This business is quite a strain. I wish I could get into port. It looks as if there is no chance today,' he lamented. Little did he realise the nature of the welcome awaiting him that Bank Holiday weekend, as 250,000 people thronged Plymouth's waterfront to salute one man's courage, dogged determination and endurance. Millions more watched on black and white TV at home as Sunday Night at the

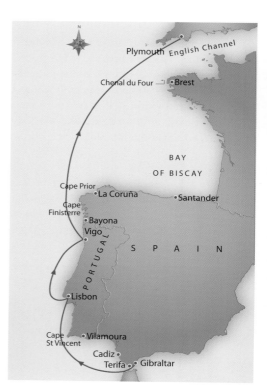

London Palladium was postponed to broadcast the news to the nation. Even in 1967 the papers reported that 'the police, with their usual sense of occasion, appeared to devote their time to towing cars away.'

Chichester plugged on and late that afternoon the breeze quickened and he called the Royal Western Yacht Club to assure them he would be there. 'Make no mistake,' he said. 'I'm coming in tonight!' Eventually, he crossed the finishing line to a hero's welcome just before 9pm, nine months and one day after setting off from the historic port.

Forty years on, following in Chichester's wake, skipper John Jeffrey, on his eighth *Gipsy Moth* leg – if you include the heroic 200-mile South Pacific hop to Tahiti, from the reef where she was salvaged – was under no illusion about the importance of arriving on 28 May, even down to the appointed hour of 2pm at the breakwater! But unlike the frustrating calms Chichester endured, John battled with too much wind – and from the wrong direction. Unusually strong northerly winds put *Gipsy Moth*'s scheduled arrival time in Plymouth in doubt. History repeated itself.

Since leaving Gibraltar almost 15 days before he and his six-strong crew had faced gales and headwinds. 'I'll never sail to a timetable again!' he promised, adding: 'Wasn't it President Kennedy who said something like

"We choose to do these things not because they are easy but because they are hard"? The people who come on board *Gipsy Moth IV* haven't chosen an easy option, they are following in Chichester's footsteps along a path of adventure.'

Those aboard included three teenagers: Kerry Prideaux, 18, a catering student from Lynton, North Devon, whose father, Nigel, had died of cancer when she was 14. 'It hit her very hard,' said her mother Kay, and to help her through her grief and to build her confidence she went on an Outward Bound adventure course and was later nominated by the Sir Francis Chichester Trust to sail on *Gipsy Moth*. The other teenagers were Grant McCabe, 16, an art student from Plymouth, and Glen Austin, 19, a watersports instructor from the Isle of Wight. The crew leader was Chris Whitwam, 32, a marine engineer from Yorkshire, who worked for the UKSA.

Gipsy Moth *battled gales and headwinds as she raced home for a 40th anniversary appointment on 28 May.*

Glen Austin cradles an orphan from the storm. Bird's blown off course in strong winds often landed on the ketch to regain their strength

'The weather has definitely got a sixth sense,' said first mate Anson Lane, 64, a retired Portsmouth software engineer. 'It was blowing from the west when we wanted to sail west and then from the north when we headed up the Portuguese coast.' The forecast was Force 5, 6 and 7, with worse to come.

Waves broke over the boat like riot police water cannons. The boat ran uphill over mountainous seas and crashed into the trough on the other side, with a shudder and a clatter of crockery from the galley. Two constants were the drone of the engine and wind on the nose. Chichester had described the ketch's progress even against small waves as 'like a charging elephant being stopped by a flywhisk.'

All those sleeping in the fo'c'sle were thrown from their bunks as *Gipsy Moth IV* plunged north. 'I'd like to thank the inventor of leecloths, who has saved my life quite a few times!' said Glen. For Grant, struggling to sleep in the forepeak, it was like being on the big dipper or a runaway roller coaster. Nearly every time John came off watch he found Grant fast asleep in the skipper's more comfortable quarter-berth, by the cockpit companionway. 'But he always jumps out to let an old man rest!' added John.

In one squall, Grant was thrown across the cockpit and got a black eye when he hit his head on a winch. John made an unscheduled stop in Portugal, at Cascais Marina, near Lisbon, so Grant could get medical treatment. To the youngsters' credit, they all turned out for their watches (four hours on, eight off) whether feeling sick, tired, cold, wet or hungry.

On 18 May, when John went off watch at midnight, *Gipsy Moth* had all but stopped making any progress up the coast. Winds of up to 40 knots were ripping sheets of spray from the tops of the waves and pushing the yacht around like a toy. Battering against rough seas and motoring along at just two knots, with a forecast of Force 9 to come, John decided to stop at Vigo, Spain, to give the exhausted crew a break and review the options.

Two days later he wrote in the log book: 'We'd be guaranteed to miss the celebrations in Plymouth if we stayed in Vigo waiting for better weather to come to us – so we're going out to look for it!'

It was over 500 miles to Plymouth, even as the crow flies, which it couldn't against these headwinds. All day, gale-force winds whipped up large waves and every once in a while, a rogue wave filled the cockpit.

'*Gipsy Moth* was a wild west rodeo horse,' wrote Anson. 'Rearing half way up the waves and then sitting in the trough with a mighty crash.'

Chichester, too, had once compared *Gipsy Moth IV* to a horse, when his criticisms of her were countered by Sheila reminding him 'she's bought you further and faster than any other small boat has sailed on a passage.'

His reply was: 'Let me say at once that she is a very handsome boat and if she is controlled she can go fast.' He recalled Lisette, a horse ridden by General Mabot, ADC to Napoleon, which had had saved Mabot's life by her great speed and by running down Russian soldiers brandishing bayonets. 'I admire Lisette, but I do not think I could ever have been fond of her... She had a bad habit of killing her grooms,' said Chichester.

Meanwhile, five jerry cans of diesel fuel lashed to the guardrails were washed overboard when an express train of a wave sluiced down the side deck. Luckily they were all strung together and trailed in the water alongside, allowing Anson and Chris to drag them back aboard. 'Just as well they did, too. We're likely to need that fuel to get to Plymouth on time!' said John.

On 22 May it proved impossible to cook, so the crew had sandwiches for supper. Heading north-westwards two days later, they hoped to find friendlier winds, having have put *Gipsy Moth* in the middle of a lot of empty ocean. They didn't expect to see land until spotting the Lizard. Force 7s and 8s had made progress to windward patchy, under deep-reefed main and staysail. Then came forecasts of Force 9 and 10. 'We expect to arrive for the party – there is a party, isn't there?' was the good-humoured message from *Gipsy Moth* on Friday 25 May.

Three days from landfall, Grant was looking forward to sleeping in a bed that didn't rock, with a roof that didn't leak. A bonus of the calmer seas was an astonishing display of dolphins. The first sign was a flock of birds swooping around a patch of sea. Then dozens and dozens of dolphins appeared, whirling and leaping as they corralled fish. 'What made this special was the number involved and that they stayed for more than two hours. Then, suddenly, they were not there any more,' said John.

After 20 months away from British waters, *Gipsy Moth* was 90 miles south-west of Cornwall's Lizard Point, the southernmost tip of Great Britain, at 49°57'N – a landfall familiar to dozens of generations of seafarers. 'Wonderful to be able to relate a position to a UK landmark – and not just any landmark – after the best part of two years circling the world,' said John.

After 1,000 miles at sea, they were ending leg 31 as they began it. 'We are battling on against a relentless northerly! Spirits are high and, under a soggy exterior, the crew are nursing a very positive sense of achievement,' John emailed. Several days of waves breaking over the deck had taken their toll on the navigation lights, which had finally given up. But they had them working again before dark.

On Saturday at midnight, 26 May, John went off watch knowing they were making good speed. Luckily, he had reefed the mainsail

'*Gipsy Moth* was a wild west rodeo horse, rearing halfway up the waves and crashing in the troughs, said Anson.

Richard Baggett gives a breakfast briefing for the crew in Fowey before departing for Plymouth

before dark, which helped reduce the impact of 'an explosion of wind that hit the ketch at 0400 hours.' John and Chris handed the main and for a while *Gipsy Moth* ran under bare poles in 38-40 knots. But canvas was needed forward to help keep control in the large following seas, so the staysail was set. By the time John and Chris were back in the cockpit it was time to watch a spectacular sunrise. Mid-morning Sunday, the wind had backed and was on the nose again, plus they had an adverse tide. They were heading for Fowey, a quick pit stop where John would hand over command on Monday morning to Richard Baggett, the UKSA's lead skipper, for the final hop to Plymouth. They were joined by *Yachting Monthly*'s Dick Durham.

Writing his last ever log entry, John, an ex-RAF flying instructor, who had sailed *Gipsy Moth* more miles than anyone else since Sir Francis, said: 'There's nothing left to say, except what a delight it's been to sail with so many different people and watch them change on the legs from Australia, Indonesia, Sri Lanka, the Maldives, Djibouti, Egypt, Crete and

Malta. Chichester was a great Englishman. It's common for people of my generation to say that there are no more coming along, and that the country has gone to the dogs. Through this project, it's been my privilege to see a lot of young people with the courage, determination and energy to prove that's not true.'

The morning of Bank Holiday Monday 28 May, turned out to be a perfect sunny day in Cornwall and Devon. Rain clouds parted, split by the summer sun, following three days of gale-force winds, torrential rain and even snow on the Chilterns, all of which had turned the weekend into a wash out with newspaper headlines: 'Holiday misery for millions.'

Ten yachts followed *Gipsy Moth IV* out of Fowey and by the time she rounded Rame Head, that rocky, wild and windswept headland on the westward edge of the entrance to Plymouth Sound, an armada of welcoming craft awaited her, with a TV helicopter overhead. The headland, now a popular picnic spot, is the first and last sight of land seen by sailors and fishermen leaving Plymouth and is part of the sea shanty *Spanish Ladies*.

Barry Pickthall/PPL

After 610 days and 28,264 miles, Gipsy Moth's epic odyssey is almost over.

Mark Lamble

The pride of Plymouth makes waves as thousands welcome her back home.

Dick Durham/Yachting Monthly

of champagne to celebrate, while surrounding vessels blasted sirens and fire boats sprayed red, white and blue water. Chichester was met on shore by the Lord Mayor of Plymouth and other dignitaries and driven to the Guildhall where, at a press conference, he was asked what he would like to do now. 'After four months of my own cooking I'd like the best dinner from the best chef in the best surroundings and in the best company,' he declared.

In 2007 another blast of foghorns echoed around the harbour as a fire tender sprayed an arc of water and the pride of Plymouth, *Gipsy Moth*, sailed inside the breakwater accompanied by nearly 200 boats. She made a brave sight, beating northwards under jib and double reefed main in a brisk northwesterly. RIBS from Plymouth Youth Sailing acted as guard boats, deterring over-eager spectator yachts from getting too close. I was onshore with Giles Chichester, who wiped a tear from his eye, as we watched dinghies, jet-skis, a lifeboat, classic yachts and even a rowing gig, join the flotilla of well-wishers. Spontaneous applause

By the time Gipsy Moth rounded Rame Head an armada of welcoming craft began to appear. BELOW: Thousands cheered and clapped on Plymouth Hoe

A fly-past by the original Gipsy Moth bi-plane which met Sir Francis in 1967 had been cancelled because of strong winds. But the pilot, Nigel Reid, who had flown over *Gipsy Moth* at the Plymouth start in September 2005, was among the crowds to watch the homecoming.

In 1967, Sir Francis had welcomed his wife Sheila and son Giles aboard *Gipsy Moth* at Plymouth breakwater, as they bought bottles

Mark Lamble

broke out from a 5,000 strong crowd on the Hoe as *Gipsy Moth* moored to a buoy, assisted by former skipper Steve Rouse in a RIB.

At 1500 hours, just as planned, *Gipsy Moth*'s young crew, led by Baggett, transferred by tender to the steps of West Hoe Pier, where Sir Francis had stepped ashore on a twilight evening 40 years ago. Then, the hilltops of Devon and Cornwall, blazed with fire beacons, just as they had 400 years ago for his predecessor and kinsman, Sir Francis Drake.

Now *Gipsy Moth*'s tattered red ensign, which had flown at her mizzen masthead, was handed to the Deputy Lord Mayor of Plymouth, Ken Foster. The welcoming party included Giles Chichester, his wife Ginnie and their son Charlie, plus Jon Ely, CEO of the UKSA, Basil Butler, commodore of the Royal Western Yacht Club and Vivien Pengelly, the leader of Plymouth City Council.

On this sunny afternoon the crowds of spectators had been invited to join a celebration of the Swinging Sixties era. After all, 1967 had been dubbed 'the Summer of

Dick Durham/Yachting Monthly

Love'. Flower power had arrived in Britain, along with hippies, drop-outs, and the rallying call 'Make love not war', as the Vietnam conflict continued. Mini-skirts, flared trousers, long hair and bare feet were all the rage and four days after Chichester's homecoming, the Beatles released their iconic album, *Sgt. Pepper's Lonely Hearts Club Band*. Noel Gallagher, later of Oasis fame, was born the day after Chichester's homecoming and 1967 films *The Graduate* and *Bonnie and Clyde* became cult movies.

John Jeffrey points to the mooring buoy off West Hoe Pier, where Sir Francis stepped ashore on a twilit night in 1967.

The Beatles Sgt Pepper album was released in 1967 and Sandie Shaw's Puppet on a String won the Eurovision Song Contest.

Mark Lumble

The crew took Gipsy Moth's tattered red ensign ashore to present to Plymouth's Deputy Lord Mayor.

Forty years on a Beatles tribute band, The Fab Beatles, played on stage on Plymouth Hoe, and a giant 40 square-metre TV screen showed archive black and white film of Chichester's 1967 arrival, as well as relaying live colour pictures from camera boats on Plymouth Sound of her arrival this glorious day.

Gipsy Moth's safe homecoming after her second circumnavigation had been the climax of a magical three days in Plymouth, following a concert by Elton John and the city's half marathon.

A pub landlord marked the return of *Gipsy Moth IV* by renaming his pub in her honour and bringing back 1967 prices. Nigel Ledger, renamed the Yard Arm, on Citadel Road, the *Gipsy Moth* for a week, displaying the name on a huge banner draped across the pub.

Late that afternoon, the ketch motored around to the Royal Western Yacht Club's HQ at Queen Anne's Battery Marina for a reception. Many of her ten different skippers, and crew were there, including Linda Crew-Gee and Emmanuel Oladipo, who had been aboard when she struck the reef in the South Pacific. It was the first time they'd seen her, since they stepped off her that fateful night on Saturday 29 April, as she lay at a crazy angle on the coral ledge, waves breaking over her cockpit, a gaping hole smashed in her hull.

In the evening, at a dinner, sponsored by Corum Watches, Giles Chichester said his father would have been proud to see a new young generation benefit from challenging adventures aboard *Gipsy Moth*.

Twenty-five-year-old Elaine Caldwell, from Glasgow, with whom I'd sailed from Plymouth 20 months ago on the first leg of the circumnavigation, spoke movingly about the *Gipsy Moth* project being like a stone thrown in a pond with the ripples spreading beyond anyone's imagining ... it had been a voyage around the soul as well as across oceans.

'We have just taken part in this on the back of a man who sailed around the world at the age of 65, and kept going. He could have stopped when he got to Sydney – and we could have stopped when *Gipsy Moth* hit a reef. What this has taught me is resilience. I know that inside me, something has changed forever,' she said.

The memorial plaque marking Chichester's landing place in 1967.

RIGHT:
Gipsy Moth's ensign presented to the Deputy Lord Mayor by Glen Austin

Paul Gelder/Yachting Monthly

Paul Gelder/Yachting Monthly

Plymouth to Cowes

Final Homecoming

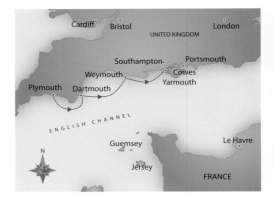

For her 'last charge' from the West Country to her new home in Cowes, *Gipsy Moth*'s skipper Richard planned three overnight stops at Dartmouth, Weymouth and Yarmouth. 'You know you're on a famous yacht when everyone waves,' said Steffan Meyric Hughes, news editor of *Classic Boat* magazine, as they headed out to sea from Plymouth breakwater. 'Like minor, dishevelled royalty, we waved back, some raising heads from sick buckets while suffering the infamous *Gipsy Moth* roll!'

A 0600 start next morning the ketch motored across Lyme bay in a light north-east wind with clear skies. They missed the last of the favourable tide to get around Portland Bill's notorious race, the graveyard of many vessels, but surfing through the standing waves was thrilling, with the log reading 12 knots. Taking the inside passage, close to the red-striped lighthouse – 'not a place to be in any wind,' noted Richard – they made slow, comfortable progress.

Until, that is, they ran over an unseen lobster pot, wrapping its rope around the prop and killing the engine. 'A very bleak picture of the next few days ran through my head in a flash,' said Steffan, who had been on the helm. '*Gipsy Moth* voyage stopped by *Classic Boat* magazine!' Luckily, Richard made a heroic leap overboard, knife clamped in teeth, to cut the rope away.

Day three saw *Gipsy Moth* sailing along Dorset's Jurassic coastline, England's first natural World Heritage Site. The sun shone as they poked the ketch's bow into Lulworth Cove for a quick glimpse, before motor-sailing on past Anvil Point and across Christchurch Bay in time to witness the spectacular sight of the

Leg 32

Distance:
160 miles

Skipper:
Richard
Baggett (35)

Mate:
Chris
Whitwam (32)

Crew Leader:
Jackie
Wigglesworth (33)

Crew:
Steffan Meyric
Hughes (32)
Charlotte
Pudney (18)
Joe Aziz (17)

Leg sponsor:
Isle of Wight

Mark Lamble

Gipsy Moth
*reaches the final
finish line of her
lap around the
planet.*

*BELOW:
A final salute
from the bi-plane*

*From Bali
to Bayona
and Kupang to
Cowes,* Gipsy
Moth*'s bow has
been a platform
to wave to crowds.
Ellen MacArthur
joins the
young crew*

Needles revealed as the sun burnt off a veil of sea mist. The breeze filled in and the cruising chute went up as they sailed up the Needles Channel, buzzed by Nigel Reid in his bright red Gipsy Moth bi-plane. At Yarmouth, *Gipsy Moth* joined the Old Gaffers' Rally, anchoring outside the harbour, the crew heading ashore to join the festivities. On Sunday 3 June, Britain's most famous young solo sailor, Ellen MacArthur, arrived by RIB to join the crew for the ketch's final homecoming to Cowes. They were accompanied by a growing armada of vessels, including the *Solent Scene*, chartered by the UKSA, and packed with staff, family, friends and supporters.

As *Gipsy Moth* sailed around Egypt Point, a canon salute was fired by the Royal London Yacht Club.

A few days later, Princess Anne visited the UKSA to launch a new yacht science degree and stepped aboard *Gipsy Moth IV*, to meet the project team for a final time, including skippers Richard Baggett and John Jeffrey, John Walsh, who managed the re-fit at Camper & Nicholsons, David Green and myself.

When Jon Ely introduced me as project founder with the time-honoured phrase: 'This is the man we have to blame for starting all this!' The Princess, at last, countered: 'You can't go on blaming him forever!'

Gipsy Moth IV's arrival in Cowes, marked a proud and poignant conclusion to the project and the beginning of a new era.

She had voyaged voyaged 28,264 miles, during her 610-day circumnavigation and been sailed by 10 skippers, 19 mates, 32 crew leaders and 96 crew. Together they had visited 32 countries in which more than 11 languages were spoken. Crews had needed inoculations from nine potentially fatal diseases.

Sailors aboard had included young people recovering from cancer, drug addicts who had kicked the habit, ex-prisoners, millionaires, a Princess, a Dame and a Duke.

It had been a life-changing journey for scores of youngsters. And the man they all looked up to was a 65-year-old legend – Sir Francis Chichester, who, somehow, did it all completely alone and with just one stopover in 226 days.

But *Gipsy Moth* would not be resting on her well-earned laurels. In a few days she would be starring in the JP Morgan Asset Management Round the Island Race, one of the world's biggest races with 1,500-plus boats. She also had a date at Southampton Boat Show in September and London's Earls Court Boat Show in December, where she would be a centre-piece attraction in the pool.

Meanwhile, she would continue to take young people sailing in the Solent and beyond. The Isle of Wight, a premiere partner in her restoration and circumnavigation,

had sponsored 15 island youngsters as crew on the circumnavigation and more than 100 others had undergone training development at the UKSA.

'We have enriched and developed young people's lives – not just the 90 that crewed on *Gipsy Moth IV*, but thousands more who stepped aboard her at ports of call around the globe and followed her adventures,' said Jon Ely, the CEO of the UKSA.

The plan for the future is for *Gipsy Moth IV* to be the centrepiece of a proposed new Isle of Wight Maritime Heritage Centre, to be built in East Cowes, where she will continue to inspire the next Robin Knox-Johnston or Ellen MacArthur.

Princess Anne meets the Gipsy Moth *project team for the final time, including Ed Dolling from BT, skipper John Jeffrey and David Green*

A welcoming flotilla escorts Gipsy Moth *home off Cowes*

My thanks to the Gipsy Moth IV supporters

The dream to see *Gipsy Moth* sailing again was a project that took over the lives of many – for some it was weeks and for others it was months and years. It would be impossible to thank everyone who helped me along the way, but there are many to whom I owe a debt of gratitude.

My biggest debt is to David Green who, as Global Project Manager, delivered a near-miracle, overseeing the restoration of *Gipsy Moth IV* in record time (twice!) The contribution of David's wife, Pat, should not be under-estimated, along with many other wives and partners who endured long hours as *Gipsy Moth* stole time and hearts.

Others at the UKSA who played a major role include CEO Jon Ely, whose patience and persistence saw the project through to a spectacular and fitting conclusion. Anna Symcox worked tirelessly for more than two and a half years. Frank Fletcher, now with the Ellen MacArthur Trust, was a big help at the start. John Walsh oversaw the restoration for the UKSA, helped me check facts for the book and is now skippering the *Gipsy Moth IV* 'experience sailing days'. Skippers Richard Baggett and John Jeffery sailed the ketch more miles than anyone since Chichester and were both there on the reef in Rangiroa when tragedy turned to triumph. Both were also superb ambassadors for the project. John's 'blog' on the website was invaluable. Global Voyage Co-ordinator Dewi Thomas, with Lynn O'Byrne, gave generous help in checking facts for the book.

Long before *Gipsy Moth* touched salt water for the first time in 38 years, the consent of her custodians at The Maritime Trust was needed. CEO Richard Doughty and Marie-Helene Bowden worked many hours to make this happen. Anna Somerset was also enthusiastic and their chairman, Sir Julian Oswald, Admiral of the Fleet, gave his blessing.

The Blue Water Round the World Rally's logistical support made a second circumnavigation so much easier. Peter Seymour and Chris Mounsey agreed to waive the entry fees for *Gipsy Moth* to join the rally and paid for her transit of the Panama and Suez canals. Later one of their directors, Stephen Thomas, made the first substantial donation. Tragically, Stephen died in an accident a few weeks later, but his widow, Catherine, and son, James, continued to support the project and set up a bursary in Stephen's memory. Peter and Annette Seymour provided many photographs for this book and helped check accuracy. Rally co-director Tony Diment and his wife Christine, plus Richard Boot, also assisted.

Giles Chichester and his wife Ginnie, together with our patrons and supporters, Ellen MacArthur, Emma Richards and Sir Robin Knox-Johnston were all very generous in offering tangible support.

At Camper & Nicholsons, MDs Pat Lilley and later Giorgio Bendoni, plus chief shipwright, Bill Shaw, gave many hours to the project before *Gipsy Moth* even left Greenwich dry dock. Martyn Langford was C&N's project director for most of the refit. All the C&N workers gave 110% in skills and determination to beat the clock for launch day in June 2005.

After reading accounts of the 150-plus crew who sailed *Gipsy Moth*, 'known as the vomet comet', I should have invested in Stugeron shares (the seasickness remedy).

Skippers and crew who helped check facts in the manuscript, and provided photos, included John Jeffrey, Antonia and Ray Nicholson, Tim Magee, Sam Connelly, Andrew Eccleston, plus crew Lucy Scales, Alistair Buchan, Linda Crew-Gee, Chris Bray and Claire Frew.

At *Yachting Monthly* I had support throughout the project from my publisher Simon Owen, deputy editor Miles Kendall,

features editor Dick Durham and consultant editor James Jermain, who all sailed on *Gipsy Moth*. Past publisher Jessica Daw and former assistant publisher Nicia Carter-Johnson also helped in the early stages.

YM photographer Graham Snook kept a photographic 'diary' of the restoration and photographers Lester McCarthy and Mark Lamble also contributed. In the magazine's art department, Holly Ramsay's design skills and Maxine Heath's charts of *Gipsy Moth*'s circumnavigation helped tell the story. Editorial Assistant Jane Fenton and Geoff Pack Scholar Sam Brunner assisted with research.

During my travels, I was made to feel at home in Sydney by Andrew ('Oz') Bray his wife Vicky and son Chris. Alex Whitworth sailed us to welcome us past Sydney Heads in *Beramilla*. In Tahiti Dimitri Zoellin offered support in the crisis and in New Zealand, Steve Philp, YM's former art editor, and his wife Angie, and Rufus assisted me.

Murlo Primrose and her son Dan, plus Sandy Illingworth, son of designer John Illingworth, and Colin Sylvester, who had worked in the Illingworth-Primrose design office, at 36 North Street, Emsworth, all shared their memories, and in some cases, invaluable papers and memos on the *Gipsy Moth* history. Naval architect Nigel Irens, surveyor Paul Jeffes, plus Martin Thomas and Alan Taylor, present and past Commodores of the Ocean Cruising Club, were all enthusiastic supporters.

David Palmer, my book editor, offered patience and encouragement, while Grzegorz Filip, the long-suffering designer, pored over thousands of photographs with me to make the final selection for the book. Barry Pickthall let me burn the midnight oil in his design studio and photo library.

In the race against time to finish the manuscript, my wife Anne was an eagle-eyed proof reader as well as a calming influence and our daughter Laura began to wonder if a writing career was too much of a sacrifice with 'lost weekends' at a word processor. You hear about journeys which change people's lives and wish you could discover one. For me it's been a privilege to be a part of *Gipsy Moth's* second voyage

Paul Gelder
Emsworth, September 2007.

GIPSY MOTH IV PROJECT PARTNERS

UKSA United Kingdom Sailing Academy

The Maritime Trust

YACHTING MONTHLY

GIPSY IV MOTH
YACHTING MONTHLY · UKSA · MARITIME TRUST

Premier Partner

ISLE OF Wight

Global Partners

BT

CORUM
SWISS TIMEPIECES
OFFICIAL TIMEKEEPER

Classic Platinum Partners

- British Marine Federation
- Camper & Nicholsons Yachting Limited
- www.solent.TV
- Royal Navy
- splash broadcast
- Royal Air Force
- Blue Water Round the World Cruising Rally
- Red Funnel
- offshore challenges sailing team
- SEEDA South East England Development Agency
- skandia
- Crusader Sails
- King of Shaves
- B&G Racing Performance
- Pindar
- Peter Harrison Foundation
- Rotary International
- Army
- NERA
- Francis Chichester Limited

Charity Partners

- columba 1400 Community & International Leadership Centre
- Ellen MacArthur
- Classic Boat Museum Isle of Wight
- University of Plymouth
- Save the Children
- newsround
- Portsmouth City Council
- RYA Sailability
- the brightside trust
- crime concern working for safer communities
- Prince's Trust
- hft Supporting People with Learning Disabilities
- The Sir Francis Chichester Trust
- Somerset College of Arts and Technology so many fields of expertise
- Maroochy Shire Council
- the inventure trust
- Barnardo's Giving children back their future

Technical Partners

- Seafresh Desalinators
- C-MAP UK
- Sundog eyewear
- inCAM digital surveillance
- AVON
- Geolink
- J. Shirlaw
- Broadblue Catamarans
- Simrad
- Lewmar
- International yachtpaint.com
- Ocean Safety
- Spencer Rigging Ltd
- SP
- Mastervolt Tailor Made Energy
- Yanmar marine
- Bainbridge International
- Ormiston Wire Ltd
- Turner Designs
- Navtec Rigging Solutions
- AXIS Communications
- RS Aqua
- Aqua Marine
- cover guard
- theyr
- OCENS
- Sweden Yachts
- Kidde
- YSI
- GMN
- reach mobile interactive text messaging
- Tiflex
- Henri Lloyd
- Tek-Tanks Solutions in Plastics
- Admiralty Charts and Publications
- Toughbook Computers for the Outside World
- Marlow
- BHG marine
- Barrus
- C-Guard
- esendex

Business Partners

- Cowes Yacht Haven the home of international boating since 1800
- Beken of Cowes Marine Photographers
- Lester Aldridge
- The Moorings The Best Sailing Vacations In The World!
- Plymouth Gin since 1793
- matrix ebusiness
- Parcelforce Worldwide
- npower
- ppi
- Kelvin Hughes
- mca Maritime and Coastguard Agency
- Volvo
- Medina Yard
- marriottdesign
- upix the virtual tour providers
- Oceanassist
- Mount Gay Rum Barbados
- Benzie of Cowes The Yachtsmen's Jeweller
- KOS Picture Source Ltd
- currencies direct

Gipsy Moth IV circles the world twice

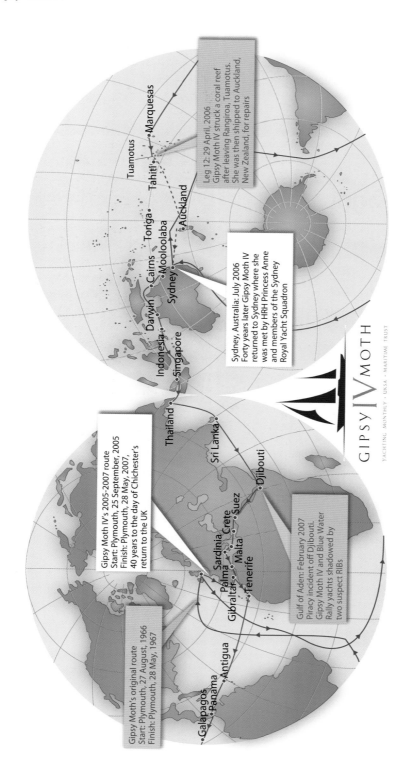

Marquesas

Tuamotus

Tahiti

Auckland

Tonga
Cairns
Mooloolaba
Sydney

Darwin

Indonesia
Singapore

Thailand

Sri Lanka

Djibouti

Suez
Crete
Sardinia
Palma
Malta
Gibraltar
Tenerife

Galapagos
Panama
Antigua

Leg 12: 29 April, 2006
Gipsy Moth IV struck a coral reef after leaving Rangiroa, Tuamotus. She was then shipped to Auckland, New Zealand, for repairs

Sydney, Australia: July 2006
Forty years later Gipsy Moth IV returned to Sydney where she was met by HRH Princess Anne and members of the Sydney Royal Yacht Squadron

Gipsy Moth IV's 2005-2007 route
Start: Plymouth, 25 September, 2005
Finish: Plymouth, 28 May, 2007,
40 years to the day of Chichester's return to the UK

Gipsy Moth's original route
Start: Plymouth, 27 August, 1966
Finish: Plymouth, 28 May, 1967

Gulf of Aden: February 2007
Piracy incident off Djibouti. Gipsy Moth IV and Blue Water Rally yachts shadowed by two suspect RIBs

GIPSY IV MOTH

YACHTING MONTHLY • UKSA • MARITIME TRUST

Gipsy Moth IV made her first epic passage from Plymouth to Sydney, Australia, and back to Plymouth in 1966-67, via the three Great Capes of Good Hope, Leeuwin, and Horn. Forty years, in 2005-07, a more leisurely circumnavigation seemed fitting for the grand old lady.

The Blue Water Round the World Rally circles the globe every two years, providing support and safety for a fleet of cruising yachts. It follows the trade winds route from the Canaries to the Caribbean, through the Panama Canal and across the Pacific to Australia, and home via Indonesia, Phuket, Sri Lanka and the Suez Canal. Gipsy Moth's shipwreck in the Pacific saw her shipped to Auckland, New Zealand and Sydney, before rejoining the fleet in Cairns. Chichester may well have approved of trade wind sailing: 'Wild horses could not drag me down to Cape Horn and that sinister Southern Ocean again in a small boat,' he said, back on dry land after his 29,000-mile adventure.

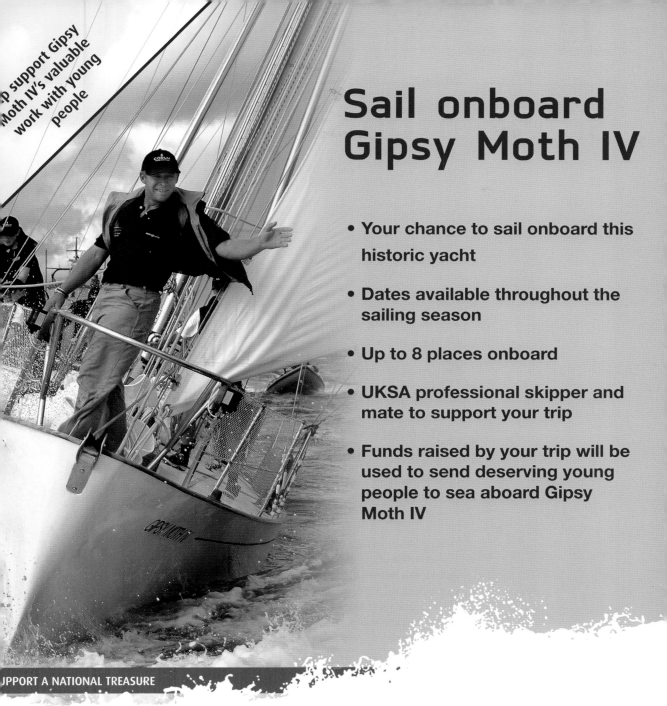

Sail onboard Gipsy Moth IV

- Your chance to sail onboard this historic yacht

- Dates available throughout the sailing season

- Up to 8 places onboard

- UKSA professional skipper and mate to support your trip

- Funds raised by your trip will be used to send deserving young people to sea aboard Gipsy Moth IV

Gipsy Moth IV is available for you or your company to charter with a choice of one day, or weekend, or five day Gipsy Moth sailing experiences

Book now, Call us
0800 781 1080
or visit
www.uksa.org/gipsymoth

UKSA
The Maritime Academy

0800 781 1080
www.uksa.org

UKSA
West Cowes, Isle of Wight PO31 7PQ

Registered Charity Number 299248
Patron HRH The Princess Royal

Single-handed sailor

By Mark Knopfler
From Dire Straits
album *Communique*

Two in the morning, dry-dock town
The river rolls away in the night
Little Gipsy Moth she's all tied down
She quiver in the wind and the light

Yeah and a sailing ship just held down in chains
From the lazy days of sail
She's just a lying there in silent pain
He lean on the tourist rail

A mother and her baby and the college of war
And the concrete graves
You never wanna fight against the river law
Nobody rules the waves
Yeah and on a night when the lazy wind is a-wailing
Around the Cutty Sark
The single-handed sailor goes sailing
Sailing away in the dark

He's upon the bridge on the self same night
The mariner of dry dock land
Two in the morning, but there's one green light
And a man on a barge of sand
She's a gonna slip away below him
Away from the things he's done
But he just shouts 'hey man, what do you call this thing?
He could have said 'Pride of London'
On the night when the lazy wind is a-wailing
Around the Cutty Sark
Yeah the single-handed sailor goes sailing
Sailing away in the dark

Little Gipsy Moth she's all tied down
She quiver in the wind and the light

Chris Laurens/PPL

© Mark Knopfler and Dire Straits (Recorded December, 1978)